PILATE TO CONSTANT[INE]

KT-419-523

PILATE TO CONSTANTINE

by

JAMES BULLOCH

THE SAINT ANDREW PRESS
EDINBURGH

1981.

First published in 1981 by
THE SAINT ANDREW PRESS
121 George Street, Edinburgh EH2 4YN

Copyright © J. Bulloch, 1981

ISBN 0 7152 0453 X (Limp)
ISBN 0 7152 0460 2 (Cased)

All rights reserved. No part of this publication may be reproduced or transmitted in any form or by any means, electronic or mechanical, including photocopy, recording, or any information storage and retrieval system, without permission in writing from the publisher. This book is sold subject to the condition that it shall not, by way of trade or otherwise, be lent, re-sold, hired out or otherwise circulated without the publisher's prior consent.

Printed in Hong Kong by
Permanent Typesetting & Printing Co., Ltd.

CONTENTS

Chapter 1

The Kingdom of God and the Church

1

Until the Arabs realised that their oil gave them a stranglehold on the economy of the industrial west the Semitic peoples had only twice made an impact on world history, though each time with massive consequences. Palestine lay in a quarter of the Roman empire which had economic importance but otherwise, Semitic in race and culture, it was part of a Third World of the time which, unless when it made trouble, counted for little. Here the life of Jesus was spent. It consisted of a spell as joiner in a hill-top village, two or three years of sporadic teaching, and death on the rubbish tip outside a city wall. No other literature has been so assiduously combed as the scanty records of his life but despite this, without that personal decision which he in his time demanded of men, they remain as enigmatic as himself.

His dates are uncertain. We count the years from his birth, but the calculation was the work of Dionysius Exiguus[1] in the sixth century and is only approximate. An exhaustive enquiry[2] concludes that he died on Friday 3 April A.D. 33, but A.D. 30 is more widely accepted.[3] Roman officials paid no more heed to the innumerable summary executions among subject peoples than did the men in Whitehall who dealt with the Victorian outposts of the empire. At least two other executions took place in Jerusalem that day, probably on related charges. While he was a child in Nazareth, over 2,000 were crucified in the suppression of a minor rising.[4] Yet it is from his birth that most of the world now reckons time, an unconscious admission that this is the watershed of history.[5] In the same way his life is generally seen as the origin of the Church.

It has been said that the word *Christianity* is first used by Ignatius,[6] but the Greek word which he coined was in contrast with *Judaism* which referred in the first instance, not to a set of doctrines, but to the community which held them. For its modern meaning as a pattern of beliefs there is no equivalent in the New Testament. Instead we read of Christ and the Kingdom of God; and we are confronted with the Church and the Gospel. Why then do we speak of Christianity and not of the Kingdom of God? And why are sectarianism and individualism thought to reflect the mind of Christ when the visible and indestructible outcome of his life and the most astonishing phenomenon of our time is the world-wide Church? There is another way of looking at the matter which, though often forgotten, has deep roots in Christian thought.

At Skara Brae and Jarlshof in treeless and windswept Orkney and Shetland, Bronze Age men inhabited huts of dry stone masonry, but normally in Western Europe their presence is traced from their artifacts and burial places. However in southern Iraq, where the great rivers flowed down to the gulf through vast swamps and banks of mud and sand, Bronze Age men built houses. As the earlier mud brick hovels decayed, first villages, and then towns, were built upon the debris until the mounds rose high above the level countryside and on their summits appeared cities, Erech, Eridu, Lagash, and Ur. Excavation there unearthed streets, houses and temples, exposed mosaics, metalwork, and musical instruments; the long-lost luxuries of a vanished civilization.

There was a citizen of Ur who deliberately left its comforts to return to the nomadic life and thus separated himself from the religion of Sumeria[7]. He carried with him the traditions of his people concerning the great flood which had left a deposit of eight feet of sediment over the earlier remains and beneath the city which he knew, but he had chosen to be solitary and landless because in the world of his time it was impossible to be a member of a community without sharing its religion. Religion was a relationship, not between God and the individual, but between society and its gods. Morals and conscience had no part in it. Worship was a communal act integrated with daily life, seedtime and harvest. Its ritual conduct was held to guarantee prosperity and its disavowal involved ostracism, if not some greater penalty.

Unfortunately our language employs the same word to describe the God of Abraham and the gods of paganism. Comparative religion has been concerned with similarities between the faith of the Bible and the ethnic religions, but the Bible presents Abraham as a man who made a breach with his ancestral religion. Its gods were humanised beings who met the universal urges of mankind and were to be dreaded or placated; but Abraham had been called to serve the invisible God,[8] the Creator of all, who was inexorable justice as well as infinite love, and to enter into covenant with him. In return he was promised that his descendants would become a great nation, that they would inherit the land where he was a wanderer, and that in him all nations of the earth would be blessed.

It is a commonplace to say that Jehovah developed from a tribal God into the one omnipotent God. Israel saw it otherwise. They had become a nation because the one God had called them. To vary a saying of Pascal, you pay your money and you take your choice. From Abraham onwards the continuing existence of the believing community is a fact of world history, and it is in this light that the Church has seen herself. By its very nature polytheism is capable of a generous tolerance, willing to absorb any divinity to whom men pray. Hinduism is hospitable and so, up to a point, was classical paganism. Israel's God, on the other hand, was notoriously a jealous God. His people scorned the cults of greater civilizations.

Like Israel the Church has seen her existence as springing from the acts of God in history and owing nothing to the ethnic religions. This exclusiveness, as much resented in the modern world as in the ancient, is part of the offence of the Gospel. When any statement of the faith fails to give offence to the outsider there is cause to suspect that it is defective and inadequate. The greatness of the divine community, says Ignatius,[9] lies in its being hated by the world, not in its being convincing to it.

There are theologians who regard this interpretation of the Church as naive, but on this basis arguments as to whether Jesus did or did not intend to found a Church are irrelevant, for the early Christians saw themselves as the Israel of God, the community of faith which had at last received the promise made to Abraham.[10] They were the heirs of the covenant. Since God made man he had not ceased to call men to himself and so there had always been a Church in the world; the Fathers even traced her origins past Abraham to Abel, past history into myth and legend. 'The Church', said Aquinas, 'is universal in time, and those are wrong who allow it a limited space, for it began with Abel and will last even to the end of the world ... and after.'[11] In the same way a standard document of the Reformation says that 'the Church has always existed and will always exist'.[12]

All that went before Christ was a preparation for his coming. In him the promise made to Abraham was fulfilled and the believing community which began with one man and had been confined to one nation became world-wide. They had come from the east and from the west, from the north and from the south, and had sat down in the Kingdom of God.[13] So the Church saw herself. As the Bible contains both Old Testament and New, so it is a paradox that in A.D. 33 the Church was quite new and also very old.

On the other hand, writing at a time when most Jews had rejected the Gospel and the Church was committed to the mission to the Gentiles, the evangelists never concealed the disquieting words in which it is made plain that Jesus restricted his ministry to his own nation.[14] It has been suggested that if ever Jesus declared the world mission of the Church before his passion[15] it was when, at the cleansing of the temple, in the court of the Gentiles, he used the words of Isaiah 'My house shall be called of *all* nations a house of prayer . . . .'

At his trial and at Calvary the saying 'Destroy this temple and in three days I will raise it up', which St John[16] associates with this incident, was cited against him. These words are ambiguous. Later his disciples interpreted them in the light of his resurrection while his opponents thought that he anticipated the end of the temple. Possibly both were correct.

Sacrifices are meaningless and repellent to the modern mind, and though the state of Israel has regained control of the temple site it is hard to imagine any renewal of the ancient rites. If the lords of the chain stores and the real estate market are ready to hand over their millions for Zionism, they are unlikely to do so to renew the sacrifices of lambs on Mount Moriah. This is not so much a consequence of the ruin of the temple in A.D. 70 or the anticipation of a furious reaction from the Arabs, as of the new world of thought created by Christ. There can be no going back. Through disasters which might have ended greater nations, Israel had not merely preserved its identity, but had upheld its unique faith. Now, with the coming of Christ, that faith burst its confines to influence the world.

Such things do not happen by inadvertence. There is no truth in the 'Cleopatra's nose' theory[17] according to which the course of history is diverted by trivialities. Every event has a cause proportionate to it and whatever previous developments may have contributed, the magnitude of this one is some measure of the stature of Jesus.

Written above the cross in three languages, the charge against him symbolised the cosmopolitan environment of the dozen working men from Galilee. Rome ruled them, but their traditions were Hebrew and their milieu Hellenistic; and in this pluralist society the Church was to emerge from the chrysalis of Judaism to become Catholic or universal.

In 1904 before the rise of Zionism Sir Leonard Wolley noted how paradoxical it was that Palestine had so compulsive an attraction for a people whose hold on it had been so discontinuous. They did not claim to have been its first inhabitants. In the time of Ezra the phrase, *the people of the land*, had the same alien and hostile sense as in the time of Joshua.[18] Modern Israel, which also has its feud with the Palestinians, the people of the land, is the third of Israel's occupations of the land where Abraham was a stranger. Each commenced from small beginnings and steadily grew. As the name shows, the children of Israel began as the tightest and most primitive of all communities, a family. For centuries after the entrance into Palestine under Joshua the tribes knew no central administration and no secular authority other than the judges called to office in time of emergency and, like Harry Truman, going back to their home town once their term was done. Israel did not form a state. But when, in the eleventh century B.C., the Philistines threatened to overwhelm them, the Israelites saw their only hope of survival in a kingdom like those of the nations around them. Full of foreboding, since he regarded it as a rejection of God's purpose for them, Samuel reluctantly granted their demand.[19] It is difficult to overestimate the significance of this for the future of Israel and the understanding of the Kingdom of God. Israel had been chosen, not to be yet another small state in the Middle East, but to be the divine society, the people of God. Nevertheless Saul was to rule his people under the law of God and his kingdom was to have a constitutional character. His authority was never to be absolute. Yet he was *the Lord's anointed*. This title has been translated in the Bible and Christian thought in three forms so that its content is at once expressed and also concealed. By *the Lord's anointed* is meant the king who once reigned in Israel; by *the Messiah* the coming king of Jewish expectation; and by *Christ* the fulfilment in the person of Jesus.

Saul failed in his obligations. David was seen as the ideal king, not because he was perfect, which he obviously was not, but because he tried to reign as God's servant. When he sinned, he repented and accepted his punishment. There are hints that the brief greatness of his kingdom was seen as a sign of the greatness of Israel's God, but it is also possible that the division of the kingdom after Solomon was due in part to an uneasiness that the monarchy had become too powerful and was a threat to the covenant between God and his people. Chapter after chapter of *I* and *II Kings* tells how the failure of the monarchy to obey God led in the end to disaster and exile. In the last years of the northern kingdom Hosea dated Israel's decline from the day when she chose to be ruled by a king. Her transformation from a society into a state had been a communal sin and an insult to the God whose sovereignty she had repudiated. Biblical accounts of the monarchy are shaped by the prophets' conviction that Israel's destiny was that of a people in covenant with God rather than that of a state, and when the Babylonians stormed Jerusalem they found Jeremiah in prison because he had forecast the end of the monarchy.[20] Nevertheless the kingdom of David left an abiding memory and a recurrent dream which has been fantastically realised, at least in one respect, by modern Israel, not a kingdom in name but in fact a centralised state, the most ruthless and efficient in the Middle East. Despite concessions to orthodox Jews, she is a secular state.

When the first occupation ended in the suppression of the kingdom and the transportation of its people to Babylon, some 45,000 survivors, it has been reckoned,[21] were left in Judaea to till the soil and endure the inroads of their martial and predatory neighbours. Some Israelites had remained after the fall of the northern kingdom and, according to Nehemiah, had friendly relations with the priestly aristocracy of Jerusalem. Gentile settlers brought in by the Assyrian kings were said to have introduced them to a syncretistic worship.[22] If so, the Samaritans, as their descendants were called, got rid of heathen elements, accepted the Pentateuch alone as their Scripture, and had their great shrine at Mount Gerizim. It was this last, rather than doctrine, as the woman at the well explained to Jesus, which divided them from the Jews.[23]

At first the returning exiles occupied only Jerusalem and some fifteen miles round about,[24] but before the fall of the Persian empire they had spread into Galilee and across the Jordan into Gilead.[25] Thus, apart from the obnoxious Samaritans, there were now two Jewish groups. One lived on the bare soil of Palestine. Scattered across the former domains of the Persians, the other, the Jews of the Dispersion, *the Diaspora,*[26] richer and more numerous, less hidebound by the Law if still loyal to it, contributed to the worship of the distant temple and hoped at some time to participate, but were content to remain in the land of their exile. It was a division not unlike that between modern Jews in Israeli kibbutzim and those of Long Island and Palm Beach.

When Jerusalem was captured the extinction of the monarchy and the transportation of its people might have been expected to wipe the Jews from the pages of history, but Israel retained its identity in exile, not as a nation but as a community of faith, and in this setting the concept of Israel as the divine society rather than as a national state reasserted itself. This called for reconsideration of the nature of the Davidic kingdom. Ezekiel saw the place of the king filled by a prince whose function was that of a spiritual ruler. Though sprung from the line of David he was to be no more than God's servant. By the time that *Deutero-Isaiah* was written God alone was recognised as the ruler of his people and the role of his servant was seen as one of suffering. Some, like the priestly writers, envisaged the destiny of Israel in terms of the service of God in the ritual of a reconstructed temple.

When the returning exiles commenced the rebuilding of the temple Joshua, the High Priest, shared the leadership with Zerubbabel, a man of Davidic descent whom the Persians had appointed as governor much as the Japanese appointed Henry Pu Yi, a cadet of the ancient Manchu dynasty, as their puppet in Manchukuo. Haggai and Zechariah regarded Zerubbabel as the Messiah, the branch out of the stem of Jesse, but it was not to be. About 515 B.C. his name disappears from the record.

Throughout this second occupation, with the exception of the years between the heroic revolt of the Maccabees and the capture of Jerusalem by the Romans in 63 B.C., the Jews were under alien rule and did not form an independent state. So long as tribute was paid and recruits provided for the army, the Persians left their subject peoples pretty much to run their own affairs. But with the coming of Alexander of Macedon this unmanageable empire, hampered by inadequate communications over vast distances, collapsed. After the battle of Issus in 333 B.C. Syria and Egypt fell to Alexander at once. When he died without an heir in 323 B.C. his conquests fell apart as rapidly as those of Persia while, as *Daniel* 11 oracularly tells, his generals fought among themselves to establish the succession kingdoms.

Alexander brought more than a change of masters. With him came Greek settlers and, even more importantly, their language, literature, ideas and culture. No greater contrast could have been found than that between the Jew with his fanatical monotheism, his intense absorption in the sovereignty of God and the destiny of God's people on the one hand, and, on the other the open-minded curiosity of the classical Greek whose religion was a mythology and a civic observance, whose intellect was more assured than his will, and who believed that to see the truth was to attain it, that evil was only ignorance and virtue knowledge. These qualities remained, but Greek and Levantine were to affect each other. By now Plato, Euripides, and Phidias were numbered with the dead and the great days of Greek philosophy and art lay in the past. There came a mingling and cross-fertilization of cultures. Among the Jews, and especially among their upper classes, there was a growing readiness to accept the hellenizing policy of their rulers both in language and religion; and the inevitable counterpart to this was an increasing determination among others that Israel should stand apart from all other nations, upholding the faith in Israel's God and the observance of his Law.[27]

Palestine, after some vicissitudes, had become part of the succession state of Syria, and when Antiochus Epiphanes came to its throne in 175 B.C. he deposed the High Priest to make way for another more amenable to Hellenization. This was the signal for wild disorders and in 169 Antiochus occupied Jerusalem, looted the temple, and massacred many in the streets. Circumcision and observance of the Sabbath — the most obvious aspects of the Law — were made punishable by death. Sacrifices to the heathen gods were to be offered in every town and anyone with a recently circumcised child or a scroll of the Law was to die. In December 167 a heathen altar was set up in the temple on the site of the great altar of burnt offering. Ten days later the first sacrifice — *the abomination of desolation* of Daniel — was offered on it.[28] At this crowning outrage the revolt of the Maccabees broke out and, contrary to all expectations, succeeded. In 141 B.C. the citadel in Jerusalem, the last Syrian stronghold, capitulated to the High Priest Simon.

> As long as Simon lived, Judaea was at peace. . . . He extended his nation's territories and made himself master of the whole land. . . . Old men sat in the streets, talking together of their blessings; and the young men dressed themselves in splendid style. . . . His renown reached the ends of the earth.[29]

Independence was short lived. Sooner or later Roman occupation was inevitable, but the rulers of Judaea, quarrelling among themselves, were foolish enough to invite Roman intervention. Jerusalem surrendered to Pompey in 63 B.C. without a blow, but a minority held out against him on the temple rock. When the three months' siege was over, twelve thousand had died and the priests had been slaughtered at the altar.

Resistance to Antiochus had been powered, not by nationalism, but by religious fanaticism. Rome, as the New Testament shows, did not interfere with the temple or the Law and so for long provoked no major outbreak of rebellion. Both in the *Diaspora* and in the homeland Israel survived, not as a secular state but as the people of God, the community of faith. As such, it has been called a theocracy[30] and, as we have seen, the roots of this go far back.

Evidently the synagogue originated in the exile and was introduced to Palestine by those returning as the normal Sabbath worship, so that ordinary Jews became accustomed to the weekly reading of the Law and came to understand that the priesthood derived its authority from the Law, rather than the other way about.[31] In the days before the revolt when Hellenism seemed in the ascendant there were those known as the *Hasidim*, the godly or devout, who stood for the uncompromising observance of the Law. After a momentary hesitation they threw in their lot with the revolt and in so doing rallied the mass of the people both to it and to their own stand for every jot and tittle of the Law. Had it not been so Judaism might have degenerated into no more than an ethical monotheism, lacking exclusiveness and so interesting enquirers, but probably also lacking the conviction to survive. So far as is known, this is the only example of an eastern religion resisting by force the influence of Hellenism.[32]

Even in the days of the fanatical Maccabees the *Hasidim* held that a theocracy[33] where the high priests ruled was not quite identical with one where God alone ruled. Tension existed. By the time of Christ the strict observance of the Law for which the *Hasidim* stood had been transmitted to the Pharisees. As a class they stood aside from the great priestly families whose own supporters, the Sadducees, while they stood for the Law, lacked that passionate zeal and the craving for righteousness which can be seen in a former Pharisee like Paul and which alone made tolerable the burden of a rigorous Law.

Theirs was the religion of the cultured and prosperous, the members of the establishment, the Pharisees, of the masses.[34] For both, the state as they knew it, from the customs desk where a publican named Levi sat, to the judgement hall where the governor sat, was an evil to be endured. 'Is it lawful to pay tribute to Caesar?' Those who posed the question were the most aware of its awkwardness. Though they lacked the adroitness to reply frankly and with safety in public, neither Pharisee nor Sadducee had any doubt what the answer should be. For the Sadducees the alternative to the Roman state was one where government was in the hands of the hereditary priesthood; for their opponents the alternative was the ideal of a people living under the Law of God. Whatever the leadership may decide no resistance movement is ever sufficiently uniform to control its underground associates and among the masses there was a continuing measure of support for guerillas, active or potential, who could think of the attainment of independence by no other method than violence. For the men of Qumram — and many others — the deliverance of Israel, the new age, and the Messianic kingdom were to be brought in by warfare,[35] an expectation occasionally glimpsed in the New Testament and from which there came the risings which ended only with the second expulsion of the Jews from Palestine. At Qumram the divergent concepts of the Messiah created the hope of two Messiahs, one the warrior king who would win freedom for his people in battle, and the other the coming High Priest who would preside over their obedience to the Law.[36] 'They shall be ruled by the first laws with which the men of the community began to be disciplined until the coming of a prophet, and the Messiahs of Aaron and Israel.' While they looked forward to these two, the Church looked back to Jesus as the Messiah who had come, combining in himself the roles of prophet, priest, and king, and forward to his second coming when he would bring this present age to an end.

From start to finish the Gospels are concerned with Jesus as the one who brings in the Kingdom of God in fulfilment of the ancient promise. Peter's vivid memory of his first day with Jesus has shaped the first chapter of *Mark*. It tells of the startling impression made by his person, his calling of the first disciples, and his acts of power and healing; it sums up his teaching in the words, 'The time is fulfilled and the Kingdom of God is at hand'. Even after the resurrection the question, 'Lord, wilt thou at this time restore again the kingdom to Israel?'[37] shows the conviction that this was the message of Jesus and the persistent misunderstanding of it. Few concepts have been so lucidly and memorably described as was this one in the parables and aphorisms of Jesus; few have given so much cause for debate.

Roman historians wrote for the upper classes of the imperial race and in Palestine alone do we see a province through the eyes of the subject people and their working class. Within a century Rome suffered two terrible defeats. Crassus, who looted the temple in 54 B.C., next year had his army slaughtered by the Parthians at Carrhae — Abraham's Haran; and Varus, who crucified the two thousand Jews in A.D. 6 when legate in Syria, lost his legions in A.D. 9 in the German forest. Their opponents left no record for us to read, but in the Gospels it is as though we learned the hopes and fears of the men who followed Spartacus and Boadicea; there is no mistaking that for similar people in Israel the coming of Jesus was the coming of the Kingdom of God.

What did they expect the Kingdom to be? Fourteen generations are reckoned by *St Matthew* from Abraham to David, fourteen from David to the end of the monarchy, and fourteen more to the birth of Christ. This is symbolic. Each stage marks a transition in the history of the divine community.

'The Lord God will give unto him the throne of his father David,' said the angel to Mary, 'and he will reign over the house of Jacob for ever; and of his Kingdom there shall be no end.'[38]

'Where is he that is born King of the Jews?' was a question to disturb any ruler aware of the implications.[39]

'He hath put down the mighty from their seats, and hath exalted them of low degree. He hath filled the hungry with good things, and the rich he hath sent empty away.'[40]

This is the revolutionary manifesto of a community whose master has reversed the values of that society which in turn executed him. Compared with the confidence of the *Magnificat, The Red Flag* is a mournful dirge.

Always the office of the Messiah, the Davidic King, was bound up with the unique status of Israel as the people of God.[41] Jesus is never said to have claimed, at least in words, to be the son of David, nor did he invite the use of the title, but it is implied.

'How say the scribes that Christ is the son of David?' he asked. 'David himself calleth him Lord; and whence is he then his son?'[42]

This is told in a context of rejection, yet Mark comments that 'the common people heard him gladly'. Why? We are not told, but it is implied in the Gospels that Jesus' Kingdom is incomparably greater that that of David. Bartimaeus was not reproved for using the title but, as can be seen in *St Mark*, if the son of David who was also David's Lord had come to claim his rights, he had not come in David's way. He may have had a whip of small cords in his hand, but not a sling and a smooth stone from the brook. *St Matthew* has the strongest interest in this title with its political undertones and on Gentile soil less significance was found in it; yet *St John*, where the kingship of Christ is scarcely mentioned until the trial, recalls the question, 'Shall Christ come out of Galilee? Hath not Scripture said, That Christ cometh of the seed of David, and out of the town of Bethlehem, where David was?'[43]

All who heard Jesus knew that his message was the coming of the Kingdom of God and with time it was seen that this involved his own person and destiny. Among dissidents and supporters of the establishment the phrase had as varied political associations as, more recently, 'the dictatorship of the proletariat' had in Franco Spain, so it is surprising that he escaped official attention as long as he did. In many ways his teaching was in keeping with Israel's traditional faith but at this point his divergence was a major one, as intolerable to the Jews of his time as of ours, for he was himself the Lord of the Kingdom and his mission the renewal of God's community. In modern English *kingdom* can mean a territory, and the same is true of the Greek word in the New Testament, but behind it is a word in the Aramaic speech of Jesus; this has no ambiguity and means personal rule. Sovereignty implies a community, the people who obey that rule.[44] When the modern world speaks loosely of *the Kingdom* in terms of late nineteenth century theological liberalism it is forgotten that 'whatever social applications may be given to the teaching of Jesus, the essentially religious idea of God reigning in the lives of men and in human society lies at the bottom of it all.'[45] In which human society? Is God's sovereignty known in the secular world which crucified Jesus and has not altered since then? Any interpretations of *the Kingdom* in terms of a benevolent humanism are strangely inadequate.

As the Kingdom of God was the message of Jesus it was also the charge that brought him to death. He had not come merely to make an addendum to familiar ethics. His new wine was not to be put into old bottles; for he had set the course for a community fundamentally at odds with established society. However veiled his claim to be the Messiah, the Lord of the Kingdom, may once have been even to his disciples and however misunderstood it may have been, it could not be ignored. 'Why was he crucified?' asks the man of today. Any contemporary would have asked, 'How could he expect not to be?'

His entry on Palm Sunday was a threat to Roman authority and the cleansing of the temple an insult to the priestly aristocracy. If there was a reluctance to arrest him in any place where rioting might flare up only the briefest of intervals could pass before he was put out of the way. Three parties were involved. Herod Antipas, in whose jurisdiction most of the activities of Jesus had taken place, played only a minor part.[46] As for the other two, it was members of the Sanhedrin, whether or not that court met in formal session, who took the initiative; but it was the Roman governor whose troops were needed and whose decision was final. Presumably it was no more difficult to instigate a lynching or arrange an assassination in the Middle East then than now, and there is a certain irony that the case of Jesus was thought important enough to require — up to a point — proper legal procedure.

However anxious men like Peter or the beloved disciple may

have been to know what was happening, no known adherent of the accused stood a remote chance of following the case at close quarters through its various stages. Court procedure has always been something of a mystery to the uninitiated and none of the evangelists can have had a detailed grasp of it but, says A.N. Sherwin-White,

> the impression of a historical tradition is nowhere more strongly felt than in the various accounts of the trial of Christ, analysed in Roman terms.... Consider the close interdependence of Mark and Matthew, supplementing each other even in particular phrases, yet each with his particular contribution, then Luke with his more coherent and explicit account of the charges and less clear version of the activity of the Sanhedrin, finally John, who despite many improbabilities and obscurities yet gives a convincingly contemporary version of the political pressures on Pilate in the age of Tiberius.[47]

Life in occupied countries always has some common features. Information on what went on behind court doors reached friends of the accused in Vichy France and does likewise in Eastern Europe today. No doubt it did so in Palestine also.

First came the appearance before the ecclesiastical authorities. Until now the word *Messiah* had had a political content for the most part, but Jesus had been seen to give it a new meaning.

> Again the high priest asked him, and said unto him, Art thou the Christ, the Son of the Blessed?

> And Jesus said, I am; and ye shall see the Son of Man sitting on the right hand of power, and coming in the clouds of heaven.

> Then the high priest rent his clothes, and saith, What need we any further witnesses?

> Ye have heard the blasphemy; what think ye? And they all condemned him to be guilty of death.[48]

A comment by Caiaphas indicates that Jesus was dreaded in priestly circles as the potential leader of a popular rising doomed to be disastrous,[49] but the primary interest of the priesthood was the charge of blasphemy and despite the scepticism of Lietzmann[50] there is no sound reason to question substantially the account in *St Mark*.

While it lay within the scope of a Jewish court to declare a prisoner worthy of death, normally it was not within its legal competence to execute him.[51] Accordingly Jesus was next sent to Pilate; but here it was necessary to frame the charge in such a way that the required verdict would be given. His potential as a revolutionary[52] was stressed, a matter of no difficulty because of the ambiguity attached to the title of Messiah. 'Art thou the King of the Jews?' said Pilate, and it was for this, as the title above the cross, an undeniable non-Christian notice of Jesus,[53] that he was condemned. To the last the misunderstanding of the title *Messiah* can be seen in the mockery of those at the foot of the cross and in the exchange of words between the two men crucified with Jesus.

Who was to blame? As anyone who has read Roman comments on the Jews must know, anti-semitism is older than the rise of the Church, but whenever there have been pogroms in Christian times Jews have been painfully sensitive to the charge that they were responsible for Christ's death. No detailed accounts of the judicial arrangements laid down at the creation of Roman provinces or the demarcation between imperial and native jurisdictions have survived, in Palestine or elsewhere.[54] This has not prevented many confident assertions, but all that can be said with certainty is that it was secular authority, whether Jewish or Roman, that condemned Jesus, for the high priests held office as Roman nominees and for administrative ends.

In 1828 Joseph Salvador, a French Jew, argued on the basis of the Gospel texts as they stood — the only available premises at the time — that Jesus had been legally and justly condemned. But biblical criticism with its radical methods offered a simpler means of shaking the traditional version by manipulation of the evidence, and in 1866 Ludwig Philippson, a German rabbi, grasped it to argue that the Romans alone were to blame. Since then there has been a succession of varied interpretations. In 1908 Karl Kautsky produced a Marxist interpretation which drew the attention of Lenin. Jesus, he held, had been condemned by Pilate because of his claim to kingship and therefore for high treason. All the rest was invention on the part of 'the ignorant, silly and foolish evangelists'. The judgement of a more recent Marxist, Milan Machoveč, Professor of Philosophy at Prague from 1953 to 1970, is that to deprive Jesus of responsibility for the Church is like depriving Marx of the responsibility for Communism. 'Kautsky's Jesus,' says Machoveč,

> 'is a politically active dissident and a social revolutionary. It is not nonsense to suggest this, and we have already seen that Jesus' prophetic-eschatological thinking undoubtedly has social and political consequences. This view, however, does not go to the heart of Jesus' position, and it betrays a total lack of understanding of what his eschatological thinking really was; it contained socio-political elements but is not reducible to them.'[55]

In 1929 Robert Eisler published in German, and in 1931 in English, *The Messiah Jesus and John the Baptist*. This hit the headlines in the popular press because it contained a description of the appearance of Jesus drawn from a passage rather dubiously ascribed to Josephus.[56] Eisler's main thesis was more important. According to this Jesus had been a pacifist until he realised that his mission of delivering Israel could not be accomplished peacefully but only by the sword. Though he himself must face death[57] Simon Peter, to whom he had committed the keys of the Kingdom, would be his successor as deputy-Messiah, a viceroy on the soil of Palestine until his own return in power and glory. As for the keys of the Kingdom, these represented, not doctrinal or spiritual authority, but power over the independent state of Israel soon to be restored in more than ancient splendour.[58] Consequently Jesus was arrested as a revolutionary, passed to the Jewish authorities for a curt cross-examination, and then despatched to death by Pilate after a summary hearing.

In other words, Jesus had been an associate of the Zealots.[59] Followers of John the Baptist, possibly associated with the Essenes or the men of Qumram, were among the disciples. Otherwise Scribes, Pharisees, Herodians, and Sadducees are never mentioned among the inner circle around Jesus and of contemporary parties only the Zealots are recorded among the disciples. Sometimes known as *sicarii*, from their use of the *sica* or hooked dagger[60] still sold as a tourist souvenir in the Gulf States, this party inherited a long tradition of underground resistance and enjoyed a reputation like that of the Yugoslav partisans. As early as 81 B.C. their favourite weapon was banned by Rome in the lands around the eastern Mediterranean where she ruled.

When Archelaus was banished in A.D. 6 and Judaea reduced from the status of a client kingdom to that of a province, it was necessary for the new administration to conduct a census. Feeling ran high, for this was the prelude to a restriction of civil liberties and more intensive taxation. Guerilla war broke out. Writing in the aftermath of the disastrous rebellion of A.D. 66-70, Josephus, who knew them well, was reluctant to say more about their foremost activists than was unavoidable. Judas of Gamala in Galilee had been their first leader. When Peter and his companions were before the council, Gamaliel advised moderation and cited the precedent of 'Judas of Galilee who in the days of the taxing drew away much people after him'.[61] 'Art thou that Egyptian,' Paul was asked after the temple riot, 'who leddest out into the wilderness four thousand men of the *sicarii*?'[62]

At least one disciple had been a Zealot, for they were known as Qanna'im and we find Simon the Canaanite of *Matthew* and *Mark* described in *Luke* as Simon Zelotes.[63] While the name of Iscariot has generally been thought to be derived from a place-name, it is plausibly suggested that it is derived from *sicarius*.[64] If so, it may be that disillusion with a master who failed to meet his expectations prompted the betrayal. Similar interpretations have been offered for the names of Simon Barjona and the sons of Zebedee, nicknamed Boanerges.[65] Part of this is misplaced ingenuity, but in a land of strong Zealot traditions it would only be natural if young men were attracted to a teacher who spoke of the coming of the Kingdom of God. They could not anticipate that it was to be different from their hopes; but even on the last journey south James and John still saw themselves as the foremost henchmen of a new King in Jerusalem,[66] and in Gethsemane at least one disciple carried a sword.[67]

Though it fails to get the publicity achieved by Eisler, periodically the thesis that Jesus saw himself as destined to establish a kingdom by violence is propounded on evidence of

this sort and suppression or evasion of evidence to the
contrary,[68] often with the assurance of Prince Monolulu at the
racecourse announcing, 'I gotta horse. I gotta horse.' Thus the
gentle anarchist of the Gospels is depicted as a predecessor of
Haganah, Irgun Zvai Leumi, and the Stern Gang, and an
advocate of the methods employed with extreme success by the
modern state of Israel, with total lack of success by the Palestine
Liberation Movement and, on a much larger scale, by all the
great powers of the modern world. Since others have done so
with such different results, let us now take a brief look at what
Jesus meant by the Kingdom of God.

Jesus, we read, came from Nazareth to John the Baptist and
then spent forty days in the wilderness; but so far as his hearers
were concerned there was no gradual introduction. Almost
overnight, it must have seemed, he laid down the carpenter's
tools, emerged from obscurity, and began to preach with
imperious authority. He did not hesitate to set his own
commands above the Law and the Prophets.[69] Matthew and
Luke had before them a collection of his sayings in which is
one unrecorded by Mark and unsurpassed in audacity by
anything in *St John*. 'All things are delivered unto me of my
Father; and no man knoweth the Son but the Father; neither
knoweth any man the Father, save the Son, and he to
whomsoever the Son will reveal him.'[70] 'The Son of Man', he
said,[71] 'hath power on earth to forgive sins.' 'By what authority
doest thou these things? And who gave thee this authority?'
demanded the outraged priests, and received in reply a question
which they could not answer.[72] It was evident to outsiders. 'I also
am a man under authority,' said the military man from
overseas,[73] 'and I say to this man, Go, and he goeth.'

For a long time it has been fairly common ground among New
Testament critics that *St John* is inferior to the Synoptic Gospels
as a historical source, but what they merely tell, *St John* actually
conveys. There is a tribute to this from an unexpected quarter in
the comment of a contemporary atheist from eastern Europe.[74]

> The later literary records of the Synoptic Gospels,
> with a few exceptions, have not managed to catch
> 'this personal magic'. . . . Yet it is clear that in reality
> it was not only Jesus' teaching which played an
> important role here, but also, no less notably, the

sheer pull of his overwhelming personality, a kind of
awe in those he met. . . . Wonder is a more common
theme in the independent tradition of John's Gospel
. . . for example in the truly emphatic confession:
'We beheld his glory, glory as of the only Son from
the Father. . . . Grace and truth came through Jesus
Christ.' This is an aspect of the personality of Jesus
which will never be fully clear to us in all its details.

Since Harnack's time there has also been a popular impression
that the message of Jesus was one of love to God and one's
neighbours. So it may be worth while to note the order of *St
Mark*. It deals, not so much with what Jesus said, as with what
he did. After the initial announcement of his preaching little
more is said in detail about it, apart from a chapter of parables
and an attack on the Pharisees. Instead we are told that his first
act was the calling of the disciples, the twelve patriarchs of a new
Israel and the nucleus of the people of the new Covenant. Then
come the miracles, the acts of power which even his enemies did
not deny. Midway through the Gospel comes Peter's confession
of Jesus as the Christ. Thereafter we are told more of the
content of the Lord's teaching, but it is now concerned with his
coming ordeal. Then comes the most detailed narrative, the
story of his last days and death, and the sudden ending as the
discovery of the resurrection strikes fear into the hearts of the
disciples. In other words, we are told of the preaching of the
Kingdom of God but, as in the Epistles, its meaning is seen in the
acts and person of Jesus.

Three words, meaning acts of power, wonders, and signs, are
used in the New Testament to describe miracles. Jesus intensely
disliked the publicity involved and rejected the temptation to
impress men; but for all who had eyes to see, his acts of power
were meant to be signs of the coming of the Kingdom. *St John*,
more formally planned than the other Gospels, is written round
seven great sayings on the mystery of Christ's person and seven
miracles, seven great signs of the Lord and his Kingdom. When
John the Baptist sent messengers from his prison cell they were
told, 'go and shew John again those things which ye do hear and
see: the blind receive their sight, and the lame walk, the lepers
are cleansed, and the deaf hear, the dead are raised up, and the
poor have the Gospel preached to them.'[75]

If the mighty works done in Chorazin and Bethsaida had been done in Tyre and Sidon they would have repented,[76] for the purpose of miracles was to awaken not wonder but repentance. In one sense the supreme miracle is Christ's resurrection; in another, his presence among men. All his acts are seen in the New Testament as signs of his victory over the powers of evil in a hostile world.

> If I with the finger of God cast out devils, no doubt the Kingdom of God is come upon you. When a strong man armed keepeth his palace, his goods are in peace; but when a stronger than he shall come upon him, he taketh from him all his armour wherein he trusted, and divideth his spoils.[77]

This sense of conflict is often found in the Gospels. 'I am come to cast fire on the earth,' says Jesus[78] in a cryptic saying,

> 'and what will I, if it be already kindled? . . . Suppose ye that I am come to give peace on earth? I tell you, Nay; but rather division.'

And again,

> Think not that I am come to send peace on earth: I came not to send peace but a sword. For I am come to set a man at variance against his father, and the daughter against her mother, and the daughter-in-law against her mother-in-law. And a man's foes shall be they of his own household. He that loveth father or mother more than me is not worthy of me, and he that loveth son or daughter more than me is not worthy of me. And he that taketh not his cross, and followeth after me, is not worthy of me. He that findeth his life shall lose it; and he that loseth his life for my sake shall find it.[79]

Those who read the story of Lazarus were meant to understand that Jesus was put to death because he demonstrated not merely in word but in action his claim to be the Resurrection and the Life. He was crucified, not because he preached the love of God and the brotherhood of man, but because word and act declared him to be the promised Christ, the Lord of the Kingdom[80] which had now come. However crudely it may at

times have been expressed, the understanding of Christ's death
in the Fathers was in terms of conflict and victory.[81] They saw his
life not so much as one of teaching, but of effective action in a
hostile world. And what he did had changed the world. As Marx
said with reference to Feuerbach, 'The philosophers have only
interpreted the world; the point, however, is to change it.'

We seek in vain for a simple and detailed reconstruction of the
teaching of Jesus; this is not, as is so often suggested, because of
the lack of materials or because of their fragmentary character
or the media through which they have come down to us, but
because his words are so seminal, so many-sided, cryptic and
disturbing. His sayings on the Kingdom of God are anything but
simple; but those which declare that it has now come are explicit
and unequivocal, the most characteristic and distinctive of the
Gospel sayings, and without parallel in Jewish teaching or
prayers of the period. If therefore we are seeking the *differentia*
of his teaching on the Kingdom of God we must find the answer
here.[82] When he preached in his home town he quoted Isaiah on
the hope of Israel. 'This day', Christ said,[83] 'is this Scripture
fulfilled in your ears.' His hearers understood him better than
some modern scholars and so they tried to murder him.

When the prophets of the Old Testament had looked for the
Kingdom of God they had seen it as one that was yet to come in
judgement and vindication whereas 'the New Testament asserts
on every page that this which was spoken by the prophets has
happened.'[84] It is impossible to eradicate from the Gospels the
demands of the Kingdom on men as a present reality with which
they are confronted, but simultaneously the Kingdom has a
future reference, a consummation when the hidden reality of
Jesus as the Son of Man will be seen by all when he comes in
judgement.[85] Jesus was haunted by the vision of the future and
his own role in the impending events, but the Kingdom as he saw
it was not simply a paradise to come, despite its future element.
It was a present demand.

Prophecy and apocalyptic both had a place in Jewish
tradition. Prophecy, whatever its language, was directed to the
present situation and its understanding in the light of God;
apocalyptic, on the other hand, was a fantastic vision of
judgement. One was a call to repentance, the other an assurance
of ultimate divine vindication. Prophecy, long unknown, had
reappeared in John the Baptist, but apocalyptic literature was

current and enjoyed a vogue, and the New Testament contains a Christian example in *Revelation*. Elements of apocalyptic are found in the Gospels.[86] In 1892 Johannes Weiss argued that Jesus saw the Kingdom in terms of a coming cataclysmic act of God which could not come until the guilt of his people had been taken away by his own death, and a developed version got striking publicity from Schweitzer in 1906; but Schweitzer was more successful in destroying current interpretations than in establishing his own.

A phrase in the Lord's Prayer reminds us that Christ prayed that the Kingdom might come; yet nowhere is there the unequivocal saying, 'The Kingdom of God will come', to balance the many which speak of it as present.[87] At a point in his ministry Jesus began to tell his disciples that rejection and death awaited him.[88] Nor were they to expect anything better. 'If they have called the master of the house Beelzebub, how much more shall they call them of his household?'[89] With this warning of hostility go forecasts of disaster for Jerusalem and predictions of the end of the age, and coming of Christ in glory, and the final judgement; but never is it said that the Kingdom of God will also come at a later date. In one sense God's Kingdom would not be fully manifest until the end of the age, but basically it had come with Christ. It was announced in the words of Jesus, seen in his person and acts, and his formation of a new community. Throughout this involved a complete reversal of the expectation of his people.

Christ's Church is not the preserve of the scholars but of the downtrodden of the earth. Scribes and Pharisees do not get a good press in the New Testament. When Levi was called he invited his own kind of people — a great company of publicans, says St Luke — to a meal with Jesus. 'Why do ye eat and drink with publicans and sinners?' asked the Scribes and Pharisees, and Jesus replied, 'They that are whole need not a physician; but they that are sick. I came, not to call the righteous, but sinners to repentance.'[90]

No doubt Levi was no better and no worse than the rest of the disciples. It was left to later ages to describe them as saints. 'The publicans and the harlots,' said Jesus when challenged in the temple by the priests, 'go into the Kingdom before you.'[91] His choice of followers is described in the parables of the lost sheep, the lost coin and the lost son, and no doubt there is a picture of the Church in the parable of the supper to which the invited guests failed to come and the servant was told, 'Go out quickly into the streets and lanes of the city, and bring hither the poor, and the maimed, and the halt, and the blind.'[92]

It is the community of forgiveness and reconciliation. John the Baptist had demanded repentance, but Jesus declared forgiveness. 'Son,' he said[93] to the paralysed man, 'thy sins be forgiven thee.' And in reply to the murmurs he said, 'That ye may know that the Son of Man hath power on earth to forgive sins ... I say unto thee, Arise, and take up thy bed, and go thy way to thy house.' In return his followers were to forgive one another. Peter was to forgive his brother 'not seven times, but seventy times seven'.[94] 'If ye forgive men their trespasses,' we are told, 'your heavenly Father will also forgive you.'[95] Justice, which the greatest of the Greeks had reckoned essential in any commonwealth, which the Old Testament prophets had demanded from man, and Job from God, got scant treatment from Jesus. However long they served, no labourer in the vineyard got more than the others. 'So the last shall be first, and the first last; for many be called, but few chosen.'[96] Instead the way of Jesus is one of grace and love.

When asked for the most important commandment Jesus cited none of the ten, but the commands that men should love God and their neighbour.[97] He commended humility both by word and example.[98] Like the Essenes, his disciples provided nothing for their journeys; but the Essenes went armed against robbers while Jesus was as indifferent to security as to property.[99] It was easier for a camel to go through a needle's eye than for a rich man to enter the Kingdom of God.[100] Others had said, 'An eye for an eye, and a tooth for a tooth', but he disclaimed violence and retaliation and counselled the turning of the other cheek.[101] When a Samaritan village refused hospitality James and John wished to command fire to consume it in the spirit of an Old Testament prophet, but were told, 'Ye know not what manner of spirit ye are of. For the Son of Man is not come to destroy men's lives but to save them.' And they went to another village.[102]

Those whom the world counted unfortunate, the poor in spirit, the mourners and the meek, he counted blessed; the pure in heart would see God; the peacemakers would be called the children of God; and those who were persecuted for righteousness'

sake would enter the Kingdom.[103] When asked about the tribute
money, Jesus gave a crushing reply, but no direct answer. This
has not prevented the widespread assumption that he meant,
'Yes, you should pay.' But in hundreds of his sayings there is no
ambiguity. In the Kingdom of God as he proclaimed it there
was no place for the state or its methods.

This is the way of the Lord Jesus, and if the Kingdom of God
is his message we have here something at least of its content for
men; forgiveness, grace and love from God to man and from
man to his brothers; a new community ruled by love and not by
power, indifferent to property and repudiating violence, with
standards far transcending law and justice. All this is to be seen
in any truly Christian family and much of it in the traditional
Jewish family where the Covenant made with Abraham has not
been forgotten. Otherwise, where else is it to be found outside of
the Church of Christ? It is in the Church alone that the new life
is found. No outsider understands the Church but only those
who have known this life from within. It is clear that in the New
Testament the Kingdom of God and the Church of Christ are
essentially related, and that the question of the relationship
between them is not one that has to be imported into the New
Testament.[104] 'Four main theories have been held concerning the
relation of the Church to the Kingdom of God', William Temple
wrote.[105] He listed first what he called the Roman theory, that
the Church *is* the Kingdom, and added, 'Most if not all of what
seems to non-Romans the errors of Rome are intimately
associated with the this stark identification, which gives to an
historical and in part earthly institution a claim to absolute
obedience.'

Since Constantine, eccentrics like the Anabaptists and
Jehovah's Witnesses have identified the Kingdom of God with
the divine society in a sectarian sense, and the kingdoms of this
world with its enemies. Undoubtedly the message of the
Kingdom of God is not exhausted in the empirical Church even
though she is the body of Christ but, especially in a century
when the scope and power of the state have grown monstrously
as never before, it should be asked whether the failure to see,
first, the Kingdom of God in the people of God, the Church,
and second, the state as its enemy, may not be in practice a
greater error. Can it be — setting aside their sectarianism — that
the heretics have not been far wrong? 'They expected the

Kingdom of God,' says Machoveč of the first generation of Christians, 'and the Church came.'[106] But the Church is not the denial, as the writer supposed, but the fulfilment — at this stage — of the hope. She is the earthly face of the Kingdom of God.

However striking the transformation made in the divine society by the coming of Christ, it cannot be divorced from its roots in time gone by. Before written record there were those who, no matter how limited their faith and obedience, were drawn to God. None of his twelve disciples, as Origen noted, can fully have understood Christ; and among their number was one who denied him, and one who betrayed him. It is a paradox that this element of betrayal existed from the start among the people of God and has never been absent from the Church. Princes of the Church — for whom it should be remembered, the New Testament makes no provision — have conducted persecution and religious wars, and condoned slavery and riches in the midst of poverty; and the most bitter opponents of the Church have been, like Samuel Butler, sons of clerical families which bore the name of Christ but ignored his way; yet despite this, the Church has never ceased to be the household of faith. In the same way, Israel, called to be the people of God, preferred to be a state, a society based on power and upheld by violence. That is why she wants to hold on to the Gaza strip and the west bank of Jordan today. Yet it was as the people of God that she survived after she ceased to be a kingdom.

In Old Testament times two Hebrew words were used to describe the people of God. Although with time they came to be used fairly indiscriminately, originally one referred to the people of Israel, whether met together in one place or not, and the other referred to an actual meeting. After the exile this second word came to be used almost exclusively of the divine society, as Israel became increasingly conscious of her true calling, not as a state, but as the people of God. It was used to distinguish her from the heathen peoples. When the *Septuagint*, the Greek version of the Old Testament, was translated those who first worked on it used the Greek word synagogue for both Hebrew words, but later reserved it for the former, while they translated the latter by *ecclesia*, a word which Christians were to appropriate to describe themselves, the *ecclesia* or Church of God. So closely connected are these two words, synagogue and church, but which soon came to be contrasted.[107]

By adopting this word Christians asserted that it was their own community, and not those who had rejected their Lord, which had continuity with those whom God had called to be his people in time past. But they also applied the word, as we do the word *Church* today, not only to the whole community of Christians but to particular congregations. In doing so they gave the word two associations which cannot be explained by its Old Testament background.[108] Those who formed it had been called by God to be saints, men brought into a new relationship with God. Secondly, when the name was applied to Christians in one place its corporate sense was not lost but transferred, for the local congregation was part of a unity in which each part represented and, in fact, was the unity of the whole. Christ was fully present in each. In *Ephesians* each congregation is seen as the body of Christ and a sanctuary of God; but it is not suggested that the one universal Church is a federation of local Churches. It was not that they were grouped into a whole, for it was not congregations but individual believers who composed the universal Church. All members of local congregations were within that Church, but their relationship with it was direct and not mediated.[109] Did Christian salvation mean only the release of the individual soul from sin and death? Or did it mean salvation for the people of God of whom the convert was now a living part, a member of the body of Christ? Always the early Church took the second for granted, and here it differed essentially from the propaganda of contemporary mystery religions.[110] A believer found his place at once in a congregation which was the local manifestation of the divine society. Church organisation arose from the awareness that the universal Church was the primary reality.[111] 'We do not know,' says Harnack, to whom this was as uncongenial as it was unavoidable, 'how this remarkable conviction arose, but it lies perfectly plain upon the surface of the apostolic and post-apostolic ages.'[112]

Only twice do we find an explicit reference to the *ecclesia*, the Church, by this name in the Gospels. Modern individualism has seized on this fact to conclude that Jesus never meant to set up a Church. Against this we must place the history of the people of God in the Old Testament which is the background to all he said and did, and the fact that the Church is the outcome, not of his words, but of his life. Repeatedly he spoke of the new people of God in terms of community; as the sheep of his flock, the throng of wedding guests, the multitude of fishes gathered in the net, or the city set on a hill whose light cannot be hid. Their community is the better substitute for the home and family which his disciples must forsake, and the household of God the Father. Those who hear his word are his mother, his sisters and brothers, and it is in the fellowship of the table that the family of God is seen in anticipation of the meal of salvation at the consummation of all things.[113] In the New Testament there are no isolated Christians outside of the Church.

Immediately after the parable of the shepherd who left the ninety and nine to search for the sheep that was lost, comes the less familiar of the two references to the Church (*ecclesia*) by name in the Gospels. Jesus spoke of how any follower of his must deal with an alienated brother. Firstly, he must reason with him privately, then in the company of two or three brethren and, if that fails, he must lay the dispute before the *ecclesia*.[114] When this was first spoken, one may assume, this meant the local Jewish community, but it soon lay open to a purely Christian interpretation.

Far more notice has been given to the other reference, partly because of its place in arguments about the papacy, and partly because if the concept of the divine society is forgotten it becomes necessary to dispose of this saying.[115] According to *St Matthew* when Peter confessed that Jesus was the Christ, he replied,

> Blessed art thou, Simon Bar-Jona, for flesh and blood has not revealed it unto you, but my Father which is in heaven. ... Thou art Peter, and on his rock I will build my Church, and the gates of hell shall not prevail against it. I will give unto thee the keys of the Kingdom of Heaven, and whatsoever thou shalt bind on earth shall be bound in heaven.[116]

In its time the older Israel had been the people of God; now, having been confessed as the Son of God, Jesus was to build the divine society anew on the man whose faith first showed him as called by God to that task. When Christ had risen the task was begun at Pentecost when the apostles were the primitive *ecclesia,* the living rock on which a far larger and ever growing *ecclesia* was to be built as each new convert was added.[117] Later controversy diverted attention away from the fact that it was to the Church rather than an individual that Christ committed the keys of the Kingdom. This saying in which our Lord names the new or Christian *ecclesia* marks at once its continuity with the older Israel and its newness as his own community.[118] It marks its intimate relationship with the Kingdom of God of which it is the visible sacramental and witnessing organ.[119]

Whatever happened to the Kingdom of God? Certainly, it was not forgotten in the first century. We are told at the opening of *Acts* that the risen Christ spoke with his apostles 'of the things pertaining to the Kingdom of God', and in the last chapter we are briefly told that this was also the message of Paul during his last time at Rome.[120] Otherwise, in *Acts* and the *Epistles* the phrase is found little more than incidentally. For the most part, as in the Gospels, it is spoken of as a present reality[121] but, as on the lips of Jesus, it also has a future reference.

> 'Then cometh the end,' says St Paul, 'when he shall have delivered up the Kingdom to God, even his Father; when he shall have put down all rule and all authority and power. For he must reign, till he hath put all enemies under his feet. The last enemy that shall be destroyed is death.'[122]

When compared with the Synoptic Gospels, *St John* reflects this changed atmosphere in the scarcity of references to the Kingdom. Why did the generation of Christians who left it on record that the Gospel of the Kingdom of God was the burden of the preaching of Jesus, almost cease to speak of it themselves? Was it not because his death and resurrection placed all his words in a new setting and because they found themselves within the new community of grace and love which was ruled by their risen Lord through his Holy Spirit? They experienced the Kingdom in their common life in the Church, the earthly face of the Kingdom until its fulness should come.

Jesus had never separated himself from God's people, Israel, and neither, at first, did the apostles. They were distinguished by their faith, their preaching of Jesus as Lord, the admission of converts by baptism, and their eucharistic fellowship. It should also be noted that their first collective act after the Ascension was to perpetuate the apostolic ministry by the appointment of one to fill the place of that disciple who had defected from their ranks.[123] Otherwise, what marked them out was a communal way of life in explicit obedience to the commands of Jesus.

> All that believed were together, and had all things
> common: and sold their possessions and goods, and
> parted them to all men, as every man had need.

> Neither was there any among them that lacked; for as
> many as were possessed of lands or houses sold them,
> and brought the prices of the things that were sold,
> and laid them down at the apostles' feet; and
> distribution was made unto every man according as
> he had need.[124]

After all, it was merely a continuation of the practice of Jesus
and his disciples, an instance of the principle enunciated by
Bakunin in 1870 and Marx in 1875, 'From each according to his
ability, to each according to his needs.' One immediate failure to
act sincerely, recorded in *Acts* 5:1-11, does not detract from the
fact that the Church set out to observe this primitive
communism which is still taken for granted within the Christian
home, though disregarded by Christian society at large.

However real the continuity between the older Israel and the
young Church, the rejection, first of Jesus in his earthly life, and
then of the risen and ascended Lord, made a breach between the
two inevitable. There was an uneasy interval, an uncertain calm
before the storm until hostility exploded. Peter and his
companions did not dissociate themselves from the temple
worship any more than did Jesus; and Paul, who had a clear
view of the new situation, many years later spent his last
moments of liberty in the temple courts paying his vow in the
traditional manner.[125] But more than tradition was involved;
Israel was the people of the Covenant and the direction of
Christian evangelism, to the Jew first and only later to the
Gentile, was inherent in the nature of the Church.[126] 'The God of
Abraham, and of Isaac, and of Jacob, the God of our fathers,'
said Peter,

> 'hath glorified his son Jesus: whom ye delivered up,
> and denied him in the presence of Pilate, when he
> was determined to let him go. But ye denied the holy
> one and the just, and desired a murderer to be
> granted unto you; and killed the prince of life, whom
> God hath raised from the dead; whereof ye are
> witnesses.'

But he went on to say,

> 'Ye are the children of the prophets, and of the
> covenant which God made with our fathers, saying
> unto Abraham, And in thy seed shall all the kindreds
> of the earth be blessed. Unto you first God, having
> raised up his Son Jesus, sent him to bless you, in
> turning away every one of you from his iniquities.'[127]

Loyalty to tradition combined with tentative efforts to express a
strong but ill-defined faith in Christ marks this as an accurate
account of the preaching of the young Church in its first days. In
the four or five years between the resurrection and the first
missionary work in Samaria Christian doctrine took shape.[128]

As the faith was clarified there came the parting from the
older Israel, but it took a little time for each to assess the other,
and the first victim of their antagonism was Stephen. It has been
surmised that he was a Hellenist and also, with less reason, that
he was a Samaritan,[129] but possibly the most that can be said is
that he was acquainted with Jewish circles where a less traditional
understanding of Israel's history was found. One of the seven
deacons but not associated with their distinctive work, Stephen
was active as an evangelist and controversialist. His speech
before his death is an account of the destiny of Israel which
develops into a bitter polemic against a nation which has
consistently resisted God in the cultus of the temple and the
rejection, first of the prophets and, ultimately, of Jesus.[130]
Resentment against him, therefore, was on purely religious
grounds and without the political nuance found in the charges
against Jesus. It would seem that Stephen saw the Law not
merely in terms of precepts to be obeyed but of God's unfailing
purpose for Israel;[131] that he did not draw a sharp antithesis, as
did Paul, between Law and Grace, and, understandably, that he
had not to face the question of the obligations of the Law for
Gentile converts. *Hebrews*, while regarding the temple as
superseded, saw in it a foreshadowing of those good things
which had come in Christ. Paul had seen the Christian
community displacing the great building at Jerusalem as the
place of God's presence among men, and the theological
significance of the older sacrificial system may have evaporated
for him, but he did not categorically repudiate the temple and its
cult.[132] Stephen, on the other hand, showed active hostility. Yet

circumcision was still for him a symbol of membership among
God's people.[133] This was a dispute in a circle which was still
Jewish, and it ended in a lynching without any of the show of
legalism at the death of Jesus.[134]

Yet it marks the parting of the ways. Aware of the significance
of Stephen's death for the world mission of the church, the
writer of *Acts* noted how those who stoned Stephen 'laid down
their clothes at a young man's feet, whose name was Saul',[135] but
after a few verses he went on at more length to tell of Philip, the
only deacon other than Stephen of whom anything is told.

In the case of Stephen hostility had been directed, not against
the older apostles, but against that new and radical element in
the leadership of the Church which was drawn from the
Hellenists. When they were driven from Jerusalem Philip found
safety among the Samaritans, a people who, like Stephen, had
rejected the temple.[136] Long-standing enmity separated the Jews
and the Samaritans. But when the Samaritans believed Philip's
gospel, Peter and John were sent down from Jerusalem to
support him in his work.[137] So the first act of persecution led
to Christian preaching, for the first time, beyond the bounds of
Israel.

A further stage came when Peter, whose priority among the
apostles was always evident, not merely baptised a Gentile
convert but broke the conventions of his people by sitting down
to eat with him.[138] This was the beginning of the end of the rigid
distinction between Jew and Gentile. Christ, in the words of
Ephesians, 'had broken down the middle wall of partition'.[139]
Further preaching among Gentiles is probably implied in the
statement that Christians now travelled to Antioch, the coastal
cities of Syria and Cyprus,[140] and there may be more than
coincidence in the fact that only now do we hear of persecution
of an apostle as distinct from interrogation.[141]

Relations between the Christian Church and the Synagogue
have seldom been creditable and often shameful, but an essential
kinship exits between the two such as neither admits with the
ethnic religions; and the breach between them, primitive and
persistent, is part of the mystery and tragedy of the Church. Too
little sympathy has been given to early believers who wished to
be Christians and yet remain sons of Israel. Bitter hostility is
reflected in the phrase, 'the synagogue of Satan'.[142] Paul
remembered that it was Jews 'who both killed the Lord Jesus,

and their own prophets, and have persecuted us',[143] but he could never escape from his own Jewish roots. Circumcision was an embarrassment to some Jews of the time and there were young men who endeavoured to have the traces removed so that they could participate naked, as was the custom, in the games. To the modern reader it seems a meaningless and ridiculous rite, but Paul's constant references tell that it had been the distinguishing mark of the people of God[144] and that the ending of it was a problem.

When Paul and Barnabas reported to the Church at Antioch on their missionary travels in Syria, Cyprus and Asia Minor, 'certain men which came down from Judaea' insisted that Gentile converts must be circumcised. After long argument Paul and Barnabas went up to Jerusalem about A.D. 49 to resume the debate among the leaders of the Church. At the close James, the brother of Jesus, who by now was presiding in the Church at Jerusalem, declared a compromise solution. Gentile converts did not need to be circumcised, but all were to 'abstain from pollutions of idols, and from fornication, and from things strangled, and from blood'.[145] Men long accustomed to the Mosaic Law found it hard, at first, to distinguish between its moral and its sanitary requirements.

According to Paul's own account[146] the decision had not been reached as easily as might be supposed from the pages of *Acts*. In his own case the parting from the ancient ways of his people had been the outcome of drastic examination of the content of the Gospel and the problems of his own inner life. Before his conversion, to use his own words, as an earnest Pharisee he had 'followed after the law of righteousness', but had not attained it because he 'sought it not by faith'.[147] His people's rejection of their Redeemer gave him deep sorrow. 'Brethren,' he wrote, 'my heart's desire and prayer to God for Israel is, that they might be saved, for I bear them record that they have a zeal of God, but not according to knowledge.' 'Hath God cast away his people?' he asked, and replied, 'God forbid. God hath not cast away his people which he foreknew.'[148] As the failure of Israel to accept Christ had ensured that the Gospel would go beyond its bounds into the wider world and not be confined to one nation, would not the fruit of Israel's conversion when, in God's good time, that came, bring all the greater fruit?

This relationship between the Church and the older Israel may be seen in three respects: community, Scripture, and faith; in each there are elements of continuity and separation. Awareness of it was always present in the minds of the New Testament writers.[149] 'All our fathers', St Paul wrote to a largely Gentile congregation at Corinth, 'were under the cloud and all passed through the sea; and did all eat the same spiritual meat; and did all drink the same spiritual drink; for they drank of that Rock that followed them; and that Rock was Christ.'[150] In other words, his Gentile converts had entered into the inheritance of Israel's long history. In particular, Christians identified the Church with 'the remnant',[151] that faithful minority of which the prophets spoke, which was to remain true to Israel's God when the rest of the nation became apostate and which, in time, was to inherit the promises. It was this identification which infuriated Stephen's judges.[152] So when second century opponents, who valued antiquity as twentieth century ones value modernity, condemned the Church as being of recent origin, the charge was consistently rejected. Hermas personified the Church as a very aged woman.[153] 'The Bible and the apostles', says a Christian sermon of about A.D. 150, 'say that the Church is not limited to the present, but existed from the beginning.'[154] A century later Origen wrote that, 'the Church existed in all the saints who have been from the beginning of time'.[155] But while the older Israel had been a national community, the Church knew from the start that she was to be Catholic and to gather all nations. Yet at the start the early Church was entirely Jewish; for a long period it was Jews and Jewish proselytes who formed the majority of her people, and only with time did Gentiles outnumber them.

A second element in this relationship is the Scripture. Part of the Church's inheritance from Israel was the Old Testament; yet she not merely added the New Testament, but placed a radically new interpretation upon the Old. Every time traditional Jews heard the Scriptures in the Synagogue, said St Paul, a veil lay over the mind of the hearers, not to be taken away until they should turn to Christ.[156] Allegorical interpretation had been developed by the rabbis,[157] especially in Alexandria, but more was involved here, for a Christian meaning was seen in the explicit words of the Old Testament. This comprehensive reinterpretation was attributed to Christ himself, for he had said that the traditional and superficial understanding of the Old Testament was inadequate.[158] It is characteristic that St Luke

tells how on the road to Emmaus the risen Christ showed how
his death and resurrection had been foretold by 'Moses and the
prophets'.[159] In the fragments of apostolic preaching in *Acts*, in
St Paul's arguments, in the elaborate system of thought and
allegory in *Hebrews*, and in the constant citation of the Old
Testament by *St Matthew*, there is the recurring assertion that
the Gospel is 'according to the Scriptures', and that Christ
himself had taught so. As St Paul[160] bluntly observed, the early
Christians were not intellectually distinguished and such a
startling and comprehensively new interpretation of so familiar
and sacrosanct a book must indeed have been the work of no
common mind. So thorough was this that the Old Testament
from the start took its place beside the apostolic witness as a
norm of Christian teaching. Consequently the Old Testament
was read in Christian worship, as in the synagogue, until the
Epistles and Gospels could be added to it. So conveniently did
the Greek text of the Old Testament, the *Septuagint*,[161] lend itself
to a Christian understanding, and so thoroughly was it annexed
by Christians, that early in the second century a fresh translation
was made, for Jews who could not read Hebrew, by Aquila of
Pontus who is said, on rather unreliable evidence, to have been a
kinsman of the Emperor Hadrian, and a Jewish convert to the
Christian faith who returned to Judaism. It has been surmised
that the *Epistle of Barnabas*, attributed to the companion of St
Paul, a work which forcefully repeats the thesis of Stephen, was
produced in reply to this new translation.[162]

The third element is the Church's inheritance of the faith of
Israel. The religions of the ancient world were syncretistic; they
were tolerant of each other, hospitable to new divinities, and
ready to assimilate. But Israel's faith was essentially intolerant
and uncompromising. Two great cultures — those of Egypt and
Mesopotamia — had been influential in the lands where Jews
had been immigrants, and it might have been expected that the
weaker nation would have been prepared to assimilate the beliefs
and cults of the two greater ones. Hebrew thought did not do so:

> On the contrary, it held out with a peculiar
> stubbornness and insolence against the wisdom of
> Israel's neighbours. It is possible to detect the
> reflection of Egyptian and Mesopotamian beliefs in
> many episodes of the Old Testament; but the

overwhelming impression left by that document is one, not of derivation, but of originality.[163]

Israel's intolerance of the ethnic religions was inherited by the Church, as may be seen in the irritation and exasperation of Paul at Athens 'when he saw the city wholly given to idolatry'.

Behind this lay the long history in which God had dealt with Israel as with no other nation and thus had made himself known in a way to which the history of no other nation offered even a remote analogy. Religion in the Orient, Greece and Rome was explicitly mythological, but Israel saw God revealed in her history. There was no suggestion that he had not worked in the history of other nations, but in no other had these events been associated with a consistent religious interpretation. 'He showeth his word unto Jacob, his statutes and judgments unto Israel. He hath not done so with any nation; and as for his judgments, they have not known them. Praise ye the Lord.'[164] This understanding — which is a unique phenomenon in world history — was essentially communal, whatever part individuals might have in it, and it was the work of a long succession of prophets whose testimony to God's purpose, rather than the events themselves, was the vehicle of revelation.[165]

Two words in the New Testament are translated as *religion*. One refers to the cultus of the temple and the other might also be translated as *superstition*. Neither is particularly respectful. When found in the New Testament they are used, as in *James*, by way of contrast or, as with St Paul, as a disparaging term for the Judaism he had abandoned.[166] Not till the time of Constantine did Christians use the word *religion* to describe the Christian faith as well as the heathen religions.

Israel's faith centred on the unity and holiness of God who dealt with men in judgement, mercy and grace. First among the great events which formed it was the call of Abraham and the covenant of promise made with him. Second in time, though scarcely in importance, came the exodus. God had brought his people out of slavery in Egypt, had given them his Law at Sinai, and renewed the covenant. Disasters such as the fall of Jerusalem and the exile in Babylon had not destroyed Israel's identity as they had those of other nations. Instead they had deepened its faith with an understanding of apparent tragedy not unrelated to the Christian faith in the Lord who had died for

men. Israel's faith was not so much concerned with the past as
with the hope that in Abraham all nations would be blessed. The
apostolic message was that this had now come to pass. 'I stand
and am judged for the hope of the promise of God made unto
our fathers,' said Paul before Agrippa, and to the Jews at Rome
he said, 'For the hope of Israel I am bound with this chain.'[167]
The fulfilment of Israel's hope was that God had given his Son.

Accordingly it was to the people of Israel that the apostles
first looked for converts. They failed to gain Palestine and so
failed to gain the Jews further to the east; yet they did not look
entirely in vain. After all, the first circle of Christians was
completely Jewish and continued so for some time, but the Jews
formed a larger proportion of the population of the empire than
the size of Palestine would suggest and most were in the
diaspora, the Jews scattered in other lands.[168] Wherever Paul
went in towns of any size he seems to have found a synagogue.
Possibly there were about 8,000,000 Jews in the time of Christ.
Of these about 1,000,000 were in Egypt, 1,500,000 in Syria and
Asia Minor combined, and 100,000 each in Italy and Cyrenaica.
These figures cannot be pressed too far. Estimates of their share
in the population of the empire run between 6 per cent and 9 per
cent, but in the eastern provinces they must have comprised
almost a fifth of the population.[169] Most were poor, none were
outstanding in the empire, but presumably they shared their
national proclivity to get on in the world. Apart from this, their
distinctive religion drew attention and many Gentile adherents.
Christian Jews ceased to be members of the synagogue and were
merged in the Christian congregation without distinction. Thus
the general assumption[170] that only a tiny minority of Jews
became Christian lacks evidence and is probably an overstatement.
If there were 120 Christians in Jerusalem at Pentecost there must
have been others elsewhere in Palestine; and that day reputedly
3,000 more were baptised.[171] Frequent conversions followed,
particularly in the *diaspora*. If the list of Peter's hearers at
Pentecost is rhetorical, in that the lands of their origin are
related to the twelve signs of the Zodiac,[172] it states in reasonable
order the dispersed settlements of the Jews. Firstly it names four
provinces of Asia Minor and two of North Africa, and then a
still further community scattered abroad. In Persia and
Mesopotamia the Jews were long established, and from them the
Jews of Asia Minor derived.[173]

But whether east or west of the iron curtain which separated the two empires, the Jews of the dispersion, while loyal to the faith and and law of Israel, had also been subject to the continual pressure of the Hellenistic thought and culture around them. Distance from the temple made the sacrificial system increasingly irrelevant for the Jew in a Gentile environment. He had been accustomed, perhaps for generations, to the synagogue and there his religion centred. On the other hand, Jewish monotheism and ethics drew enquiries from thoughtful pagans.[174] Proselytes were made. If the Jews alienated some by exclusiveness and customs such as circumcision, they had also attracted a wide fringe of enquirers. Time and again, when Paul preached in a synagogue and had to withdraw, it was these enquirers who followed him to listen and be baptised. So Jewish was the early Church that at first Romans in authority regarded riots between Jews and Christians as no more than disputes between Jewish sects.[175] At Jerusalem the local Church continued Jewish in membership and leadership until Hadrian banished all Jews from the city in A.D. 135.[176]

Here as elsewhere Christ brought not peace but a sword. We have seen the widening of the breach in the martyrdom of Stephen, the admission by Peter of a Gentile convert, the debates on circumcision and the law, and the understanding of Christ's sacrifice. As Jewish hostility increased, Christian converts received ill treatment[177] which was to be repaid a thousandfold in after years.

All the prophecies, the apostles taught, had been fulfilled and a new age inaugurated by the coming of Christ, who had been born of the seed of David, had died according to the Scriptures, had risen, and was now exalted at the right hand of God as Son of God and Lord of the living and of the dead, and would come again as Judge and Saviour of men.[178] His coming had set the law and the prophets in a secondary place, as when at the Transfiguration a voice was heard saying, 'This is my beloved Son', and Moses and Elijah were seen no more.[179] This, with the doctrine of the Holy Spirit, was the content of the *kerygma*, the Christian message for the outsider as distinct from the *didache* or teaching within the Church, and from it the Apostles' Creed still betrays its descent by its form and language.[180] Early Christians preached Christ's resurrection as witnesses;[181] they declared that he was Lord of all; and they appealed to the presence and work of the Holy Spirit in the company of believers, seen at times in abnormal phenomena but more profoundly in the intimate fellowship of worship and the sharing of resources in a free, joyful and enthusiastic fellowship.[182] To use a phrase familiar in worship but seldom understood, this was the communion of the Holy Spirit, the bond of unity. It was the new power in life and in death which the world saw in changed men that carried conviction.

Thus Church and Synagogue went different ways, for not all had responded to the good news. Where the Synagogue gave central place to the Law, the Church did likewise to the grace of the Lord Christ; where the one was national the other was catholic or universal; where the one had circumcision and the Passover the other had baptism and the Eucharist; and where the one had the Sabbath the other had the Lord's Day, the weekly anniversary of Christ's resurrection. What made this separation, in one sense, permanent, was the increasing definition of Christian doctrine, the growth of the Church in Gentile lands, and the Jewish rebellion of A.D. 66 which ended with the disasters of A.D. 70.

Relations between Jews and Romans, originally friendly, had deteriorated in the time of Christ and it needed no prophet but simply a political observer to make the forecast found in *St Mark* 13, if not in such dramatic form. There would be a rebellion; it would fail; and it would end in a massive investment of Jerusalem for a lengthy siege. Probably it was in A.D. 26 when Pilate, whose household troops were being moved up from Caesarea to their winter quarters in Jerusalem, flouted Jewish scruples on images by ordering his men, as was usual elsewhere, to bring their standards into the holy city. Such was the uproar that he withdrew his orders. Later he provoked a second disturbance by applying the temple revenues to the construction of an aqueduct.[183] These were more than stray incidents. They uncovered the latent tension between a fanatical population and a government which might not always be willing to accommodate itself to native prejudice. In addition, the Jews were widely disliked by the peoples of the empire. At Alexandria, where there was a considerable Jewish minority, the first serious pogrom of Roman times broke out in A.D. 38. Jewish premises were looted, members of the Jewish council were publicly flogged, their wives forced to eat pork, and their synagogues desecrated by statues of the emperor. This occasioned the embassy of Philo, Judaism's most distinguished contemporary spokesman, to that unsavoury character, the Emperor Caligula.[184] Meantime the governor of Syria had ordered the preparation of a statue of the emperor for erection in the temple itself, and it was only the death of Caligula in January A.D. 41 which prevented fulfilment of his orders and the violence which inevitably would have ensued.[185] Under Nero, says Josephus, 'Jewish affairs grew daily worse and worse, for the country was again filled with robbers and a gang of impostors who seduced the multitude.'[186]

When Paul returned to Palestine from his last missionary voyage, Antoninus Felix had been governor since about A.D. 52.[187] Throughout his term of office he had experienced continual trouble from the resistance and had he really credited the charge that Paul was 'a mover of sedition among all the Jews throughout the world',[188] he would have dealt with the case more decisively. But Felix had a Jewish wife, Drusilla, the sister of Agrippa who reigned over a client state in the north of Palestine and, if a verse in *Acts*[189] is to be taken at face value, he also had at least some superficial information on the nature of Christian teaching. His wife was brought to the hearing, probably to give him informed and unbiased opinion on Jewish religious disputes, and when her husband was satisfied that the charge had no political content he suspended proceedings and, to avoid irritating the Jews, left it in abeyance for his successor to settle.

After Paul had been in custody for two years Porcius Festus, the new governor, arrived to find the Jewish authorities impatient for an immediate decision. As the newcomer still had much to learn about Jewish troubles he invited Agrippa and his sister Berenice, when they arrived to pay their compliments, to listen to Paul. They confirmed the opinion of Felix and agreed that the case could have been dismissed if the accused had not already removed it from the jurisdiction of the provincial court by appealing to Caesar.[190] Festus had come to a province seething with rebellion.

> Judaea happened then to be infested with robbers, who pillaged and laid in ashes all the towns they entered. And it was now, that those named *sicarii*, a sort of robber, increased to a very great number;

these persons used small swords, not much different
from the Persian *Acinax, Sicae* among the Romans;
and from hence was given this name to these robbers,
who committed a great deal of havoc and bloodshed,
for they came on solemn days, and blending
themselves among the multitude of people, which
assembled from all parts of the city on account of
religion, they killed whom they thought fit.[191]

These were the Zealots. Felix and Festus saw that Paul was
not associated with them, but did not understand that the
Christian equally stood for an alternative society.

With the removal of Paul from Palestine, hostility next struck
at James, the brother of our Lord. When Peter escaped from
prison it was to James that he asked that the news should first
go. We are told of Peter that 'he departed, and went into
another place.'[192] Until now the Church at Jerusalem had been
under the leadership of Peter and John, but from now on we
find James as head of the community, and for this there is no
clear explanation. At the great debate on circumcision it was he
who presided and gave the decision. When Paul returned from
his last missionary voyage in A.D. 58 it was to James that he
reported. James welcomed him with some reservations and
required him to make a public demonstration of his respect for
the Law by taking, like himself, a Nazarite vow. While so
doing, Paul became the unwilling centre of the riot which led to
his arrest.[193]

At the earlier meeting he had placed James first among the
three 'pillars' of the Church,[194] but it transpires, though Luke
did not choose to say so in *Acts*, that James was a conservative
prepared to demand the observance of the Law by Christian
Jews. Some light is shed on his character by the *Epistle of
James*, the authenticity of which seems obvious except to those
who question everything in the New Testament. It is a poor
man's edition of the Sermon on the Mount, with only a mention
of Christ to mark it as other than Jewish, so mediocre that it is
hard to see how it would have been preserved if it had not come
from some person of note.[195] It has no theology. Paul and its
author were not always in agreement. James had persuaded
Peter and others to cease sharing meals and, presumably, the
Eucharist with Gentiles, and it needed strong argument to

convince Peter that the new principles of the Church were more vital than kindly concessions to Jewish scruples.[196]

Antioch, the scene of this argument, already had a Church fully conscious of being a part of the people of God, mindful to keep in touch with the Church at Jerusalem but not content to be ruled by it, Gentile in background and indifferent to the Law as Paul himself was not. Significantly, it was here that the members of the Church were so distinct from the Jews that the word *Christian* was coined.[197]

Festus died[198] in office in A.D. 62, and in the interval before a successor arrived from Rome, Agrippa took it on himself to remove the High Priest and replace him by Ananus, a man of strong character. Until this time action against the Christians had been comparatively restrained, but James and some other unnamed Christians were now seized.

All we know of James suggests that he owed his position, not to ability or any clear grasp of Christian doctrine like that of Paul, but to the fact that he was a brother to Jesus and had been given a vision of the risen Lord. He was an austere man, much respected, a vegetarian and a teetotaller, whose sanctity was made evident by the fact that he never took a bath. Apparently he was so conservative and loyal to Jewish tradition that, if forced to make a choice, he would stand by his Jewish heritage. He had never ceased to worship in the temple. At Passover time he was made to stand on the parapet and called on to tell the truth about Jesus.

'Tell us,' they said, 'what is meant by "the door of Jesus"?'

To their surprise he gave a decisively Christian answer like that of Stephen.

'Why do you question me about the Son of Man? I tell you, he is sitting in heaven at the right hand of the Great Power, and he will come on the clouds of heaven.' Some voices in the crowd cried out in support of him, but the mob threw him from the parapet and stoned him until a fuller of clothes killed him by beating him on the head with the club used in his trade. A stone nearby marked the spot with his name,[199] and in the time of Constantine the Church in Jerusalem treasured the episcopal chair in which he was reputed to have sat.[200] Some time later, for the historian on whom we depend is more sure of events than of dates in this time of crisis, the apostles met with the family of Jesus and elected as his successor Symeon, the son of that

Cleopas who met with our Lord on the road to Emmaus.[201] He was a cousin to Jesus, and for the time being, it would seem, something like a caliphate was possible in the bishopric of Jerusalem and the kinsmen of Jesus.

Long foreseen, the great rebellion broke out in A.D. 66. Relations between the Jews and the Church of the circumcised Jewish Christians in Jerusalem had long been bad, but the climax of the revolt placed an intolerable strain upon them. As the Roman army moved up to the walls of Jerusalem the Church in the city[202] had sufficient emotional detachment to anticipate the outcome, to leave before the siege began, and to settle in a body in a town called Pella to the east of Jordan. Numbers cannot have been large. Far from having much in common with the Zealots whose cause had now been accepted by the nation, Christians had repudiated violence and confidence in any regime established by it. Theirs was the community which recorded the Sermon on the Mount as the standard for living.

It is a Marxist commonplace[203] that it was the socio-economic situation of the Roman Empire, in Palestine and elsewhere, the fate of the peasants and the collapse of the risings from the Spartacists to the Jews of 66 and 134, which created the need for 'salvation' on which the Christian ideology took shape. Religion became a substitute for action, 'the opium of the people'. So for a modern Marxist a fundamental objection to the early Church is the pacifism, reconciliation and disengagement from contemporary conflict for which it stood. But it was not left to the nineteenth century to discover this. It was better, said the Church, to suffer injustice than to contribute to it. Christians placed no hope in a regime secured by bloodshed, hatred and bitterness, but saw the Kingdom of God in the way of the cross, forgiveness and love.

They did not fail to note that it was the week of Christ's passion when the Roman legions finally closed the ring around the doomed city. Josephus tells how, as the siege drew to its climax, the roofs could be seen to be covered with bodies of dead women and children for whom no burial place could be found. Old men lay dead in the streets and the young had not the strength to bury them.[204] Many fled in despair and were captured by the Romans who crucified upwards of 500 daily in sight of the walls.[205] Innumerable corpses were thrown into the gullies beneath the walls.

> Titus, by chance, was walking round the walls, and
> came to see the valleys filled with the dead bodies,
> and a deep flood of gore, with innumerable carcases
> floating in it; he fetched a vast sigh at the miserable
> spectacle and, with uplifted hands, called the most
> high God to witness that the deed did not belong to
> him.[206]

After the fall of the city the soldiers grew weary of slaughter, as farm cats get tired of killing mice when old stacks are burned. Survivors were herded into the temple enclosure. Zealots who had taken part in terrorism were executed; those under the age of seventeen were sold, while the best-looking over that age were sent to Rome for the triumphal procession of Titus, and the rest to hard labour in Egypt or to serve as victims in the arenas of provincial cities. According to Tacitus 600,000 died in the siege;[207] according to Josephus 1,100,000.[208] It is unlikely that anyone knew exactly. Whatever the total, the numbers were vast and the disaster unparalleled until Dachau, Belsen and Auschwitz. Not till the spring of A.D. 73 were the last fires of rebellion finally extinguished by the fall of the grim fortress of Masada in the wilderness of Judaea.[209] Grief and terror must have reigned in every Jewish heart from the eastern frontier of the Persian empire to the western shores of the Roman. Judaism had presented Rome with her most obstinate problem, but an even more formidable successor was at hand.

Otherwise, the fall of the city and the ending of the temple sacrifices did not mean as much as might have been expected, for in the *diaspora* the synagogue and the Law controlled Jewish life. But Jewish Christians must have reconsidered their position when they saw that the charge that 'Jesus of Nazareth shall destroy this place'[210] was literally true. Few facts of history are more remarkable than the absolute rejection given first to Christ, and then to the Church, by all but a fraction of his own nation, the original people of God. Probably the fall of Jerusalem only increased the concentration of the Church on the mission to the Gentiles. 'Get thee out of thy country, and from thy kindred, and from thy father's house, and I will make of thee a great nation.'[211] God's words to Abraham might have been addressed to the Church at this moment of parting.

No disjunction so drastic could be quite clear cut, and a

natural reluctance to abandon the Law and customs of the Old Testament survived among some groups of Jewish Christians. Without spokesmen of note and settled in remote places, Christians who strove to maintain their Jewish practices seemed, to the few Christian writers aware of them, to be curious anomalies. Some were regarded as orthodox Christians who, inconsistently, observed the Sabbath, circumcision and other Jewish customs, but others known as Ebionites[212] regarded Jesus as no more than the last and greatest of the prophets.

'They regarded him,' says Eusebius,

> 'as plain and ordinary, a man esteemed as righteous
> through growth of character and nothing more, the
> child of a normal union between a man and Mary;
> and they held that they must observe every detail of
> the Law — by faith in Christ alone, and a life built
> upon that faith, they would never win salvation.'[213]

Eusebius listed a second group which, like the Church as a whole, acknowledged the Virgin Birth, but did not hold the divinity of Christ. They emphasised the Law, dismissed the epistles of St Paul as the work of a renegade, and used 'the Gospel according to the Hebrews' alone.[214] Yet they also celebrated the Eucharist on the Lord's Day. Associated with them was Cerinthus, an eccentric of whom it was told that when St John in his old age met him in a bath house he left and said, 'Let us get out of here, for fear the place falls in, now that Cerinthus, the enemy of the truth, is inside.'[215] Also associated with them was Nicholaus who was blamed, perhaps unjustly, for loose views on sex and whose followers were pilloried in *Revelation* as Nicolaitans.[216]

In the half century after the fall of Jerusalem, Jewish risings in Egypt, Cyrene and Cyprus continued. Two events precipitated another among the Jews still found in Palestine. Hadrian[217] prohibited circumcision throughout the empire and he determined to rebuild Jerusalem, which had lain waste since the siege. It was to be known as Aelia Capitolina and on the summit of the temple rock was to be a temple of Zeus. Probably his humane mind never dreamed of what this meant for fanatical Jews. A sudden revolt under Bar Kochba took the Roman garrison by surprise. For a short time Bar Kochba was master of Judaea and coins were minted with messianic inscriptions. This

time the Jews, like the Vietcong, relied on guerilla tactics, but
Mao Tse-tung's assurance of the inevitable success of guerilla
wars against civilized powers did not prove true in this case. By
A.D. 135 they had been flushed out of their last stronghold and
all was lost. Over 500,000 were said to have died in the fighting
and, says Dio Cassius, 'All Judaea was almost a wilderness.' It
ceased to be a Jewish country. Jerusalem was rebuilt as Aelia
Capitolina and no Jews were permitted in it under pain of death.
From now on they were 'aliens in a heathen world'.

'And to Jerusalem, thy city,' said the Jewish prayer book for
centuries,

> 'return in mercy, and dwell therein, As thou hast
> spoken; rebuild it soon in our days as an everlasting
> building, and speedily set up therein the throne of
> David. ... Let our eyes behold thy return in mercy to
> Zion.'

Almost nineteen centuries were to pass until in the Six Days'
War the Israeli troops reached the Wailing Wall and their
chaplain drew out the ram's horn and sounded it once again
above the gunfire in the city of David.

Meantime the Church took little interest in Jewish Christians
who had not been absorbed in its greater fellowship. Ignatius,
writing late in the first decade of the second century, wrote, 'If
we live according to Judaism we confess that we have not
received grace.'[218] Apparently those whom Justin Martyr knew
half a century later were orthodox on the main points of the
faith. He saw no harm in their observance of the Jewish Law,
provided they did not seek to impose it on other Christians.[219]
Irenaeus, who came from Smyrna in Asia Minor to Lyons in
Gaul, had less chance of knowing them directly than Justin, who
had been born in Palestine. Writing a few years later he called
them Ebionites, and knew that some of them denied the Virgin
Birth, used only *St Matthew*, and would have nothing to do with
St Paul.[220]

Always few in number, if some held opinions condemned in
the Church at large, it is probable that most of them should be
seen, not as sectarians or heretics but sometimes as Christians
who refused to part from old customs, and sometimes as Jews
with a deep reverence for Jesus.[221]

The Church was to destroy the Greek and Roman religions so

completely that they have never since been living alternatives to the Christian faith, but Judaism, the matrix of the Church, survived in full vitality and has ever since maintained its separate being from Moscow to Johannesburg, a living witness to the fact that the children of Abraham are still within the covenant. Often shamefully and brutally treated both by the Church and by secular society, the Jews have been forced by the odds of a harshly discriminating environment to exert themselves; often, as in modern Israel, in the sweat of their brow, and often, as in western countries, by intellectual ability. Out of this has come great success in many fields. Their capacity for making fortunes has been equalled only by their generosity. They have advanced the cause of civilization far beyond what their numbers might warrant, as is to be seen in their pre-eminent share of Nobel Prizes. While many, like Marx and Freud, have abandoned the faith of Israel, they have not been able to deprive themselves of the heritage of their race. Their suffering and achievements as a people are those of the Suffering Servant of Isaiah. They are a minority which has refused to conform, witnesses to the truth, however unfashionable, that there is a righteous and compassionate God who revealed himself in their history and who will raise them and all men above their despairs.

Notes to Chapter 1

1. J.B. Bury, *History of the Later Roman Empire*, I, p.466n.
2. G. Ogg, *Chronology of the Public Ministry of Jesus,* pp.244-277.
3. *ibid.* p.281. M. Grant, *The Jews in the Roman World,* p.107.
4. Josephus, *The Jewish War,* II, v.
5. O. Cullmann, *Christ and Time,* pp.17-19.
6. Ignatius, *Romans,* III. *Philadelphians,* VI. *Magnesians,* X.
7. Sir Leonard Woolley, *Abraham,* pp.250-255.
8. M. Machoveč, *A Marxist Looks at Jesus,* pp.57-60. Confirmation from an atheist.
9. Ignatius, *Romans,* III.
10. *Barnabas,* XIII, XIV. *cf.* O. Cullmann, *Christ and Time,* pp.132-134.
11. St Thomas Aquinas, *Theological Texts,* ed. T. Gilbey, p.340.
12. *Second Helvetic Confession*, XVII.
13. *St Luke* 13:29.
14. *St Matthew* 15:21-28.
15. R.H. Lightfoot, *The Gospel Message of St Mark,* pp.63-67.
16. C.H. Dodd, *The Parables of the Kingdom,* p.48.
17. Pascal, *Pensées,* II, 162. R.G. Collingwood, *The Idea of History,* p.149.
18. *Ezra* 10:2. *Numbers* 14:9.
19. *I Samuel* 8.
20. *Jeremiah* 34-38.
21. W.O.E. Oesterley, *A History of Israel,* II, pp.51-59.
22. *II Kings* 17:34.
23. E. Bevan, *Jerusalem Under the High-Priests,* pp.14ff. *St John* 4:20.
24. Oesterley, *History of Israel,* II, p.72.
25. E. Schürer, *History of the Jewish People in the Age of Jesus Christ,* 1, p.142.
26. H. Lietzmann, *History of the Early Church,* I, pp.75-87.
27. M. Grant, *The Jews etc.,* pp.23-25.
    S. Sandmel, *The First Christian Century in Judaism and Christianity,* pp.14-23.
    R. McL. Wilson, *The Gnostic Problem*, pp.5-9.
28. *Daniel* 11:31. Schürer, I, p.155.

29. *I Maccabees* 14:4-11.
30. Josephus, *Against Apion,* II, xvii-xxiv.
31. Bevan, p.8. Wilson, p.14.
32. Schürer, I, p.146.
33. *cf.* M. Grant, *The Jews etc.* p.20. Cullmann, *The State in the New Testament,* p.9.
34. Bevan, pp.124-126. H. Maccoby, *Revolution in Judaea,* p.9.
35. T.H. Gaster, *Scriptures of the Dead Sea Sect,* pp.258ff.
36. M. Burrows, *The Dead Sea Scrolls,* pp.355, 361.
    Gaster, pp.15, 67, 310.
    W.D. Davies, *Christian Origins and Judaism,* pp.114ff.
37. *Acts* 1:6.
38. *St Luke* 1:32ff.
39. *St Matthew* 2:2.
40. *St Luke* 1:51-53.
41. C.H. Dodd, *The Founder of Christianity,* p.93.
42. *St Mark* 12:35-37. J. Jeremias, *New Testament Theology,* I, p.259.
43. *St John* 7:4ff.
44. Cullmann, *The Early Church,* p.120.
45. Dodd, *Parables,* pp.29ff.
46. A.N. Sherwin-White, *Roman Society and Roman Law in the New Testament,* pp.29-32. *St Luke* 23:7-15.
47. Sherwin-White, pp.191ff.
48. *St Mark* 14:61-64.
49. *St John* 11:49-51.
50. Lietzmann, I, p.60.
51. Sherwin-White, pp.36ff., 46.
52. Jeremias, *NT Theology,* p.78.
53. W.G. Kümmel, *The Theology of the New Testament,* p.72. Cullmann, *The State in NT,* pp.41-49.
54. J. Blinzler, *The Trial of Jesus,* p.7.
55. Machoveč, p.217.
56. Eisler, *op.cit.* p.393.
57. *ibid.* p.375.
58. *ibid.* p.380.
59. Cullmann, *The State in NT,* pp.10-23.
60. G. Kittell, *Theological Dictionary of the New Testament,* vol. 7, pp.278-82.
61. *Acts* 5:37.
62. *Acts* 21:38.
63. *St Matthew* 10:4. *St Mark* 3:18. *St Luke* 6:15.
    S.G.F. Brandon, *The Fall of Jerusalem and the Christian Church,* pp.104ff.
64. Maccoby, p.172.

65. *ibid.* pp.172, 301.
66. *St Mark* 10:35-44.
67. *St Mark* 14:47.
68. S.G.F. Brandon, *The Trial of Jesus of Nazareth,* pp.140-150.
69. *St Matthew* 5:17, 21-24.
70. *St Matthew* 11:27. *St Luke* 11:22.
71. *St Mark* 2:10.
72. *St Matthew* 21:23-27.
73. *St Luke* 7:8.
74. Machoveč, pp.79ff.
75. *St Matthew* 11:4-5.
76. *St Matthew* 11:21.
77. *St Luke* 11:20-22.
78. *St Luke* 12:49-51.
79. *St Matthew* 10:34-39.
80. W. Manson, *Jesus the Messiah,* p.39.
81. Gustav Aulen, *Christus Victor,* pp.35-51.
82. Dodd, *Parables,* p.40. R.H. Lightfoot, *St Mark,* p.31.
83. *St Luke* 4:21.
84. J.S. Whale, *Christian Doctrine,* p.67.
85. Kümmel, p.183. Cullmann, *State in NT,* pp.87ff.
86. *St Matthew* 24. *St Mark* 13. *St Luke* 21.
87. Dodd, *Parables,* p.43.
88. *St Mark* 8:27-38.
89. *St Matthew* 10:25.
90. *St Luke* 5:27-32.
91. *St Matthew* 21:31.
92. *St Luke* 14:15-21. Jeremias, *NT Theology,* I, pp.176-178.
93. *St Mark* 2:1-11.
94. *St Matthew* 18:22.
95. *St Matthew* 6:14.
96. *St Matthew* 20:16.
97. *St Mark* 12:28-34.
98. *St John* 13:1-15.
99. Josephus, *Against Apion,* II, viii. *St Matthew* 10:9ff.
100. *St Luke* 18:25.
101. *St Matthew* 5:38-42.
102. *St Luke* 9:51-56.
103. *St Matthew* 5:1-12.
104. Cullmann, *Early Church,* p.108.
105. W. Temple, *Citizen and Churchman,* p.55.
106. Machoveč, p.194.
107. F.J.A. Hort, *The Christian Ecclesia,* pp.3-7.
108. Sir E. Hoskyns and N. Davey, *The Riddle of the New Testament,* pp.24ff.

109. Hort, p.168.
110. A.D. Nock, *Conversion*, pp.114-119.
111. R. Bultmann, *NT Theology*, I, p.93.
112. A. Harnack, *The Mission and Expansion of Christianity*, I, p.432.
113. Jeremias, *NT Theology*, pp.167-170.
114. *St Matthew* 18:15-17.
115. Kümmell, pp.38, 129ff.
116. *St Matthew* 16:16-19.
117. Hort, p.17.
118. Hort, p.226. T.M. Lindsay, *Church and Ministry in the Early Centuries*, p.5.
119. C.T. McIntyre, *God, History, and Historians*, p.36. *cf.* St Augustine, *De Vera Religione*, VI, iii.
120. *Acts* 1:3; 28:23.
121. *I Corinthians* 15:24.
122. *Romans* 14:17. *I Corinthians* 4:20. *Colossians* 4:11.
123. *Acts* 1:15-26.
124. *Acts* 2:43ff.; 4:32-35.
125. *Acts* 21:26.
126. *Romans* 2:10.
127. *Acts* 3:13-26.
128. Robinson, p.85.
129. M.H. Scharlemann, *Stephen: A Singular Saint*, pp.17-22.
130. *Acts* 7.
131. Scharlemann, pp.117-133.
132. Scharlemann, p.123.
133. *Acts* 7:51.
134. M. Grant, *The Jews etc.*, pp.115ff.
135. *Acts* 7:58.
136. Cullmann, *Early Church*, pp.185-192.
137. *Acts* 8:14.
138. *Acts* 10:11-18.
139. *Ephesians* 2:14.
140. *Acts* 11:19-30.
141. *Acts* 12:1-19. Harnack, I, p.48.
142. *Revelation* 3:9.
143. *I Thessalonians* 2:15.
144. *Colossians* 2:11. *Ephesians* 2:11-22.
145. *Acts* 15:20.
146. *Galatians* 2:1-21.
147. *Romans* 9:31ff.
148. *Romans* 10:1; 11:1-2.
149. A. Richardson, *An Introduction to the Theology of the New Testament*, pp.266-281.

G.A.F. Knight, *A Christian Theology of the Old Testament,* pp.335ff.
150. *I Corinthians* 10:1-4.
151. *Romans* 9:27. *Isaiah* 10:22.
152. *Acts* 7:22-54.
153. Hermas, *The Shepherd,* II, iv.
154. II Clement. J. Quasten, *Patrology,* I, pp.53-58.
155. Origen, *Commentary on Canticles.* H. Bettenson, *Early Christian Fathers,* p.339.
156. *II Corinthians* 3:14-18.
157. R.P.C. Hanson, *Allegory and Event,* pp.34-36.
158. *St Matthew* 22:29-33.
159. *St Luke* 24:27.
160. *I Corinthians* 1:26.
161. Tertullian, *Apology,* XVIII.
162. M. Grant, *The Jews etc.,* p.244.
163. H. and H.A. Frankfort, *Before Philosophy,* p.241.
164. *Psalms* 147:19-20.
165. A. Richardson, *Christian Apologetics,* p.140.
166. *James* 1:27. *Acts* 26:5. *Galatians* 1:13.
167. *Acts* 26:6; 28:20.
168. Harnack, I, p.8.
169. M. Grant, *The Jews etc.,* p.60.
170. K.S. Latourette, *A History of the Expansion of Christianity,* I, pp.74, 83.
171. *Acts* 1:51; 2:41. *I Corinthians* 15:6.
172. S. Benko and J.J. O'Rourke, *Early Church History,* p.15.
173. R.H. Pfeiffer, *History of New Testament Times,* pp.166-196.
174. Harnack, I, pp.9-18.
175. Suetonius, *Claudius,* XXV, iv.
176. Eusebius, *Ecclesiastical History,* IV, v.
177. Harnack, I, pp.57ff.
178. Dodd, *The Apostolic Preaching and its Development,* p.28.
179. *ibid.* p.113.
180. *ibid.* p.176.
181. Harnack was very cagey in acknowledging this. Harnack, I, pp.43ff.
182. Dodd, *Apostolic Preaching,* pp.134-139.
    Richardson, *Introduction,* pp.109-111.
183. Josephus, *Antiquities,* XVIII, iii.
184. M. Grant, *The Jews etc.,* pp.128-132.
185. Josephus, *Antiquities,* XVIII, viii. *Jewish War,* II, x.
186. Josephus, *Antiquities,* XX, viii.
187. Tacitus, *Annals,* XII, liv.
188. *Acts* 24:5.

189. *Acts* 24:22.
190. *Acts* 26:32.
191. Josephus, *Antiquities*, XX, viii.
192. *Acts* 12:17.
193. *Acts* 21:17-40.
194. *Galatians* 2:12.
195. Robinson, pp.118-139.
196. *Acts* 11:2-18. *Galatians* 2:12-16.
197. Harnack, I, p.54.
198. Josephus, *Antiquities*, XX, ix.
199. Eusebius, *Ecclesiastical History*, III, xxiii.
200. *ibid.* VII, xix.
201. *ibid.* III, xi. *St John* 19:25. *St Luke* 24:18.
202. Eusebius, *Ecclesiastical History*, III, v.
203. A. Kalthoff, *The Rise of Christianity*, pp.33-58.
     K. Kautsky, *Foundations of Christianity*, pp.258, 264ff.,
     323-325.
204. Josephus, *The Jewish War*, VI, xii.
205. *ibid.* V, xi.
206. *ibid.* V, xii.
207. Tacitus, *History*, V, xiii.
208. Josephus, *The Jewish War*, VI, ix.
209. *ibid.* VII, vi.
210. *Acts* 6:14.
211. *Genesis* 12:1.
212. The word *Ebion* means poor.
213. Eusebius, *Ecclesiastical History*, III, xxvii.
214. *cf.* M.R. James, *The Apocryphal New Testament*, pp.1-7.
215. Eusebius, *Ecclesiastical History*, III, xxviii.
216. *ibid.* III, xxix. *Revelation* 2:6, 15.
217. Oesterley, *History of Israel*, II, pp.459-463.
     Spartianus, *Hadrian*, XIV.
218. Ignatius, *Magnesians*, viii.
219. Justin Martyr, *Trypho*, XXXVII, i.
220. Irenaeus, *Against Heresies*, III, xi, 7.
221. B.J. Kidd, *A History of the Church to 461*, I, p.96.
     L. Duchesne, *Early History of the Christian Church*, I, pp.85-96.

Chapter 2

Lord Christ and Lord Caesar

2

Jesus died at the hands of the Roman military. Rome had begun as a cluster of iron age forts on the little hills above the marshy banks of the Tiber, near enough to reach the sea and yet beyond the reach of seaborne raiders. First by alliances and victories she attained supremacy in Italy, then in the most desperate struggle of her history she wrested control of the western Mediterranean from the North African city of Carthage, and in the two centuries before Christ she occupied those lands around the eastern Mediterranean which had been part of Alexander's conquests. Unlike Alexander, Rome did not go on to conquer Persia and reach the frontiers of India, a fact of great importance for the future spread of the Christian Church. Except for some outlying acquisitions such as Britain in the west, Dacia beyond the Danube in what is now Rumania, and parts of Mesopotamia, her domains had reached the natural limits of an empire in the Mediterranean regions; and here, for the most part, they halted.

From early republican days the city had inherited a constitution in which the powers of the magistrates and of the senate were balanced. Theoretically a democracy, in practice it had become, like Athens in its great days, an oligarchy. All her administrators, statemen and soldiers of ability were members of the senate and capable of being assembled at short notice. For a time this provided the senate with a marked ascendancy, but as great armies were raised to subdue the Levant and as the booty of the conquered lands flowed in, the oligarchy proved unable to breast the rising tide of war and internal tensions. From 167 B.C. onwards there were signs that the consent of the working class and the loyalty of the great magistrates and commanders were failing. While the conquest of new lands enriched the nobles and the commercial classes the peasant farmers were approaching despair. Few of them recovered from the devastation caused by Hannibal's marches through Italy, and as

European farmers were hit in the late nineteenth century by wheat from North America and frozen meat from Australia, New Zealand and the Argentine, so the small Italian farmers could not compete with the flow of cheap cereals from North Africa. When the ship bringing Paul and his guard to Rome was wrecked on Malta, it was not merely because of ill weather but because the cargo of wheat in the open hold had shifted. Small scale farming ceased to pay while great estates, worked by slave labour, continued to prosper. Peasants drifted into Rome to swell the ranks of an urban proletariat largely maintained by the bounty of the state and entertained by the free shows of the arena. 'We must go hence,' says the dispossessed peasant in Virgil,

> 'some to the thirsty Africans, and some must come to Scythia and the swift Oaxes in Crete, and to the Britons, utterly parted from the world. Shall I ever again, long years hence, see my country's bounds, and my poor cottage with its thatched roof? Shall I ever again delighted see this patch of corn, once my kingdom? Will a godless soldier own these well tilled fields, a barbarian these crops? See to what civil war has brought our wretched citizens!'[1]

Their fields and vineyards might go waste, but more often were swallowed up in great estates. None of this was evident to provincials who saw only the efficiency and ruthlessness of Roman administration. After a century of civil war when ambitious magnates exploited the discontent of the lower classes, Julius Caesar emerged as sole ruler four years after he crossed the Rubicon in 49 B.C. He had laid the foundations of a new pattern of government. 'The republic,' he said, 'was only a name, without form or reality.'[2] When he died a comet shone in the sky for seven nights and so popular superstition confirmed the decree of the state.[3]

Augustus retained the formalities of the republic, but from 27 B.C. until his death in A.D. 14 he ruled the empire alone. Word of the most notable event of his reign never reached his ears. All was changing. 'Nothing remained of ancient manners, or ancient spirit,' said Tacitus.

> Of independence or the equal condition of Roman citizens, no trace was left. All ranks submitted to the

> will of the prince, little solicitous about the present
> hour; while Augustus, in the vigour of health,
> maintained at once his own dignity, the honour of his
> house, and the public tranquillity.[4]

When he died the administrative and military structure of the empire was so securely established that it could function without serious interruption under his brutal successor, Tiberius, whose reign began and ended with murder, and Caligula, of whom nothing good is said beyond the shameless flattery of the Jewish embassy under Philo.

Few hated the Romans as did the Jews. Provincials knew nothing of the scandals at Rome which fill the pages of Tacitus. Whatever their loss of liberty, there was every reason why they should respect the empire. No such thing as a colour bar existed, and prosperous provincials could move into the upper circles of Roman society with acceptance until some even reached the imperial throne. From Arabia to the North Sea the subjects of the empire saw the gifts and bounty of Rome in great cities, prosperous farmland, open roads, great trading ships upon the sea, peace, justice and order. Many of them had never had it so good.

Paul differed from most of his countrymen in having great respect for Roman authority, perhaps because he came from Tarsus and the *diaspora* and not from the homeland, and he had consistently good relations with officials on the strength of his Roman citizenship. When first converted and in some danger he was sent for safety to Caesarea, the normal centre of Roman administration where Jews were not admitted to citizenship of the town.[5] Early in his travels he had hopes of converting a Roman official in Cyprus.[6] When the Jews charged him at Corinth with disrespect for the Law, Gallio, a typical civil servant, fulfilled Paul's expectations by dismissing the case since religious matters were outside his remit.[7] At Philippi he stood on his dignity and received an apology of sorts from the magistrates for the misuse of a Roman citizen. Had he been a provincial like Jesus and the twelve he would have been flogged when arrested in the temple. 'With a great sum obtained I this freedom,' said the officer of the guard; Paul replied, 'But I was born free.'[8]

This is reflected in his letters. He told Timothy to pray 'for kings, and for all that are in authority',[9] and Titus to remind his converts 'to be subject to principalities and powers, to obey magistrates, to be ready to every good work.'[10] Elsewhere he speaks of 'the princes of this world' in a manner more in keeping with the rest of the New Testament for, he says, 'had they known it, they would not have crucified the Lord of glory'.[11] In the same letter he tells Christians that they are not to make use of the civil courts.[12] Part of this is no more than the requirement that Christians should be law-abiding, peaceful and dissociated from the violent elements in society; but more is involved. Writing to the Church in Rome which had more intimate knowledge of the imperial circle than any other, he gave the state a sanction not found elsewhere in the New Testament and without support in the words of Jesus:

> Let every soul be subject unto the higher powers.
>
> For there is no power but of God; the powers that be are ordained of God.[13]

No Old Testament prophet had given such unqualified approval to royal authority. At the end of his course Paul chose to appeal to Caesar in the confident expectation of impartial justice. 'Rulers,' he had written,

> 'are a terror not to good works, but to the evil. . . . Do that which is good, and thou shalt have praise of the same: for he is the minister of God to thee for good. But if thou do that which is evil, be afraid; for he beareth not the sword in vain; for he is the minister of God, a revenger to execute wrath upon him that doeth evil.'[14]

We are not told what those 'of Caesar's household' thought when they read this. Contrasting past legends with present realities Sallust wrote that the Roman state had once been a model of justice but had become intolerably brutal.[15] Paul had forgotten, but was to discover by experience, that 'government is at once the source of order and the root of injustice'.[16]

A well-known verse in *I Peter* suggests the same outlook: 'Honour all men. Love the brotherhood. Fear God. Honour the king.'[17] This is an echo of *Proverbs* 24:21, which is a caution against rebellion. All this is in keeping with the passive reaction of Christians to social and economic violence and injustice which infuriates political activists. His disciples had been told by

Jesus not to reply in kind. If they had no choice save to live under the existing social regime, they found no hope in rebelling just to replace it by another as fallible.[18] Servants — and this includes slaves — were to obey their masters and masters were to treat them humanely.[19] Injustice was inherent in secular society. Many years later Marx taught that so long as there was a state it would be the agent of class oppression and not the guardian of the weak and oppressed, a diagnosis confirmed today from East Germany to Vietnam. Roman justice proved no more reliable for Paul than for his Master. When he reached Rome he was not to be vindicated. 'I am now ready to be offered,' he wrote to Timothy in a very different key when he saw how the land lay,

> 'and the time of my departure is at hand. I have fought a good fight. I have finished my course. Henceforth there is laid up for me a crown of righteousness, which the Lord, the righteous Judge, shall give me at the day.'[20]

Paul had assessed Rome too highly. She owed her empire to military genius and discipline, and retained it by a capacity for law and administration. Yet there were weaknesses. Augustus recognised but could not remedy the loss of the ancient rigour of Roman morals. It does not seem to have occurred to Tacitus or Suetonius that the regime they despised would not always be tolerated by its subjects. Too much rested on the personality of the emperor. Neither Augustus nor any of his successors solved the constitutional problems of a state which lacked the machinery to resolve internal class conflicts or provide a legal alternative to incompetent despotism. Injustice permeated Roman life; her provinces were exploited for the benefit of the idle rich and the equally idle poor of the Roman slums. Labour can cripple modern society by strikes, but the ancient *lumpenproletarier* did not work at all.

> What he wanted was a share in the pleasures of the rich ... he wanted to plunder the rich, not to change the mode of production. The sufferings of the slaves in the mines and the plantations left him as cold as the sufferings of the packhorses.[21]

Rome's social system, weighed down by the decadent plutocrats depicted in the *Satyricon* of Petronius Arbiter, rested on slavery. Her economy had been shaped in an age of colonial expansion and was self-destructive. It must either expand or perish. Problems of logistics, the failure to draw a steady flow of recruits from the civilised provinces and the burden of maintaining armies on remote frontiers, meant that the empire could no longer expand, either in Britain or in Parthia. Not every stranger in Rome, looking at the aqueducts, the Colosseum, and the walls of Aurelian, realises that this enormous masonry was built by slave labour. Constant importation of luxuries from the East without sufficient alternative products to export created an insoluble deficiency in her balance of payments which could only be met by export of specie. This led to inflation. It was all quite modern. Industrious and saving elements in society were continually plundered and an ever-growing and rootless proletariat demanded to be placated with bread and circuses. In the absence of effective trade unions there were no strong pressure groups in industry to press their claims, but the military unfailingly disregarded the advice of John the Baptist that they should be content with their wages and had the means to enforce their demands.

Thus Gibbon's historic verdict[22] that the fall of the empire was the triumph of religion and barbarism is an appropriate comment from a complacent age which did not know that the French Revolution was about to come upon it. No man concerned with the well-being of the Roman state could afford this blindness, for Rome always lived in the memory of past revolts and the fear of new ones. Her government was therefore intensely suspicious of any association which might form a nucleus of revolt. Oddly enough, Rome experienced no social revolution. Such revolutions as she knew were palace ones in which one autocrat was replaced by another. Yet it was in this light that she saw the Church almost as soon as she became aware of her existence, and not altogether incorrectly. When the end came classical society was destroyed by 'the victories of the moribund society's own external and internal proletariats'.[23]

Apart from the brief glory of the Augustan age Roman achievements in literature were limited. Her culture depended on the legacy of Greece in arts, science and speculative thought, and in none of these did she show any marked advance. Roman religion, like Greek, was unrelated to morals, at least so far as the temples were concerned, and there the flint knives used at the sacrifices told of their primitive character. With the advance of scepticism this worship became largely a matter of the state, though the conviction that the service of the gods had been rewarded by the greatness of the Roman state was lapsing into the opinion that proper religious observances inclined the superstitious working class to accept the social order.[24]

Into the vacuum thus created came the mystery religions with their lurid rites offering immortality to their initiates. Popular they undoubtedly were, but their importance may well have been exaggerated in modern times, for the Christian Apologists pay scant attention to them. They do not seem to have been regarded as enemies worth their powder and shot. Mithraism, the best known of them, produced no literature worth the name because it had no intellectual content. It was explicitly mythical and had no historical basis. It gained initiates but never converts. It neither invited persecution nor produced martyrs. Nobody in his senses would propose to become a Mithraist today. Despite what has been written at times it is to be compared, not with the Church, but with the Elks or the Masons, a male society with some conventional ideals and a colourful ritual to brighten drab lives. From time to time Renan's dictum that Mithraism was the great rival to the Christian Church is repeated at second or third hand, but a sounder judgement is that of A.D. Nock, who can never be charged with viewing the subject too much through Christian eyes. 'It is wholly unhistorical,' he said,

> 'to compare Christianity and Mithraism as Renan did, and to suggest that if Christianity had died Mithraism might have conquered the world. It might and would have won plenty of adherents, but it could not have founded a holy Mithraic Church throughout the world. A man used Mithraism, but he did not belong to it body and soul; if he did, that was a matter of special attachment and not an inevitable concomitant prescribed by authority.'[25]

These mystery religions had entered the Roman world from the east much as Hindu gurus have penetrated the western world today. As for more conventional cults, from the *Lares* and *Penates,* the small gods of the household altar, to Jupiter, father of gods and men, the traditional deities of the classical world were dismissed with contempt by Christians. To find a parallel to this among classical writers one must go to Lucretius who, despite acceptance of their existence, is certain that they have no effect on the world in which we live. 'Look at the things you call gods,' says the *Epistle to Diognetus,*[26] 'Here is a wooden one, rotting away; and here is a silver one that needs a guard to protect it from theft.' Consequently Christians were popularly regarded as atheists.

Tertullian,[27] a forceful writer from the militant Church in North Africa, repudiated the charge and then went over to the attack with sardonic abuse of the idols. Pagan gods, he says, get their heads nailed on or fixed with glue. Christians are sent down the mines but ore for the heathen gods is brought up from them. Household gods get pawned when cash runs short. Battered ones are recast as frying pans. They are put up for auction in the salerooms or taken on tour round the pubs to raise funds.

Arguments of this sort have been disparaged on the grounds that the heathen knew perfectly well that the idols merely portrayed, and were not to be identified with, the divinities, but probably the Apologists found that the ordinary devotee made little distinction. When occasion arose, they knew and could deal with the subtler view of the educated pagan.

It is not quite correct to say that the Christians denied the existence of the pagan gods. Belief in demons was widespread throughout the world of the first century and was not challenged by the Church.[28] Not merely cases of epilepsy and mental derangement were ascribed to demonic agency, but many other kinds of phenomena, and it was in this way that the Church regarded the pagan gods. 'We do not honour with sacrifices and floral garlands the objects that men have fashioned,' wrote Justin Martyr,

> 'set up in temples, and called gods. We know that they are lifeless and dead and do not represent the form of God — for we do not think of God as having the kind of form which some claim that they imitate to be honoured — but rather exhibit the names and shapes of the evil demons who have manifested themselves to men.'[29]

'The demons which haunt matter,' Athenagoras wrote,

> 'eager for the smell and blood of sacrifices, and ready to lead men astray, avail themselves of these

capacities for fantasy in the souls of the multitude.
Occupying their minds, they pour visions into them,
making it seem as if these came from idols and
statues.'[30]

'All the gods of the nations are demons,' wrote Origen[31] as he
argued with Celsus, and Augustine returns to the same theme. It
had great practical importance for all Christians of the time.

Conversion meant, among other things, that the new believer
was delivered from the power of evil spirits, and exorcism was
an important element in baptism. 'It was as exorcists,' says
Harnack,

'that Christians went out into the great world, and
exorcism formed one very powerful method of their
mission and propaganda. It was a question not
simply of exorcising and vanquishing the demons
that dwelt in individuals, but also of purifying all
public life from them. . . . Nor was this mere theory;
it was a most vital conception of existence.'[32]

When Celsus and Origen debated, the argument was one
between two men, one pagan and the other Christian, on the
highest level of contemporary culture. Celsus recognised the
effectiveness of Christians but ascribed it to incantations and the
invocation of demons. Origen retorted that it was done by the
name of Jesus. He had in mind more than the recitation of the
names of power as used in pagan exorcism, for he speaks of the
recounting 'of the narratives which relate to Jesus' and says
that, even when told by unbelievers, this has power.[33]

Christians had an overwhelming confidence in victory when
dealing with the pagan gods. In later times it was not the Bible
from which Christendom derived the popular image of Satan
with horns and hoofs, but Pan the goatfoot, the rustic god of
field and hill, worshipped by the most backward of the
countryside when the Church had displaced paganism in the
cities. When Gregory Thaumaturgos sheltered in a temple
during the storm he observed that the priests found themselves
hindered in their rites, and as he went out he left a note on the
altar saying, 'Satan, you may come back.'[34] Other Christians
fastened on the story in Plutarch of the crew of the ship passing
a volcanic island and hearing the despairing cry, 'Great Pan is

dead.'[35] This story lies behind the lines, now seldom understood, in Milton's *Ode on the Morning of Christ's Nativity*: 'The Oracles are dumb; No voice or hideous hum Runs through the archèd roof in words deceiving.'

But it took the Roman world some time to learn the name of Christ. Not one of the New Testament documents was written simply to provide posterity with an historical source — an oversight which has provided generations of scholars with their academic bread and butter — but even those Roman scholars who were ostensibly historians were very shaky, by modern standards, on chronology. Quite a number of dates in Roman history would be difficult to sustain if exposed to the intensive examination applied to the New Testament, since they depend on a single statement or little more. It may be remembered that on the opening page A.D. 33 was cited as one dating of Christ's death along with the reminder that A.D. 30 was more generally accepted. This lack of precision on exact dates pervades the first quarter of a century of the young Church, but when we make contact with the main stream of Roman history more exact dating becomes possible.

After the murder of Caligula, Claudius became emperor in A.D. 41 and immediately had to deal with Jewish disputes left over from the last year of his predecessor.[36] He is mentioned in *Acts* when a prophet named Agabus foretold the famine which came in his reign about A.D. 46,[37] and again when Paul met Aquila and Priscilla at Corinth, 'because that Claudius had commanded all Jews to depart from Rome'.[38] Unhappily, those who provide a timetable for Paul's journeys do so with more confidence than agreement,[39] but probably this was in A.D. 49. According to a curt sentence in Suetonius the Jews were expelled because they had been making trouble 'on the instigation of Chrestus'.[40] We know from Tertullian that this was a common pronunciation of the name of Christ among pagans, and while there is always the possibility that the rioting was because of some other claimant the likelihood is that this tells of disputes between Jews and Christians. Shortly afterwards in *Acts*, Aquila and Priscilla appear as very active Christians and the presumption is that they were so when they arrived from Rome. When Paul wrote to the Church at Rome it contained a surprisingly long list of Christians already known to him. It is dangerous to exaggerate the rapid spread of what must, as yet, have seemed a negligible minority among the sects and religions of the empire, but it is remarkable that from small beginnings in a remote province the Church had now established a foothold in the imperial city itself.

What mattered more to Christians than the mystery religions or the temple cults was the intimate association at the summit of official life between Roman religious rites and the government of the empire. Those who received the highest offices of state by that very fact held priesthoods and participated in sacrifices. To this was now added the imposition of emperor worship which, like Shintoism in one stage of Japanese history, became a symbol of loyalty to the state. At this point the Christian Church and the Roman state were to meet in a clash where there could be no compromise. At first, as may be seen in the phrase from Suetonius, the government was slow to assess such a new and insignificant gathering. Something of this is seen again when Tacitus says that in A.D. 57 Pomponia Graecina, whose husband had commanded the Roman troops who invaded Britain in A.D. 43, was tried for 'a foreign superstition'.[41] Although unspecified, this has generally been identified with the Christian faith. Her husband and the senior members of the family sat in judgement on her and pronounced her innocent. Yet her life was seen to be changed. According to contemporaries she lived in lifelong mourning for Julia, the daughter of Drusus, but perhaps as a Christian she chose to retire from Roman society. Spasmodic and uncertain acts like this were replaced in A.D. 64 when Nero — in whose judgement as one ordained by God Paul had placed such confidence — needed a scapegoat for the fire of Rome and found it in the Christians.

'Nero,' says our first reliable account of the Christian Church from a Roman source,

> 'punished with exquisite torture a race of men detested for their evil practices who are vulgarly known as Christians. The name was derived from Christ, who in the reign of Tiberius Caesar suffered under Pontius Pilate, the procurator of Judaea. By that event the sect, of which he was the founder, received a blow which for a time checked the growth of a dangerous superstition, but it revived soon after and spread with renewed vigour, not only in Judaea,

the soil that gave it birth, but even in the city of
Rome, the common sink into which everything
infamous and abominable flows like a torrent from
all quarters of the world. Nero proceeded with his
usual artifice. He found a set of profligate and
abandoned wretches who were induced to confess
themselves guilty and on the evidence of such men a
number of Christians were convicted, not indeed
upon any clear evidence of their having set the city on
fire, but rather on account of their sullen hatred of
the whole human race.[42] They were put to death with
exquisite cruelty, and to their sufferings Nero added
mockery and derision. Some were covered with the
skins of wild beasts and left to be devoured by dogs;
others were nailed to crosses; numbers were burned
alive; and many, covered over with inflammable
matter, were lighted up, when the day declined, to
serve as torches through the night. For the
convenience of seeing this tragic spectacle the
emperor lent his own gardens. He added the sports of
the circus and assisted in person, sometimes driving
a curricle and occasionally mixing with the rabble in
his coachman's dress. At length the cruelty of these
proceedings filled every breast with compassion.
Humanity relented in favour of the Christians. The
manners of that people were, no doubt, of a
pernicious tendency and their crimes called for the
hand of justice; but it was evident that they fell a
sacrifice, not for the public good, but to glut the rage
and cruelty of one man only.'[43]

Though Tacitus says, 'one man only', behind the action of the
emperor must lie the reports of agents and spies and the
decisions of bureaucrats. Official circles had taken cognisance
of the Church and considered it a menace. Tacitus did not know
the names of the victims nor did he distinguish the apostles from
the converts, but Peter and Paul were among the martyrs.[44]

'Peter and Paul,' wrote Dionysius, Bishop of Corinth, about
170, 'sowed in our Corinth, and taught us jointly; in Italy they
also taught jointly in the same city and were martyred at the
same time.'

'I can point out the monuments of the victorious apostles,' wrote an early Christian writer quoted by Eusebius, 'If you will go as far as the Vatican or the Ostian Way you will find the monuments of those who founded this Church.'[45]

St Paul's outside the Walls marks the site where Paul died and was buried, and recent excavation has revealed what is almost certainly the tomb of St Peter beneath the high altar of St Peter's. These apostles left a name behind them, but the great majority were obscure and unknown. Tacitus suggests that their numbers were considerable. Their astonishing assurance that a community of such limited beginnings would conquer the world is matched by the endurance with which men and women recruited from the depths of a depraved society willingly faced their ordeals. An early symbol of the faith is the cross surrounded or surmounted by the victor's wreath. It was an image drawn from the wreath bestowed upon the victor in the games and the general returning from the wars, but for Christians it was one gained by suffering. This had been their Master's way but, if the martyrs understood, the Church in time was to forget.

Whatever its date, the book of *Revelation* leaves no doubt about the feelings of Christians. There was no suggestion now that the Roman state had divine warrant.

> And there came one of the seven angels which had the seven vials, and talked with me, saying unto me, Come hither; I will shew unto thee the judgment of the great whore that sitteth upon many waters ... and upon her forehead was a name written, MYSTERY, BABYLON THE GREAT, THE MOTHER OF HARLOTS AND ABOMINATIONS OF THE EARTH. And I saw the woman drunken with the blood of the saints, and with the blood of the martyrs of Jesus.[46]

Christians had been charged with a specific crime — arson — and admissions had been extracted by torture. Nero's act marked the adoption of persecution of the Church as normal Roman policy. Later the very confession of the Christian faith, apart from any crime,[47] became grounds for the death penalty. Apparently an administrative order had been issued against Christians as such.[48] Henceforth, subjects of the empire became Christians at the risk of their lives. Q. Lollius Urbicus was a

Roman soldier who served against Bar Kochba in Palestine and from 140 till 145 was governor of Britain. Under him the boundary with the northern barbarians was moved north from Hadrian's Wall to the Antonine Wall between Forth and Clyde, and Limes Road in modern Falkirk commemorates the fact that here he fixed the *limes*, or limit, of the empire.[49] About 150 he became prefect of Rome and in 152 or slightly later, he heard a case in which a Christian was denounced. When he was condemned a bystander protested that he had committed no crime save that of being a Christian. Urbicus observed, 'You almost seem to me to be such a one.' The man answered, 'Most certainly I am,' and was immediately condemned as was another who did likewise.[50]

There has been a tendency to disparage the risk of martyrdom.[51] Persecution, it is true, was neither general, in the sense that it took place everywhere at once, nor consistent, in the sense that it was always applied. It was intermittent or spasmodic, and the Church could expect intervals of comparative security when government was negligent or inefficient, for the Roman state did not have the efficiency of the Gestapo or KGB even though the intention was much the same.

Why, the modern reader asks, did Rome persecute a society which is now generally regarded at best as beneficent and at worst as innocuous? Several reasons may be given, beginning with some which were temporary and incidental and passing into that more fundamental reason which has brought persecution to some branch of the Church in every century.

In the first instance, while the Jews, who were thoroughly disliked in any case, at least held a national religion of long standing, Christians held a faith which was new, unrecognised by authority and strange ... it had never received official approval; it was a *religio illicita*.[52] Secondly, vague scandals such as infanticide, incest and cannibalism were attached to the Church, many arising from misunderstanding of the Eucharist. Thirdly, while paganism was syncretistic, Christians refused to compromise. Jove was not the God and Father of the Lord Jesus Christ under another name. This could neither be understood nor accepted.

When the altar of Victory was removed from the senate house in 382 at the emperor's command, the spokesman of paganism pleaded that, 'there is no single way by which we may attain to so great a mystery.'[53] But Ambrose replied, 'The Christian God ... alone is the true God, who is to be worshipped from the bottom of the heart. "As for the gods of the heathen, they are but demons," as Scripture says.'[54] Christians held that there was but one way.

Fourthly, Rome persecuted, not an ideology but a community, the Church. Aware of her unstable social order, Rome was ever suspicious of any groups which might cloak rebellion. The Younger Pliny wrote to Trajan that a fire had caused great damage as the town had no fire brigade. Might one be formed? But the emperor who left behind him a name honoured, according to Gibbon, beyond the suspicion of flattery,[55] replied that the risk was too great. 'Whatever name they bear it is almost certain that men so united will become a political club.'[56] It was better to tell people to fight their own fires. Even burial clubs were carefully watched. To Roman eyes Christians formed such potential underground groups.

Fifthly, the effects of conversion were seen and disliked. Men's lives were changed; their minds were given an unalterable bent; they were distinct from the rest of society, whatever ties bound them to it, and they drew to the company of their own kind.

Sixthly, the inscrutable Christian refusal to participate in any way in emperor worship was seen as an acid test leading to a tacit admission of disloyalty.

Behind all lay a spiritual fact. Roman religion was irrelevant to morals, the deepest longings of the human spirit, and to social life except where it was subservient to it; but the Roman state had seen in the Church a society transcending the state both in its bounds and its demands, possessing a spiritual and organisational unity, compelling authority, and marked effectiveness.[57] Roman hostility was not a misunderstanding or an accident, for the Church was a community independent of the state, holding its people by a stronger loyalty, and able, as later events were to show, to survive when civil government had broken down. By its own standards the Roman government was entirely justified in persecution, for the Church was a state within the state, the alternative society bent on the overthrow of the existing social order, potentially a greater menace than the Parthians in the east or the wild tribes on the German frontier. It spoke for those classes who were ignored by the classical historians. It can be argued that until 1789 so-called revolutions merely sought to change those in control of society whereas the French Revolution and others since have aimed at changing society itself. In this sense the early Church was revolutionary.

There is no record of any who made the token sacrifice to the genius of the emperor and yet claimed to have remained a Christian. All such had defected. To the Roman the refusal to sacrifice revealed sedition and a vicious mind; so the magistrate was not concerned to prove a specific crime, but simply to apply the test and pass sentence on an enemy of society. Persecution was widespread, savage, and brutal and had it been general and continuous it is hard to see how the Church could have survived.[58] At best it might have lived on as a tiny minority, as did the Japanese church before Japan was opened to the world.

How it appeared to a magistrate can be seen in the letter written to the Emperor Trajan about 112 by the Younger Pliny[59] when governor of Bithynia. He did not go out of his way to search for Christians, but he dealt with all who were delated to him. Some of those charged were lapsed Christians who readily sacrificed. Others told how they had shared in the Eucharist, and torture extracted from them 'no more than a depraved and extravagant superstition', no doubt faith in Christ as the Son of God, his sacrificial death, his resurrection and second coming. It was in the towns that the Church was strongest, but she was spreading into the countryside, and her growth could be seen in the neglect of the temples. Strong measures, Pliny hoped, would remedy this.

Persecution was particularly aimed at the bishops once it was realised that the life of the Church revolved around them. Under Trajan, who reigned from 98 to 117, Symeon, the kinsman of Jesus and successor of James as Bishop of Jerusalem, was tortured and killed.[60] Ignatius, the Bishop of Antioch, whom tradition described as the child whom Jesus set upon his knee, was taken to Rome, probably a year or two before 110, to die in the arena. Writing letters to the Churches as he made the slow journey, he protested to the Roman Church that no influence should be used to prevent his martyrdom.

> May I enjoy the wild beasts that are prepared for me.
> ... Nothing shall move me, visible or invisible,
> that I may attain to Christ Jesus.[61]

Martyrdoms made a deep impression on the surviving Christians and records of them were kept, some no more than a name and a date, but others were fuller, as in the case of Polycarp, Bishop of Smyrna, who died on 22 February 156. In youth he had known the last surviving apostles[62] and his life provided Irenaeus with an instance of the continuity of the Church's witness and tradition.[63] Strong efforts were made to make him recant. 'What harm is there in saying "Lord Caesar" and in offering incense?' As he was led into the stadium a voice was heard calling, 'Be strong, Polycarp, and play the man.' The proconsul renewed the attempt to make him recant. 'Eighty and six years have I served Christ,' said Polycarp, 'And he has done me no wrong. How then can I blaspheme my King who saved me?' So he was burned, and in the end had to be finished off with a sword thrust.[64]

Pliny wrote from Asia Minor, and it was there that Polycarp died, but Christians had now spread far to the west. In 177 the Churches of Vienne and Lyons in Gaul sent their sister Churches in Asia and Phrygia an account of their martyrs which is vivid in its simplicity. After mob violence a number of Christians were marched to the forum and accused. At this a fellow Christian, Vettius Epagathus, came forward. Evidently a man of education he was, says the record, a man 'untiring in service to his neighbour, utterly devoted to God, and fervent in spirit'. When he asked to speak on behalf of the accused the mob howled him down and the governor asked if he, too, was a Christian. Vettius replied, 'I am', and he too was martyred.

> He was called 'the Christians' Advocate', but he had in himself the Advocate, the Spirit . . . as he showed by the fullness of his love when he gladly laid down his own life in defence of his brother Christians; for he was and is a true disciple of Christ, following the Lamb wherever he goes.

His companions did not desert the accused, but stayed with him. Some were firm to the end, but ten recanted,

> causing us great distress and inexpressible grief, and damping the enthusiasm of those not yet arrested. . . . At that time we were all tormented by doubts about their confessing Christ; we were not afraid of the punishments inflicted, but looked to the outcome

and dreaded lest anyone might fall away. But the arrests went on. Those who were worthy filled up the number of martyrs so that from two dioceses were collected all the active members who had done most to build up church life.

Many deaths are described in detail, such as that of Blandina, a servant girl, who after long torture only said, 'I am a Christian; we do nothing to be ashamed of.' Of Sanctus, a deacon from Vienne, it was written, 'His poor body was a witness to what he had suffered — it was all one wound and bruise, bent up and robbed of outward human shape, but, suffering in that body, Christ accomplished most glorious things.' Many, especially the young, died in prison before they could be brought to the arena. Some were elderly, like Alexander, a physician from Phrygia, who was arrested when he was seen encouraging Christians; others were young, like Ponticus, a boy of fifteen. Knowing the Christians' care for the bodies of their dead, the persecutors threw some remains to dogs, burned the rest, and threw the ashes into the Rhône. 'And this they did as if they could defeat God and rob the dead of their rebirth.'[65]

Originally the meaning of the word *martyr* had been that of a witness, and its antecedents were Jewish.[66] Eleazer, an aged scribe, and the seven sons of one mother, are recorded in *Maccabees*[67] as having suffered a brutal death rather than break the Law. To this extent they were martyrs, but to the concept of the martyr as one who gave total witness by his death in agony and humiliation, the Church added that he thus, paradoxically, won an eternal victory. Jewish martyrs had looked to the resurrection and vindication by God, but their deaths were incidents in the suppression of an armed rising. Christian martyrs never contemplated this kind of resistance; they saw their suffering as their warfare, the way of the cross which led to victory. How intense was the emotion thus aroused can be seen in the book of *Revelation*:

After this I looked and saw a vast throng, which no one could count, from every nation, of all tribes, peoples, and languages, standing in front of the throne and before the Lamb. They were robed in white and had palms in their hands, and they shouted together; 'Victory to our God who sits on the throne, and to the Lamb!'

And all the angels stood round the throne and the elders and the four living creatures, and they fell on their faces before the throne and worshipped God, crying:

'Amen! Praise and glory and wisdom, thanksgiving and honour, power and might, be to our God for ever and ever! Amen.'

Then one of the elders turned to me and said, 'These men that are robed in white — who are they, and from where do they come?' But I answered, 'My lord, you know, not I.' Then he said to me, 'These are the men who have passed through the great ordeal; they have washed their robes and made them white in the blood of the Lamb. That is why they stand before the throne of God and minister to him day and night in his temple; and he who sits on the throne will dwell with them. They shall never again feel hunger or thirst, the sun shall not beat on them nor any scorching heat, because the Lamb who is at the heart of the throne will be their Shepherd and will guide them to the springs of the water of life; and God will wipe all tears from their eyes.'[68]

In later times the Church was to create many martyrs. Judaism created the concept, but it was the Church which gave it to the world. Christian martyrs did not die as so many have done since, for what they believed, but for a person, their Lord. He, as they well knew, had led the way. Many have since portrayed his pain, but none have shown the utter loneliness of his suffering or its gross obscenity. Thousands willingly followed in his way. Justin Martyr remembered that Socrates had died for a cause[69] but this is hardly an exact precedent, for Socrates, as Plato tells, died in comparative dignity and painlessness. Not everyone was favourably impressed by the sufferings of the martyrs. Marcus Aurelius dismissed them as no more than theatrical gestures.[70] While the beginnings of a cult of martyrdom can be seen, the Church discouraged any urge to seek it needlessly or to treat it as a sure path to eternal glory, for she had not forgotten how at Gethsemane Christ had prayed

that the cup might pass from him. Caution was always urged
except where the choice lay between death and denial of the
Lord.[71]

There is reason to think that in Persia the total offensive
against a small Church rooted in minority racial groups virtually
swept Christianity away,[72] but in the Roman empire Christians
were more numerous and not associated with distinctive racial
communities; and they were martyred not, as seems to have been
the case in Persia, in the streets and houses where they lived, but
in the public gaze in the arena. Far from halting the growth of
the Church in the empire, this furthered it, as many narratives
tell. Christian conviction at times was found in unexpected
quarters. Time and again it can be seen that strong Christian
faith, prepared to die rather than deny, was to be found among
men who had never been closely associated with the visible
Church. Consequently the Church had to make provision in her
thought for what was called 'baptism in blood', the admission
that there were those who had not been received into the
sacramental fellowship but were yet of the true company of
believers.[73]

This Christian witness was given in a predominantly urban
civilization, for one of the most striking facts recorded —
without comment — in *Acts* is the sudden passage of the Church
from a rural environment to the cities. Their accent marked the
apostles. 'Are not all these which speak Galileans?'[74] But from
Pentecost they had to speak Greek, the language of
cosmopolitan towns.

That Hellenistic culture which Alexander and his successors
had spread derived originally from the city states of classical
Greece; the eastern half of the Roman empire, and many parts
of the west, might have been regarded as an aggregate of cities,
each surrounded by its dependent territory.[75] These largely self-
governing communities were held together by the autocratic
power of the emperor, with the senate as his advisory body, the
imperial bureaucracy, and the army; but it was the commercial
and administrative classes of the cities, the bourgeoisie, who
provided a foundation for the whole structure which was, with
time, to prove inadequate to cope with the strains upon it.
Depending on the labour of the lower classes, the peasants of the
countryside, and the industrial proletariat of the cities, the
urban middle class of the empire, like the aristocracy of wealth

still further up the social scale, was reluctant to admit the lower orders into its own privileged ranks.

Social tensions steadily grew and in the end took the form of antagonism between town and country; the strength of the middle classes was broken in the inflation[76] which destroyed the value of their assets, the oppressive taxation which deprived them of the fruits of their enterprise, and the disorder of the third century; the aristocracy was largely eliminated or reduced to prestigious insignificance; and there succeeded the oriental despotism of Constantine and his heirs with its basis in the army, the bureaucracy, and the mass of the peasants.[77] But any reader of the Gospels can see for himself that although Christ visited and died at Jerusalem, the Palestine which he knew best was a land of villages and peasants, primitive in its social development and uncapitalised. His parables belong to a culture not dissimilar to that depicted in another parable which Nathan had once told to David. For Christ and his friends the temple was not the great banking establishment which it was to the aristocracy and landowners, but the shrine where the widow gave her mite.[78] Only in one brief incident did he see it in the former light, and then with fury. His disciples were out of their element in the big city. But at Pentecost the dynamic character of the Church concentrated her work in the cities, the centres of vitality and communication. We are given a glimpse of the beginnings in Antioch, but of the start of the Church in the other great metropolis of the eastern empire, Alexandria, we know nothing. Paul travelled from city to city; the bishoprics of the Church were established in the cities; and, despite the greater difficulty of imposing Christian standards upon large centres of population, this is an example to which the Church has consistently adhered.

Thus the Church was obliged to make the passage from the comparatively undeveloped social order of the Palestinian countryside to a commercial and urban environment, and to an economy with state ownership established in some fields such as mining and quarrying alongside much large-scale private capitalism.[79] In particular, she had entered a society where class distinctions were wide, deep and oppressive.

At the base of the pyramid was a mass of slaves, victims of the long series of wars and conquests which preceded the comparative peace of Augustus. Above this were free citizens

with various degrees of privilege. There was a constant
movement towards increasing the numbers of those with the
much envied rank of full Roman citizenship to which, as Paul
condescendingly told the centurion, he had been born; but the
extensions of the franchise granted by the state were prompted
not by egalitarianism, but by financial policy or the need to
conciliate depressed elements.[80] Above the unskilled labourers,
the unemployed, and the craftsmen who made up the proletariat
of the swarming city alleys, were the merchants and civil
servants and, above them all, the great landlords, the equestrian
and senatorial aristocracy.

It was a society which took injustice and inequality for
granted; and which placed so low a value on human life,
whatever the teaching of its moralists, that the pages of its
historians are full of crudity, brutality and murder. A Roman
noble waited in the next room while Augustus raped his wife.[81]
Having told of the homosexuality of Augustus, who aspired to
restore the rigour of ancient morals, Suetonius says, 'Not even
his friends could deny that he often committed adultery though,
of course, they said he did it only for reasons of state and not for
simple passion.'[82] Worse is told of Tiberius.[83] Sadism ran
through Roman life from the howling mob at the arena to those
who ruled the empire. Caligula ordered men to be killed slowly:
'Hit him so that he feels he is dying!'[84] He compelled parents to
attend their son's execution and, when a father pleaded ill-
health, he sent a litter to carry him to the spot. When the price of
meat for feeding the beasts at the arena was high he ordered
criminals to be fed to them instead.[85] When the New Testament
tells that Herod slaughtered the innocents at Bethlehem on the
strength of a rumour it is of a piece with his murder of his wife,
Mariamne, and his sons Alexander and Aristobulus.[86] And there
is no reason to suppose that the vices of Graeco-Roman society
were the monopoly of those sufficiently eminent to attract the
notice of historians. It remains a question why, when her hour
of triumph came, the Church did not repudiate the state as — to
use Augustine's phrase[87] — no more than injustice erected into a
system, and why she reacted so much more strongly against its
sexuality than against its violence.

She came into secular society, not as the product of a class
struggle[88] nor as a movement directly concerned, in the first
instance, with communal disorders, but as a community whose

life was turned to God, and to forgiveness, reconciliation, and eternal life. In the last days of the Roman republic Cicero[89] had recognised the acute division in public life between those who sought to conciliate the masses and trade upon their support, and those whom he regarded as the most dependable citizens, those with full citizenship, the senators, landowners, businessmen and their dependents. This second group, he held, had good moral standards, were solvent, balanced in judgement, and reliable. They were the true conservators of the state, defending the pillars of social security provided by official religion, Law, the senate, the courts, and the military, and so securing the rights of property which were the basis of civil liberty.[90]

This liberal dream contrasted sadly with the illiberal facts of the dying years of a republic shattered by the ambitions of Marius, Sulla, Pompey, Caesar and lesser men, and with Cicero's own death as he looked out of the litter to the pursuers who were to cut his throat.[91] When he set aside the regime which had passed away in the century of disorder, Augustus intended to provide anew a social order which would give men security, peace and freedom through political action and, above all, through submission to a beneficent ruler. And the new regime was meant to be permanent. 'May it be given to me,' he wrote,

> 'to restore the republic safe and sound, and to receive the fruit of my desire to be known as the author of the perfect state, and dying to bear with me the hope that the foundation which I have laid will be permanent.'[92]

But Cicero, who did not live to see this settlement, had contrasted with the reliable and propertied citizens, the underworld eager for revolution, deep in debt, prepared to see society at large go up in flames rather than that they themselves should be consumed.[93] Christians never shared the hope that the state would provide the conditions for the good life. Engels was quite correct when he said that, like the labour movement, 'Christianity was at first a movement of the oppressed; it began as a religion of the slaves and the freed, the poor and outlawed, of the peoples defeated and crushed by the force of Rome.'[94] But he was quite wrong when he went on to say that whereas socialism sought deliverance on this earth, the Christians sought it in the next. They made the best of both worlds. In the New Testament and the accounts of the martyrs we see how much eternal life meant to them; the New Testament, however, is mainly concerned with this life and the Church of the first century was very earthy, convinced that the Son of God had worked as a joiner and that she was, in sober fact, his body on this earth.

Three courses might be thought to have lain open before the Church as she was confronted with Roman society. As far as the first was concerned, the words and example of Christ precluded her from violence and revolution as they had withheld Christians from throwing in their lot with the Zealots of Israel. From those first days to this, a gulf has existed between the Church and the political activists who despise pietism, as they see it, and practise violence; a gulf which cannot be crossed except by surrender.

As to the second, the exclusion of Christians from public office barred any possibility that she might become a reforming body, gradually improving conditions by political action. When office was inherited, as it sometimes was, its associations with temple duties must have brought acute embarrassment to converts.[95] When Flavius Clemens was consul of Rome in A.D. 96 his problems as a Christian, if he really was one, must have been insoluble until his arrest. It was the duty of Christians, Celsus urged when the empire was under stress, to uphold the state by accepting public office, administering justice and serving in the army; a few Christians are known to have done so, but Origen, answering the charge, did not refer to these exceptions which were only early signs of defection from the Christian standards or an indication that those concerned were still only enquirers. His reply was that Christians supported the state by their prayers and exemplary lives.[96] It was a lame excuse.

Instead the Church took the course dictated by her own nature and formed a community within the community, in it but not of it. Christians had no alternative other than to live within the existing social structure, but they absented themselves from it as much as they could, like some of the Christian Brethren in Britain today, Jehovah's Witnesses in the USSR or the Amish in America. They looked, not for improvement, but for conversion, and they expected the Church to form a new community living its own life in the midst of a secular society. To be baptised as a Christian did not mean the acceptance of an individualistic ethic,[97] privately practised. Troeltsch's statement to the contrary is a consequence of his inability to free himself from the preconceptions of Liberal Protestantism. Rather it meant deliverance from the power of evil, the coming of the grace of Christ, and entry into a community which created its own ethic and supporting it by inner discipline. At this point all Christians differed from moralising Stoics and from disciples of Epictetus whose way of release aimed only at the salvation of the individual.[98]

A more obvious difference lies in the fact that most pagan moralists, though Epictetus himself was a notable exception, were drawn from the more comfortable and leisured groups of society. It is odd to find the wealthy Seneca discoursing on the evils of riches or Marcus Aurelius writing in the imperial palace on the indifference of the philosopher to food or clothing.[99] Such academic pontifications had no point of contact with the hungry poor. On the other hand, while the Church contained a complete spectrum or cross section of society, she was so deeply rooted among the lower classes that her defenders continually had to rebut the charge that the Gospel was fit only for the scum of society. Paul, who had to deal with such cases as that of Onesimus, the runaway slave of Philemon, was particularly sensitive on this score.[100] His own background seems to have been a comfortable one, with more in common with that of Philemon than of the runaway.

A visitor to the USSR once told the writer that he had seen only 'shawlies', old women of the poorest class, in numbers at church while the young and prosperous were few. On the other hand, academicians of Christian conviction have been prosecuted as dissidents. Something like this existed in the early Church. There was a wide circle of sympathisers and enquirers but the hard core was made up of those with little to lose, and a small number of those with the courage and independence to confront authority. We do not know their numbers.[101] Probably they resembled the Communist Party in Britain which has a few dyed-in-the-wool, paid-up, card-carrying members, and a much larger number of fellow travellers, and can make more trouble than its statistics suggest. Christian witness was unceasing. Plutarch advised young wives to shut the door against men with tracts for foreign religions.[102] One is reminded of Jehovah's Witnesses.

It was taken for granted in the *Epistle to Diognetus* that
Christians were poor.[103] An opponent complained that 'most
Christians are paupers and the very dregs of humanity', and the
Apologist could only reply that it was no disgrace to be poor.[104]
Most inhabitants of the empire were poor, but the Church was
the only representative organisation to reflect the fact. Classical
historians ignored the victims of society, the toad under the
harrow; but the Church did not. Those who ruled had good
cause for anxiety when they found in their midst a body rooted
in the distressed proletariat but with intellectual leadership.
Celsus saw the poorer working class as representative
Christians.[105] A survey of Christian inscriptions included
pigkillers, gravediggers and ragpickers; some, such as ivory
workers and goldsmiths, craftsmen in luxury trades yet not well
paid themselves; and some, such as architects, lawyers and
physicians from the professional classes;[106] and there must have
been many too poor to have a tombstone. *Kyrie eleison,*
surviving in the liturgy till this day, tells that the Roman Church
used the Greek spoken by the immigrant poor and a few
intellectuals. It has been argued on fourth century evidence that
in the late empire most Christians were middle class,[107] but until
the middle of the third century in North Africa — and not only
there — most Christians were 'from the lower classes and
women',[108] while in Europe and the east the strength of the
Church 'lay predominantly in Greek-speaking urban areas
among the lower classes'.[109]

A few moneyed and aristocratic Christians had been found
from the start, and when persecution relaxed for the time being
with the death of Marcus Aurelius and the accession of
Commodus, his worthless son, in 180 their numbers were seen to
be on the increase. Large-scale persecution had first broken out
in the reign of the notorious Nero and, possibly because of this,
the Christian Apologists nourished the illusion that it was the
bad emperors who had persecuted while the good had been
tolerant. 'Of all the emperors,' Melito of Sardis wrote,

'the only ones ever persuaded to misrepresent our
doctrine were Nero and Domitian, who were the
source of the unreasonable custom of laying false
information against the Christians. But their
ignorance was corrected by your religious

predecessors, who constantly rebuked in writing all who ventured to make trouble for our people. It is clear, for instance, that your grandfather Hadrian wrote to many of his representatives, in particular the proconsul Fundanus, governor of Asia; and your father, while you were associated with him in the government of the world, wrote to the cities, for instance, Larissa, Thessalonica, and Athens, and to all the peoples of Greece, forbidding them to make trouble for us. You, sir, hold the same views on this matter as they did, but with more human sympathy and philosophic insight; so we are the more convinced that you will wholeheartedly accede to our request.'[110]

This was addressed to Marcus Aurelius. Unfortunately for Christians the truth was quite contrary. Under able and conscientious emperors the law against seditious and proscribed societies, among which the Church was now foremost, was enforced, while under dissolute and incompetent rulers the pressure was relaxed as oversight of provincial officials was neglected. Nero was an exception; he enjoyed cruelty.

Nero died in A.D. 68 in his thirty-first year, the last emperor of Caesar's house and, says Tacitus, 'a new political secret was then for the first time discovered ... an emperor might be invested with the imperial power elsewhere than in Rome.'[111] Under Augustus the seizure of power by military means had been decently veiled but after Nero's death it was nakedly exposed, as in some former African colonies once they had obtained their freedom from colonial rule. Three emperors in quick succession, Galba, Otho and Vitellius — whom Tacitus described as a degraded animal — were acclaimed in turn by the army, and after a short and undistinguished reign each of them met a violent death. In A.D. 67, a year before he died, Nero had despatched Vespasian, one of the most competent of his generals, to take command in Palestine where the Jewish revolt had had its first resounding success in the capture of Jerusalem. 'All over the Orient,' wrote Suetonius,

'there was an old and standing belief that the time had come when those from Judaea would conquer the world.'[112]

As the news of the disorders in Italy reached the fighting men, the members of his staff urged Vespasian to take power into his own hands.[113]

> Between Syria and Judaea stands a mountain known by the name of Mount Carmel, on the top of which a god is worshipped under no other title than that of the place and, according to ancient custom, without a temple, or even a statue. An altar is erected in the open air, and there adoration is paid to the presiding deity.[114]

Today the flats and villas of Haifa incongruously stand among little gardens on the spot where the fierce Elijah put to flight the prophets of Baal. Tacitus does not tell us, but presumably the altar was dedicated to Elijah's antagonist, vanquished but surviving, for when Vespasian offered sacrifice he was rewarded with an oracle promising him greatness. On 1 July A.D. 69 he was hailed as emperor by two legions; he delegated the last stages of the campaign to his son Titus and set off for Rome where, after the fall of Jerusalem and his triumph, the arch of Titus portrayed for posterity the looted treasures of the temple, the seven-branched golden candlestick[115] and the table from the sanctuary, brought to adorn a Roman temple until in 455 Genseric the Vandal carried them off to be lost for ever in the sands of North Africa.

Until A.D. 79 Titus shared the throne with his father and in the two remaining years of his life, when he reigned alone, he completed the Colosseum. Its great central pavement, now broken open, covered the long alleys off which led the quarters for the gladiators, the cages for beasts, and the cells for prisoners. Today a large but simple cross at one end tells the visitor that this was for Christians what Belsen was to be for Jews, but with this difference, that the slaughter was done in public for the entertainment of the spectators on the crowded terracing.

However deep their sorrow for their kinsmen who fell in the war and for the ruin of Jeusalem and the temple, the Jews of the *diaspora* did not suffer many personal consequences because of the disaster in Palestine, save in one important respect. Until now all Jews, wherever they lived, had paid an annual contribution towards the temple. Now that the temple no longer stood Vespasian decreed that the payment should not lapse but that it should become a tax paid to the Roman exchequer through a board known as the *Fiscus Judaicus*.[116] No parallel existed for a tax levied on a community scattered throughout the empire with no local basis, so it recognised them as a community. Formerly the payment had been made by adult males, but now it was to be paid by all, without exception of age or sex. Worst of all, it could be seen as a vindictive and humiliating response to the rebellion, since it was specifically to be applied to the maintenance of the temple of Jupiter on the Capitol.

When Titus died in A.D. 81 he was succeeded by his younger brother Domitian, who had not shared in the Jewish campaign and had been in danger in Rome when his father's claim became known. No other subjects of the empire had shown such ineradicable hatred for Roman rule as the Jews, and the sons of Vespasian can never have regarded them with other than a wary eye. It may be that the temple tax was evaded, but early in his reign Domitian took steps to end this.[117] Not all the worshippers in synagogues were children of Israel by descent, for, as in the days of Paul, Gentile enquirers drawn by Jewish morals and monotheism were still to be found in every synagogue. In addition there were also Jewish Christians, most of them probably outside the synagogue and some of them possibly not, some circumcised and others not. It was small wonder if Roman tax-collectors found it hard to know where to draw the line, where to credit protests and where not. Suetonius wrote that he remembered as an adolescent being present in the court when a man of over ninety was stripped to determine whether or not he was circumcised.

If we are to believe what we are told, Domitian at first made a good impression by the reconstruction of the temple of Jupiter on the Capitol and the enforcement of the laws against luxury and vice, but later forfeited it by greed, despotism and vindictiveness; but any emperor who escaped such a reputation did so merely because he was fortunate enough to lack an historian with a mordant pen. According to Suetonius he was the first, whatever earlier flatterers had said, deliberately to assume the title of *Dominus et Deus Noster* — our Lord and our God.[118] Orientals had used this kind of phrase, but it was offensive to older Romans and shockingly so to Jews and Christians.

'Many were the victims of Domitian's appalling cruelty,' wrote Eusebius.

> At Rome great numbers of men distinguished by birth and attainments were executed without a fair trial, and countless other eminent men were for no reason at all banished from the country and their property confiscated. Finally he showed himself the successor of Nero in enmity and hostility to God. He was, in fact, the second to organise persecution against us, though his father Vespasian had had no mischievous designs against us.[119]

From a non-Christian standpoint Suetonius appears to give general confirmation to this, but possibly only because Eusebius in part relied on Suetonius. Any son of Vespasian had cause to remember the Jewish threat, but Domitian may well have had reason to distrust the Roman nobility. He became morbidly suspicious. Tacitus looked back on these years much as a survivor of Stalin's purges may have remembered them.[120] In A.D. 96 the emperor ordered the execution of his own cousin, Flavius Clemens, consul of Rome in that year, and the sending into exile on an island of his wife Flavia Domitilla, also a kinswoman to himself. According to Eusebius she was sent to Pontia, an island in the Gulf of Caeta; according to Dio Cassius to the even more forbidding island of Pantelaria. Not long before, Domitian had adopted their two sons as his heirs, renaming the one after his father and the other after himself.[121]

Our accounts of these events are inconsistent in details and probably confused. Suetonius despised Flavius Clemens for 'contemptible inertia', which probably means that he was reluctant to accept office, and so may be some confirmation of the tradition, handed down to Eusebius, that he and his wife were Christians. They had been charged, Dio Cassius tells, with 'atheism and Jewish customs'. About the same time Acilius Glabrio, who had been consul with Trajan in A.D. 91, was either sent into exile or put to death on the same charge and also because he had fought with beasts in the arena.[122] It is possible that in him we have the name of another Christian, but no Christian would have taken part in the games of the arena of his own free will. Possibly this is a confused account of his death. More recently it has been suggested that Flavius Clemens and his wife were among the Gentile enquirers at the synagogue,[123] but if it is surprising to find Romans of this rank in the Church it is even more so to find members of the family of Vespasian and Titus attending the synagogue so soon after the great rebellion and while lesser ones were still smouldering. Probably Roman officials found the distinction between Gentile sympathisers with the synagogue and Christians beyond their understanding; possibly some of the worshippers still drew no clear distinction. This is only one of the instances where too definite conclusions have been stated on inadequate evidence, by both sides, as though they were established.

Domitian, and possibly others after him, continued his father's policy of tracking down descendants of David as possible Messiahs. 'There still survived of the Lord's family,' says Hegesippus, whose work survives in extracts preserved by Eusebius,

> 'the grandsons of Jude, who was said to be his brother, humanly speaking. These were informed against as being of David's line, and brought ... before Domitian Caesar, who was as afraid of the coming of Christ as Herod had been. He asked them if they were of David's line, and they admitted it. Then he asked them what property they owned or what fortune they had. They replied that between them they had 9,000 denarii, half belonging to each; this was not in money, but was the estimated value of twenty-five acres of land from which, by their own labour, they supported themselves and raised the money to pay their taxes.'[124]

As proof, they showed their horny hands and sinewy shoulders. Domitian's interest was in no sense religious. He wished to meet the family of David the king and not that of Jesus the joiner, for he was concerned with possible threats to the peace of the empire. He asked what the Kingdom of Christ — the Messiah — was like, and where and when it would appear. Faced with the same problem as New Testament scholars the two working men explained that it was not of this world or anywhere on earth but angelic and in heaven, and

would be established at the end of the world when he would
come in glory to judge the quick and the dead and to reward
every man according to his works. So Eusebius words it, but
their answer satisfied Domitian that the Kingdom of which they
spoke had, for him, no practical relevance. He dismissed them
as beneath his notice. Probably no more than this example of
imperial contempt underlies the statement of Eusebius that he
also gave orders to relax the persecution of the Church. If
Revelation, as Irenaeus and Eusebius say, was written in this
reign, its fiery language tells another story.[125] Returning to
Palestine the two became leaders in the Church by virtue of their
kinship with Jesus and their courage as confessors.

Too much power in the hands of the military, a problem never
solved by Rome, permitted the legions to remove men from the
throne and to choose their successors; but if Caesar had not
founded a secure dynasty he had founded an institution in which
the functions of the state continued with less interference from
the vices or virtues of emperors than the historians would have
us believe. When Domitian was murdered in A.D. 96, Nerva, an
honourable, upright and somewhat undistinguished old man,
was installed in his place for a reign of less than two years. Yet
this short reign gave the state a new beginning under a succession
of emperors rightly respected both in their own time and since.
Nerva knew that if there was not another Augustus to control
the army the army would produce another Domitian to oppress
the senate and all civilian elements in the government. In
October A.D. 97 he adopted Trajan, a Spaniard by birth but
probably Italian by descent, as his son and successor.

No better choice could have been made. Trajan, an experienced
soldier whose father had won distinction under Vespasian and
Titus in the Jewish war, secured the defences of the empire and
the discipline of the army. He left little mark on the history of
the Church, as the attitude of the state to it was now well
defined. Too much weight has been laid upon his brief reply to
Pliny,[126] which leaves the impression of a busy but courteous
superior answering an officious subordinate who should have
known how to deal with the matter himself. Christians were not
to be sought out, but if convicted they were to be punished.
Anonymous letters should be ignored. But persecution still went
on steadily as the instances of Ignatius and Polycarp tell, even if
each had been permitted to spend long years as prominent

Christians. There might be much indifference towards the Church, but no security for her. A rescript of Hadrian who succeeded Trajan in 117 and reigned until 138 differs little from the reply of Trajan. It tells a provincial governor that legal action, when properly raised, must proceed against Christians but that malicious informers should be punished.[127]

Hadrian was a man of great ability and an intense sense of duty, who brought on his last illness by travelling the empire bare-headed in all weathers, but who possessed few pleasant qualities.[128] A plain man in an age of luxury, he was happy with tripe and bacon. In an age of loose morals he said that he would have divorced his wife for her bad temper, but for his public position.[129] Before his death he adopted a senator, Antoninus Pius, as his son and successor, on condition that he in turn adopted a lad of seventeen, the future Marcus Aurelius.[130] 'If a man were called to fix the period in the history of the world,' Gibbon wrote,

> 'during which the condition of the human race was most happy and prosperous, he would, without hesitation, name that which elapsed from the death of Domitian to the accession of Commodus. The vast extent of the Roman empire was governed by absolute power, under the guidance of virtue and wisdom. The armies were restrained by the firm but gentle hand of four successive emperors, whose characters and authority commanded involuntary respect. The forms of the civil administration were carefully preserved by Nerva, Trajan, Hadrian and the Antonines, who delighted in the image of liberty, and were pleased with considering themselves as the accountable ministers of the laws. Such princes deserved the honour of restoring the republic, had the Romans of their days been capable of enjoying a rational freedom.'[131]

Whatever has been written since, this still remains as the standard view of the imperial rule in the second century, though one might compare it with a view of the American colonies through the eyes of George III or of Indian nationalism through the eyes of Lord Curzon.

Christians could speak for their faith in public as Justin did when he debated with Trypho at Ephesus about 137, and their numbers were growing, but the threat, if suspended, was never absent. Popular resentment was also increasing. 'Christians,' says the *Epistle to Diognetus* midway through the second century,

> 'are treated by the Jews as foreigners and enemies, and are hunted down by the Greeks; and all the time those who hate them find it impossible to justify their enmity.'[132]

Under Marcus Aurelius new edicts made it easier and more profitable to inform against Christians. Melito of Sardis complained to the emperor that,

> what never happened before is happening now — religious people as a body are being harried and persecuted by new edicts all over Asia. Shameless informers out to fill their own pockets are taking advantages of the decrees to pillage openly, plundering inoffensive citizens night and day.[133]

Were informers granted the property of those denounced and condemned? When the martyrs of Lyons and Vienne suffered in 177 the magistrate had evidently asked advice from Marcus Aurelius,

> for Caesar had issued a command that they should be tortured to death, but any who still denied Christ should be released.[134]

It cannot be pretended that there were many Christians at this time, yet popular hostility and attacks such as those of Lucian and Celsus are signs that their numbers were increasing in response to the example of Christian life and conduct under persecution. It may be that the Apologies now appearing are evidence that Christians were aware that the mind of the reading public was responsive. A change could be seen in the membership of the Church. It was recorded that 'in Rome itself many who enjoyed the advantages of birth and wealth were moving towards their own salvation.'[135]

A famous sermon by Clement of Alexandria at the turn of the century reflects the wind of change. It is no more necessary, he says, to insult wealthy Christians than it is to cringe before them, for the rich who have learned of the Saviour's power and his great salvation have every right to be in the Church.[136] The Gospel required, not that they should give away all their possessions, but that they should set little store by them and use them well. 'We need not fling away the riches that are of benefit to our neighbours as well as to ourselves.'[137] By 250 many Christians were found at the imperial court,[138] and Cyprian attributed lapsing under persecution to growing wealth.[139] Nevertheless, though only intellectuals and the moneyed would expect any mass society to be otherwise, critics like Celsus continued to reproach the Church with having her roots among the poor and in the proletariat. Older Christians who saw the change must have felt like old stalwarts of the Labour Party when they saw Labour cabinet ministers in court dress and consorting with the aristocracy.

Until now the Church had not opted out of the common life as did the men of Qumram when they took to the desert, but within secular society she had practised a private but communal life of her own. In matters of sex she practised chastity and Christian marriage. In matters economic she practised charity. In the first days after Pentecost there was an attempt to disclaim private property,[140] but this was not general, for it may be assumed that the few acres belonging to the grandsons of Jude had been inherited. Systematic giving was part of the Christian life. Saying farewell to the elders of Ephesus, Paul quoted words of Jesus, otherwise unrecorded, 'It is more blessed to give than to receive.'[141] Christians provided for their teachers and officials, and for widows and orphans, the sick, infirm and disabled.[142] By the middle of the third century the Roman Church supported its bishop, forty-six presbyters and one hundred and eight other servants of the Church, as well as more than fifteen hundred widows and distressed persons.[143] Nor was generosity confined to their membership. Julian the Apostate attributed the growth of the Church to the kindness of Christians to strangers, their care for the dead and their manner of life. 'These godless Galileans feed not only their own poor but ours.'[144] And while Christians did this from voluntary givings, Julian could only provide a pagan substitute by a gift from the imperial revenues to the temples. Christians imprisoned or banished to the mines for their faith were special objects of charity and care; ordinary members of the Church and deacons in particular ran great dangers to aid them, so that even gaolers were impressed.[145] Similarly the Church ensured decent burial for her poor, her martyrs and even outsiders.[146] Within the Church slaves were regarded as equals with free men though there was no change in their status. In matters of sex their rights were respected as never in paganism. Christian masters were to treat their slaves with humanity and slaves were to honour their masters. Slaves could enter the ministry of the Church. Whatever may be the truth behind the scandals alleged against him, Callistus, Bishop of Rome from 217 till 222, had been a slave.[147]

Celsus complained about Christian propaganda as he saw the continual activity of the Church within the social environment through unfriendly but observant eyes. 'In private houses,' he says,

> 'we see woolworkers, cobblers, laundry workers, and illiterate and rustic yokels, who would not dare to say anything in front of their elders and masters. But when they get hold of children in private and some stupid women are with them they make surprising statements such as that the children must not pay attention to their fathers and schoolmasters, but must obey them (i.e. the woolworkers etc.). They say that the fathers and schoolmasters talk nonsense and have no understanding, and that in reality they neither know nor are able to do anything good, but are taken up with empty chatter. They alone, they say, know the right way to live; and if the children would believe them they would be happy and make their homes happy too. And if, just as they are speaking, they see one of the schoolteachers, or some intelligent person, or even the father himself, the more cautious of them flee in all directions; but the more reckless urge the children on to rebel. They whisper to them that in the presence of their father and their schoolmasters they do not feel able to explain anything to the children, since they do not want to have anything to do with the silly and obtuse teachers who are totally corrupted and far gone in wickedness, and who inflict punishment on the children. But, if they like, they should leave father

and their schoolmasters, and go along with the
women and the little children who are their
playfellows to the wooldresser's shop, or to the
cobbler's, or the washerwoman, that they may learn
perfection.'[148]

From the caustic tone one may conclude that the cobbler and
the washerwoman had not been altogether unsuccessful, and
despite Celsus and his like, these untutored Christians steadily
made converts in every class and throughout the whole range of
intellectual life.

One who was both convert and martyr wrote that pagans
became Christians,

overcome by the constancy which they have
witnessed in their neighbours' lives, or by the
extraordinary forbearance they have observed in
their fellow travellers when defrauded, or by the
honesty of those with whom they do business.[149]

As for the meaning of conversion, he wrote,

We who were filled full of slaughter and every kind
of evil, have from out of the whole earth changed our
weapons of war, our swords into ploughshares, and
our pikes into farming tools, and we farm piety,
righteousness, the love of man, faith, and hope which
comes from the Father himself through him who was
crucified.[150]

For long the numbers of Christians were tiny compared with
the millions of the empire and even after their numbers grew it is
necessary to remember that they were still very much a minority;
but a time came when they formed so numerous a minority that
the state had to choose between tolerance, with the danger of
ultimate surrender, on the one hand, and total warfare on the
other. About 212 the Christians of a city came in a body to the
magistrate; he ordered a few to be executed, but asked the rest if
they could not jump off a cliff or hang themselves. 'If we', said
Tertullian, 'should take it into our heads to do the same thing
here in Carthage ... what will you make of so many
thousands?'[151] Elsewhere he wrote that if the Christians
withdrew from it the empire would be left with more enemies

than citizens. 'We can count your armies. The Christians of one province are more numerous.'[152]

Tertullian was always of a sanguine temperament and given to exaggeration, but there is a core of solid truth in his words. In the third century this growing strength of the Church as contrasted with her earlier weakness generally inhibited state persecution, but twice provoked it on a massive scale by creating the conviction that the state must either break the Church or surrender to her. Such growth was due to the nature of the message given to the classical world, the new phenomenon of the Church as a community, the character of daily Christian life; above all, it owed a great debt to the testimony given in the courts and in the arena by thousands of martyrs, some recorded, but many more unknown, and this is something which had never happened in the world before. Behind it all lay the unceasing pressure of a community of deep conviction where every member was aware of the need to bear personal witness.

Meantime, as a minority in constant danger, Christians formed an intimate fellowship, the communion of the Holy Spirit. Symbols[153] which they created — the *Chi-Rho,* the Fish, or the Good Shepherd — told other believers of their presence while revealing nothing to the outsider. 'They recognise each other by means of secret marks and signs, and love one another,' said another critic,[154] 'almost before they are acquainted.' Pompeii was destroyed in A.D. 79, but before then the *Sator square*[155] had twice been cut on its walls. Almost certainly this anagram had a Christian content. So, despite persecution, the Church grew. All Asia Minor and Greece had bishoprics by the end of the second century; Christians were found all the way along North Africa and through Italy into France and Spain, where Paul had hoped to go. There were even, said an African Christian,[156] converts in that part of Britain — Scotland — which the Romans had not been able to conquer.

Notes to Chapter 2

1. Virgil, *Eclogue* I, 64-72.
2. Suetonius, *Julius Caesar,* LXXVII.
3. *ibid.* LXXXVIII.
4. Tacitus, *Annals,* I, iv.
5. *Acts* 9:30. M. Grant, *The Jews etc.,* pp.102, 176.
6. *Acts* 13:7-12.
7. *Acts* 18:12-17.
8. *Acts* 22:24-30.
9. *I Timothy* 2:2.
10. *Titus* 3:1.
11. *I Corinthians* 2:8.
12. *I Corinthians* 6:1-8.
13. *Romans* 13:1. Cullmann, *The State in NT,* pp.55-70.
14. *Romans* 13:3-4.
15. Sallust, *Catilina,* X.
16. R. Niebuhr, *Faith and History,* p.220.
17. *I Peter* 2:17.
18. *cf.* R. Garaudy, *The Alternative Future*, pp.21, 58.
19. *Colossians* 3:22; 4:1.
20. *II Timothy* 4:6.
21. Kautsky, pp.47ff.
22. E. Gibbon, *Decline and Fall of the Roman Empire,* lxxi.
23. A. Toynbee, *A Study of History,* IV, p.64.
24. Polybius, *Histories,* VI, lvi. *cf.* Plato, *Republic,* III, 415.
25. Nock, p.14. *cf.* F. Cumont, *Oriental Religions in Roman Paganism*, pp.158ff., 199ff.
26. *Epistle to Diognetus,* II, ii.
27. Tertullian, *Apology,* xii, xiii, xxiii.
28. Harnack, I, pp.125-146. G.L. Prestige, *God in Patristic Thought,* pp.71ff.
29. Justin Martyr, *Apology,* ix.
30. Athenagoras, *Apology,* xxvii.
31. Origen, *Against Celsus,* VII, lxv.
32. Harnack, p.131.
33. Origen, *Against Celsus,* I, vi.
34. Gregory of Nyssa, *De Vita S. Gregorii Thaumaturgi,* P.G. XLVI, col.916.

35. Plutarch, *The Cessation of Oracles,* XVII. *cf.* Ignatius, *Ephesians,* XIX.
36. M. Grant, *The Jews etc.,* pp.135ff.
37. *Acts* 11:28. Egyptian papyri show the high price of wheat. M. Grant, *The Jews etc.,* p.306.
38. *Acts* 18:2.
39. C. Buck and G. Taylor, *Saint Paul,* pp.214ff. Robinson, p.52.
40. Suetonius, *Claudius,* XXV.
41. Tacitus, *Annals,* XII, xxii.
42. *Odium generis humani* ... a phrase vaguely used to describe sedition much as *Communism* is often used in the west today and *Revisionism* in the east.
43. Tacitus, *Annals,* XV, xliv. *cf.* Suetonius, *Nero,* XVI, XXXVIII.
44. Eusebius, *Ecclesiastical History,* II, xxv.
45. Eusebius, *Ecclesiastical History,* II, xxv.
46. *Revelation* 17:1-6. Cullmann, *The State in NT,* pp.71-85.
47. Tertullian, *Ad Nationes,* III.
48. W.H.C. Frend, *Martyrdom and Persecution in the Early Church,* pp.165-168.
49. Collingwood, *Roman Britain and the English Settlements,* pp.140-149.
    S. Frere, *Britannia,* pp.141ff.
50. Justin, *Second Apology,* II.
51. R.M. Grant, *Early Christianity and Society,* p.5.
52. Nock, pp.227ff.
53. Symmachus, *Epistles,* X, liv.
54. Ambrose, *Epistles,* XVII.
55. Gibbon, iii.
56. Pliny, *Epistles,* X, xlii. xliii. Kautsky, pp.135-138.
57. W. Jaeger, *Early Christianity and Greek Paideia,* pp.16ff.
58. *cf.* J.G. Davies, *Daily Life in the Early Church,* pp.60-87.
59. Pliny, *Epistles,* X, xcvii.
60. Eusebius, *Ecclesiastical History,* XXX, xi; III, xxxii. More probably under Domitian.
61. Ignatius, *Romans,* V. Quasten, I, pp.63-76.
62. Eusebius, *Ecclesiastical History,* V, xxiv.
63. Irenaeus, *Against Heresies,* III, iv.
64. *Martyrdom of Polycarp. Letter of the Church in Smyrna.* Quasten, I, pp.77-82.
65. Eusebius, *Ecclesiastical History,* V, 1. Quasten, I, p.180.
66. Frend, *Religion Popular and Unpopular in the Early Christian Centuries,* I, pp.143-145. Tertullian, *Scorpiace,* VIII.
67. *II Maccabees* 6:18-31; 7.
68. *Revelation* 7:9-17.
69. Justin, *Apology,* XLVI.

70. Marcus Aurelius, *Meditations,* XI, iii.
71. *Martyrdom of Polycarp,* IV.
72. Sozomen, *Ecclesiastical History,* II, ix-xiv.
    Socrates, *Ecclesiastical History,* VII, xviii.
73. Tertullian, *De Baptismo,* xvi, xviii. Thomas Aquinas, *Summa Theologica,* III, Q, 68, ii.
74. *Acts* 2:7.
75. M. Rostovtzeff, *Social and Economic History of the Roman Empire,* p.129.
76. *Cambridge Economic History of Europe,* (CEHE), II, pp.54-59.
77. Rostovtzeff, IX-X.
78. *ibid.* p.249.
79. *ibid.* pp.294ff.
80. *ibid.* p.369.
81. Suetonius, *Augustus,* LXIX.
82. *ibid.* LXIX.
83. Suetonius, *Tiberius,* XLII-XLV.
84. Suetonius, *Caligula,* XXX.
85. *ibid.* XXVII.
86. Josephus, *Antiquities,* XVI, vii; XVIII, v.
87. Augustine, *De Civitate Dei,* IV, iv.
88. E. Troeltsch, *The Social Teaching of the Christian Churches,* I, p.39.
89. Cicero, *Pro Sestio,* XIX.
90. Cicero, *De Officiis,* II.
91. Plutarch, *Cicero,* XLIX.
92. Suetonius, *Augustus,* XXVIII.
93. Cicero, *Pro Sestio,* XV.
94. F. Engels, *History of Early Christianity,* p.1.
95. Tertullian, *De Idolatria,* XVII.
    Canons of the Council of Elvira. J. Stevenson, *A New Eusebius,* pp.305ff.
96. Origen, *Against Celsus,* VIII, lxxiii-lxxv.
97. Troeltsch, I, p.55.
98. S.J. Case, *The Social Triumph of the Ancient Church,* pp.7, 13. B. Russell, *History of Western Philosophy,* pp.251ff.
99. Case, p.11. Marcus Aurelius, IV, xxx.
100. *I Corinthians* 1:26-28.
101. R.M. Grant, *ECS,* pp.5-9.
102. Plutarch, *Praecepta Coniugalia,* XIX.
103. *Epistle to Diognetus,* V, xiii. Kautsky, pp.273-284.
104. Minucius Felix, *Octavius,* V, iv.
105. Origen, *Against Celsus,* III, iv.
106. Case, pp.69ff.
107. R.M. Grant, *ECS,* p.88.

108. Frend, *The Donatist Church,* p.91.
109. Benko and O'Rourke, p.114.
110. Eusebius, *Ecclesiastical History,* IV, xxvi.
111. Tacitus, *History,* I, iv.
112. Suetonius, *Vespasian,* IV.
113. *ibid.* VI.
114. Tacitus, *History,* II, lxxvi-lxxviii.
115. Josephus, *The Jewish War,* VII, v.
116. M. Grant, *The Jews etc.,* p.205.
117. Suetonius, *Domitian,* XIII.
118. Suetonius, *Domitian,* XIII.
119. Eusebius, *Ecclesiastical History,* III, xvii.
120. Tacitus, *Agricola,* II, III, XLV.
121. Eusebius, *Ecclesiastical History,* III, xviii. Suetonius, *Domitian,* XV.
122. Suetonius, *Domitian,* X. Dio Cassius, *Epitome,* LXVII, xiv.
123. M. Grant, *The Jews etc.,* pp.225ff.
124. Eusebius, *Ecclesiastical History,* III, xix, xx.
125. *ibid.* III, xvi, xviii. Robinson, pp.221ff.
126. Pliny, *Epistles,* X, lx, lviii.
127. Justin, *Apology,* LXVIII.
128. Spartianus, *Hadrian,* XXIII.
129. *ibid.* XI.
130. *ibid.* XXIV.
131. Gibbon, iii.
132. *Epistle to Diognetus,* V.
133. Eusebius, *Ecclesiastical History,* IV, xxv.
134. *ibid.* V, i.
135. *ibid.* V, xxi.
136. Clement of Alexandria, *The Rich Man's Salvation,* iii.
137. *ibid.* xi-xiv.
138. Eusebius, *Ecclesiastical History*, XII, x.
139. Cyprian, *De Lapsis,* VI.
140. *Acts* 2:44-46; 5:1-11.
141. *Acts* 20:35.
142. Harnack, I, pp.153ff.
143. Eusebius, *Ecclesiastical History,* VI, xliii.
144. Julian, *Epistles,* XLIX. Sozomen, V, xvi.
145. *Passion of Perpetua and Felicitas,* I, ii; III, ii.
146. Harnack, I, pp.165-167.
147. Duchesne, I, pp.214ff., 226-234.
148. Origen, *Against Celsus,* III, lv. *cf.* J. Daniélou, *Origen,* p.101.
149. Justin Martyr, *Apology,* XLVI.
150. Justin Martyr, *Trypho,* CX, iii.
151. Tertullian, *Scapula,* V.

152. Tertullian, *Apology,* XXXVII.
153. F. van der Meer and C. Mohrmann, *Atlas of the Early Christian World,* pp.42-44.
154. Minucius Felix, *Octavius,* IX.
155.

```
S A T O R
A R E P O
T E N E T
O P E R A
R O T A S
```

This may be solved as follows, giving the cross, the opening words of the Lord's Prayer, and *Alpha* and *Omega.*

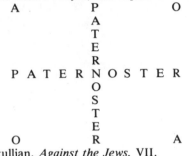

156. Tertullian, *Against the Jews,* VII.

Chapter 3

Debtor to the Greeks

3

Only a mutiny among the captains of Alexander the Great had frustrated his ambition to march to the Ganges.[1] He had started life as the son of the chieftain of a Macedonian tribe, but he ended it as lord of a vast empire stretching from the plains of the Indus to the furthest limits of Egypt on the Upper Nile. By Athenian standards Macedonians were scarcely true Greeks; they were barbarians; but Alexander saw himself as an apostle of Greek civilization. Like the renaissance civilization of Venice and Florence, this had been the culture of rich trading cities to which the surrounding countryside supplied little beyond food and slave labour. 'The country life is to be preferred,' wrote William Penn, 'for there we see the works of God, but in cities little else but the works of men.' For Greeks, this was nonsense, the exact opposite of the truth. So Alexander founded new cities. After he had sailed down the Nile he came ashore in a Mediterranean bay which so impressed him that before he left he traced the plan of the forum, temples and walls of a new trading city upon the soil with meal from his soldiers' rations.[2] He named it Alexandria after himself, as he named another near Kabul in Afghanistan, and yet another on the upper reaches of the Oxus, in what is now Russian Turkestan.[3]

In the United States north of the Mason and Dixon line and in Canada the white man, unable to use slave labour, and obliged to till the soil himself, drove out the Indians before him, thus creating a white society, and so avoiding a racial problem. His control became permanent. In North Africa and Asia, on the other hand, white soldiers, administrators, planters and business men, enjoyed a leisured and profitable life and a higher standard of living than they had known at home, through the service of a native population prepared to live in shacks and on a handful of rice. So, too, did the Greeks, and those who had assimilated to them. Throughout the countryside from the Aegean eastwards the succession states preserved much of an age-old civilization[4] with its native speech, its traditional social and economic pattern, but Greeks were settled in the cities like the Europeans in Cairo, Calcutta and Shanghai. A time came when these small groups could not maintain their power. Greek influence left its traces in early Indian art, but the Greeks themselves had gone.

Under the Ptolemies Greeks had thronged into Egypt to monopolise administrative posts[5] but here immigration was on such a scale that a racial division, though without an obvious colour bar, was created in a fashion more like that of South Africa. When the time came this was to be a factor in the acceptance first, of heresies, and later, of Islam. Meantime Greek became the language of commerce, science and philosophy from the Nile to the Danube, and from the Adriatic to the Euphrates. Beyond Mesopotamia urban development was less dominant and Greek penetration less extensive, but even here Hellenistic influence found its way to strange places. Alexander had reached the Punjab by the overland route but in early Roman times the discovery of the monsoons by Hipparchus of Alexandria opened a sea route to India. It appears that the Romans may have maintained a coastal station on Socotra off the Horn of Africa, and their traders reached out to Indo-China, Sumatra and even China itself.[6] St Thomas, it was said, made his way to India to be the founder of the Church of Mar Thoma, and despite the prejudice that no one knew anything about India till Vasco da Gama had rounded the Cape, the story has never been disproven and may well be true.

Written against this background, the New Testament distinguished between Greeks by race and Greeks by culture, calling them Greeks and Grecians or, to use other words, Hellenes and Hellenists. Saul of Tarsus was a Jew through and through, but in this sense he was a Hellenist and, to judge by their names, the seven deacons named in *Acts* were so also. So were the synagogues[7] which acted against Stephen. Thus when the New Testament was written in Hellenistic Greek it reached a wide circle of readers from Egypt to the Greek settlers in Marseilles and Bordeaux. In the middle of the fourth century Ausonius, who came from Bordeaux, could write that his father had been fluent in Gaulish and in Greek but not very good at Latin. Hellenistic Greek was the common speech of the day, related to classical Greek much as the English of the daily newspaper is to that of Shakespeare and the Authorised Version, less elegant if more useful; and, like modern English, the language in which Africans of different nationalities communicate, it was no longer the language of a nation but of a culture, a far spreading climate of opinion, and a world of thought. Of the three languages in the inscription above the cross, it was the most widely read.

Jesus read classical Hebrew in the synagogue at Nazareth and cried out in it on the cross; but Aramaic, its successor, was his daily tongue, used in prayer and in acts of healing as a few instances, quoted verbatim, in the Gospels testify. For the most part it has been assumed that he did not speak Greek. But Greek was spoken in the streets of Jerusalem[8] as in every other city of the Levant, and if there is no direct confirmation, the assumption that he did not have some knowledge of it is no better than the assumption that a man does not speak English because he comes from Skye. 'If you've only been six weeks away from Scotland,' said a shop assistant in Chicago to the writer, 'you've been quick to learn English.' Be that as it may, the Gospel was not first delivered in Greek, but from Pentecost onwards the Church had to use Greek as her main medium. Our Lord is known throughout the world today, not by his name as pronounced in Nazareth or Jerusalem, but in a form derived from a Greek rendering of it.

Set in a Hellenistic environment the Church could not have communicated her faith without using its language, but it remains an open question how far, in doing so, she may have been tempted to accept categories of Hellenistic thought. All subsequent Christian thought has been affected by her spontaneous acceptance of the precedent offered by the Septuagint for the translation of biblical concepts into Greek. A language which had never known Christian concepts had to be used to express them; elements of new meaning were injected, and the danger remained that the faith of the Church might be poured into a linguistic mould not totally in keeping with the biblical faith but subtly distorting it, a danger repeatedly met in after times by missionaries like Robert de Nobili in India, the Jesuits in China and Robert Moffat in South Africa.

Though the Church drew the line at some, many words had to be baptised into the Christian vocabulary. Classical Greek had several words for love but the Church declined to use *eros* because of its sexual connotations and preferred *agape* for the most part.[9] The very word for God, *Theos*, had to be used in the Septuagint for the God of Abraham and in the New Testament for the God and Father of our Lord, even though it was used in Homeric myths which educated Greeks dismissed as poetic fictions and Christians as degraded superstitions. But while Christians despised the cults of Olympus they had more respect for religious thought among the philosophers and dramatists. Originally the word *myth* had described any narrative, but by the time of Thucydides it had come to mean something unauthenticated and fabulous as contrasted with reality; and it was so that thoughtful Greeks saw the reputed doings of their gods. They might be thought of as representing forces in nature, but men no longer believed in them as in Homeric times.

As early as the sixth century B.C. the philosophers of the Ionian Greeks in Asia Minor began to speak of the one divine reality as an independent concept, unborn and imperishable, all-encompassing and all-governing.[10] 'One God is the highest among gods and men,' wrote Xenophanes. 'In neither his form nor his thought is he like mortals.'[11] This was the beginning of a monotheism, consistent up to a point with Christian theology though not with Christian devotion, and Xenophanes 'was the first to formulate that religious universalism which, both in later antiquity and more especially in the Christian era, was deemed to be an essential feature in the idea of God, indispensable to any true religion.'[12] Men still spoke of the gods and used the temples but simple polytheism was no longer intellectually respectable. When Plato laid down the lines on which the guardians of the state should be educated he was asked if children should be taught the fables of the gods, and replied, 'No, we shall not permit it on any account ... these are worthless stories.'[13] By way of the Stoics this contempt for the myths entered Roman thought. When Cicero discussed the existence of the gods he spoke of beings whom Christians would have described as demons and whom he would not have identified with the fullness of the divine; yet he employed a word which Christians also were obliged to use. By way of Cicero and Varro this criticism of the heathen gods passed down into Christian thought, but it was not always recognised that the ambiguity of the Greek and Latin words for the gods also applied to the God of the philosophers, a deity known only as a concept for intellectuals.

Augustine does not seem to have known the Ionian philosophers at first hand, but he gladly paid tribute to Plato. 'Socrates,' he wrote,

> 'was the first that reduced philosophy to the reformation of manners, for all before him aimed at natural speculation rather than the practice of morality.'[14]

> But of all Socrates' scholars, there was one whose glory worthily obscured all the rest, Plato,[15]

and accordingly Augustine reserved his highest praise for those who thought like him.

> Whatever philosophers they were that held this of the high and true God, that he was the world's Creator, the light of understanding, and the good of all action; that he is the beginning of nature, the truth of doctrine, and the happiness of life; whether they be called Platonists (as fittest) or by the name of any other sect ... them we prefer before all others and confess their propinquity with our belief.[16]

Augustine discussed, but decided against, the argument of some Christians that Plato must have read *Jeremiah,* and he went on with regret to note that even Plato countenanced the worship of the temples.[17]

When Christians used the Greek word for God they faced the danger of accepting a concept of the divine which was not that of the Gospel, however useful it might be in commending the faith. How could love be ascribed, with any sense of reality, to a philosophical abstraction? Paul, at Athens, knew that in Greek thought the meaning had advanced far towards a Christian understanding, but he was aware that for his hearers the word still held a content far from fully Christian. Long afterwards Pascal wrote,

> The God of the Christians is not a God who is simply the author of mathematical truths, or of the order of the elements; that is the view of the heathens and Epicureans. He is not merely a God who exercises his providence over the life and fortunes of men, to bestow on them who worship him a long and happy

life. That was the portion of the Jews. But the God of
Abraham, the God of Isaac, the God of Jacob, the
God of the Christians, is a God of love and of
comfort, a God who fills the soul and heart of those
whom he possesses. [18]

Augustine had not observed how far the thought of God in
Plato was removed from God as portrayed in the Bible and as
known in Christian life. His enthusiasm for Plato had betrayed
him into a remarkable oversight, and one many times repeated.

We have seen how the word *Christ* was used in place of a
Hebrew word, but all too soon it seems to have lost its distinctive
meaning and to have been employed as little more than a
personal name, as so frequently happens today. This acceptance
of Greek words to describe Hebrew concepts and their
adaptation to new uses was already well established when the
New Testament was written, and the most audacious instance of
this is the description of Jesus in *St John* as the Word, the
Logos. Stoicism and the Jewish philosopher Philo provided the
background for this. It was a concept ready to hand to describe
the one who 'was in the beginning with God' and 'without whom
was not anything made that was made'. Similarly, other words
had to be found to describe the Holy Spirit, the fellowship of the
people of God, the sacraments, and the grace of Christ. They
crossed the linguistic and intellectual frontiers, as words like
sputnik do today.

As the Church found herself within the community of the
secular world of classical times and yet not of it but alien, so she
was inextricably involved with the world of Hellenistic thought.
Those factors which drove the early Church beyond the frontiers
of Judaism were inherent in the Gospel, but her successful
incursion into the intellectual world of the late second and early
third centuries owed a great debt to the *preparatio evangelica*
provided by Greek philosophy. It had deprived the temple cults
of intellectual respectability and prepared the way for
monotheism.

Yet the question must arise whether, by accepting a
framework of Hellenistic thought, the Church surrendered part
of her birthright as she was obliged to enter the debate on terms
not of her choosing and in constant danger of unconscious
compromise. But if this involvement, this *détente* with

Hellenistic thought, gave the Church an entry to the thinking minds of the whole Mediterranean world, equally it proved something of an incubus when the witness crossed the eastern frontier into Mesopotamia and Persia, not to mention the Semitic land of Arabia, where early and extensive conversions would have changed the whole history of the world. To the east the Church found Jewish synagogues and Hellenistic minorities in cities such as Arbela and Dura-Europos,[19] but the door stood open to her only in minority groups alienated, to some degree, from the native majority and its culture. For that majority the Church might provide a translation into its language, but not into its world of thought.

In the event, the Church formed an amalgam of the Christian faith and Hellenistic culture which, for good or ill, has been a major formative element in the world ever since. A kingdom of the mind rather than any traced by frontiers on the map, neither identical with the Church nor coterminous with her, and certainly not with the Kingdom of God, this was known for long as Christendom; more recently it has been uncritically identified with western civilization until the rapid acceptance of technology by Asia and Africa and the fortunes of the Church in Europe have made the phrase an anachronism. Its periodical outbursts of creative and, at times, demonic energy, have produced recurrent technical and social revolutionary movements to convulse and transform the world, and since its appearance it has been responsible for virtually all the great creative urges which have shaped the changing world.

As the Church made her first contacts,

> the Greek intellect seemed to be struck with a partial paralysis, continuing for a century and a half. During that period, its activity — what there is of it — is shown only by criticism and erudition. There is learning, there is research, there is acuteness, there is even good taste, but originality and eloquence are extinct. ... From the fall of the Roman republic to the time of Trajan philosophy, like poetry and eloquence — or, at least — all philosophy that was positive and practical — became domiciled in Rome, and received the stamp of Roman character.[20]

Greece, which had given the world so much in literature, art and philosophy, had ceased to be creative. Why this should have been is part of the unanswered question as to why all civilizations have their time to be born and their time to die.

Part of the reason must lie in the Greek failure to construct any lasting social order beyond that of the city state. In Plato's time the ratio of slaves to free men in Greek cities ranged from four to one in Athens, to ten to one in Corinth.[21] Plato came from the Athenian aristocracy; in the brief interval of democracy when power was in the hands of the free citizens, Socrates had been put to death in 399 B.C., and he had been impressed by the military superiority of Sparta when she defeated his own great city. So it was to Sparta that Plato turned, though without much acknowledgement, for the model of a state. His *Republic* has nothing in common with the modern associations of that word and might more properly be translated as *The State*. It has contributed much to the spokesmen of totalitarianism in our century.[22] It was an oligarchy ruled by its austere aristocrats, the guardians, defended by strong-arm men, the auxiliaries, and maintained by the toiling masses who had nothing to contribute but their labour and who received no intellectual pabulum save the myths and propaganda with which they were fed and which, given time, they would not question. Spartan society, as described by Aristotle and Plutarch,[23] was barbarous, brutal and dedicated to making war, and Plato's idealised version of it is contrary not only to Christian standards but to the ordinary aspirations of humanity.[24] 'Plato', Bertrand Russell accurately says, 'possessed the art to dress up illiberal suggestions in such a way that they deceived future ages, which admired the *Republic* without ever becoming aware of what was involved in its proposals.'[25] Yet his pattern for the state was no mere dream; names apart, the abstractions of the *Republic* were matters of daily routine in the urban life of the first century; with this addition, that Rome provided the autocracy which held all together.

Our knowledge of Greece comes largely from those who belonged to, or wrote for, the upper classes, and is shaped accordingly. Theirs was a masculine and privileged world where women and workers had only a subsidiary place, and their ideal was that of the high-minded man, moderate, balanced, reasonable, with health, good looks, vigour, and enough means to support a comfortable life.[26] Hard work spoiled a man's looks and business cares prevented magnanimity; so the Greeks, like the nobility of eighteenth-century England, had only contempt for manual labour and trade. In each case, their income came from the land. Men of rank took it for granted that they should serve the state and stand high in its counsels. To this day their standards may be seen in their sculpture, the dignity and proportion of their architecture, and the ideal of an English gentleman. They looked for an honourable mind in a handsome body equipped with every external advantage.

Our conception of Greek religion, drawn from the philosophers and the remains of the temples rather than from Homer, is in keeping with this, but there also survived in Greece from distant times primitive rites and beliefs of a less calm and rational character. Evidently the mysteries of Eleusis were intended to ensure the fertility of the earth and its people by magic rites related to the ploughing and sowing of Autumn and the new growth of Spring. Dionysius was originally a god of fertility associated with beer and wine, and his wild rites are seen, both in their beauty and their barbarity, in the *Bacchae* of Euripides. Orphism which, if Herodotus is to be credited, had come from Egypt, had the usual rites to promote fertility and also a theology of sorts, according to which this world to which men are tied is a wheel taking them through many cycles of birth and death until they escape through ritual purification and renunciation. Ritual such as this means more to the ordinary man than doctrine, and beneath the splendid surface of Greek life there lay 'a stratum of religious conceptions, ideas of evil, of purification, of atonement, ignored or suppressed by Homer, but reappearing in later poets and notably in Aeschylus.'[27] Traces of this may be found even in Plato,[28] as in the myth of Er the son of Armenius, with its vision of the three Fates, the stern daughters of Necessity, but while mythology and the dramatists explored the stranger regions of the human soul, those who dominated philosophy had a purely abstract and rational approach. Unhesitatingly intellectual, they made no allowance for the strength of emotion, the irrationality of mankind, or the power of the subconscious. Freud may have used images from the Greek dramatists but, in more ways than one, Plato had never heard of Freud. Despite protestations of his ignorance Socrates, as described by Plato, did not think that knowledge was beyond man's reach. It was to be attained by rigorous enquiry and was of supreme importance. He held that no man chose evil willingly and with full knowledge, and that to know all would make men perfectly virtuous. Ignorance of the strength of evil and the weakness of humanity was a fatal flaw in the Greek mind.

In the same way this assurance in the abstract path of the intellect turned the Greek mind away from empirical science. Aristotle held that heavy substances fell more rapidly than light ones. Logic told him so. He did not experiment. Greece had known her golden age in the great days of Athens, but in the three centuries before Christ the centre of vitality had been shifted to Alexandria. Tertullian differed from most Christians in repudiating philosophy. 'What has Athens to do with Jerusalem?' he asked; but it was not the world of Athens with which he had to deal so much as that of Alexandria, the intellectual capital of his time. This shift had involved a change in the direction of constructive genius. [30]

Alexander's conquests had fertilised the Greek mind both with science and with superstition. It was the Assyrians, said Cicero, who first developed astronomy, and he attributed the corresponding superstition, astrology, to the Chaldeans. [31] For Horace, astrology was the Babylonian science. [32] But classical Greece had previously made more advance in mathematics and astronomy than in any other branch of science. Even so, it was the Hellenistic age which was the most fertile in superstition and the most creative in science of classical times. Euclid, who lived in Alexandria shortly after the death of Alexander, gave men a text book of geometry which held the field in many schools until the opening of this century. 'It has, of course, the typical Greek limitations; the method is purely deductive, and there is no way, within it, of testing the initial assumptions.' [33] Archimedes was a Sicilian Greek and Aristarchus came from Samos, but for more than six hundred years cosmopolitan Alexandria led the world in mathematicians, geographers, physicians and anatomists, grammarians and theologians. Rome had not created this ferment of thought; indeed, Bertrand Russell somewhat unkindly says that the Roman soldier who killed Archimedes was a symbol of the death of original thought that Rome caused throughout the Hellenic world. [34]

These men created an image of the physical universe which was to govern the minds of all educated men until the sixteenth century. According to Archimedes, his younger contemporary, Aristarchus advanced the hypothesis that the earth revolved around the sun. Seleucus in the second century B.C. taught so, but both were held to have been refuted. Eratosthenes, who died about 192 B.C., held that the world was a spheroid, that its circumference was about 24,000 miles, and that the sun was distant by about 92,000,000 miles. He conjectured that Europe, Africa and Asia formed one vast island. Seneca's surmise that the Atlantic might be divided by a great island running from north to south may have been derived from him, but it was rejected by Posidonius, whose miscalculations were generally accepted until Columbus, misled by them and using subjective assumptions, a false hypothesis, and a route abandoned by modern navigation, nevertheless discovered America.[35] Frequently one is told that the men of the first century and the middle ages conceived of the world as a flat disc, but this is a legend, for the knowledge of the spheroid shape of the earth was as commonplace in the schools of the first century as in those of the twentieth.

Hellenistic society, which brought this advance of science into being also saw its exhaustion and decay, and there is no more reason to attribute this to the dead hand of Rome, as Bertrand Russell does, than to the influence of the young Church. With the work of Ptolemy and Galen in the second century, long before the Christian Church came to be a dominating element in culture, Hellenistic science virtually came to an end so far as new discoveries were concerned. Henceforth its exponents were little more than mere compilers. Even such men as Diophantes of Alexandria, who is credited with introducing symbols into algebra in the second half of the third century, are under suspicion of merely restating what had been discovered by unrecorded predecessors.[36] Scientific discovery was no more than incidental to the life of classical antiquity, and in no way an essential element in its character as in modern Europe. As a scientific discipline and enquiry, as distinct from mere narrative, the writing of history halted with the beginnings made by Herodotus and Thucydides.[37] Similarly, by the close of the second century, the classical world had well nigh exhausted its capacity for progress in the natural sciences and there is no indication that, before its heritage was dispersed, it was moving to anything remotely resembling the scientific developments of

the sixteenth and seventeenth centuries.[38] Hellenistic science, as
it stood, was silently absorbed into Christian thinking until it
almost came to be regarded as a part of orthodoxy, but for many
centuries the seed was to lie dormant. Despite its continuity with
classical tradition, the Byzantine empire never showed any sign
of laying hold on Hellenistic science to reconstruct it into a
creative force.

When Paul reached Athens he found himself confronted with
two schools of philosophy, one named after its founder and
rightly so, since it had remained unchanged from the days when
he taught. Born about 341 B.C., Epicurus had taught in Athens
until his death in 271 B.C. He was largely a self-taught man,

> and we find in him the advantages as well as the
> defects common to self-taught men in all ages — a
> considerable freshness and freedom from scholastic
> prejudices, along with a certain narrowness of
> sympathies, incompleteness of information,
> inaptitude for abstract reasoning and, last but not
> least, an enormous opinion of their own abilities,
> joined to an overweening contempt for those with
> whose opinions he did not agree.[39]

His philosophy was essentially a practical one, not asking too
many questions, and designed to secure tranquillity.

He was a hedonist. Asked what made life worth living, he
would have answered, 'Pleasure'. Unless it meant prudence in
the pursuit of pleasure, virtue was an empty word. Hedonism
had been taken up by Plato and developed into the earliest
known form of utilitarianism, but this was a passing stage and
one left behind. Epicurus took over the cast-off ideas of Plato
and uncompromisingly denied that there were any pleasures
other than those of the senses.[40] He distinguished between active
pleasures, which were found in the attainment of a desired end
and involved pain, and passive ones, which were found in the
absence of pain or striving. Prudence and moderation were
therefore necessary for the happy life. Men should be content
with what they have and seek for no more. So far this was a
convenient philosophy for a warm climate where men could
obtain an adequate provision without much labour and without
any ambitions, a philosophy for the lotus-eaters. But it also
involved a kind of secular asceticism which might not have been

expected from his concept of pleasure. In particular sexual love, which brought desire in its train, should be avoided. His ethics centred on temperance, fortitude and justice, which consisted in the will to live and let live, a mutual agreement to abstain from aggression, not because injustice was evil, but because of the discomfort produced by retaliation and the fear of punishment. His was a radical selfishness.[41]

Epicurus was a materialist in his concept of the universe, one who explained it in terms of atoms; but since these were not entirely subject to natural law, he was not a determinist. Chance played a part in the world and in the life of man. Far from denying the existence of the gods, he asserted it, but taught that they neither knew nor cared what went on in the physical universe or in the life of man.[42] Knowledge of this set men free from religious dread and superstitious fear. Similarly death was to be accepted contentedly, since it was merely the end of consciousness and striving. There was nothing beyond. He did not believe in Providence. A true understanding of the indifference of the gods and the character of death released men from fear, which was the greatest of evils.

Notwithstanding his atomic theory, Epicurus had no interest in science. 'So far as he can be said to have studied science at all, the motive of Epicurus was hatred for religion far more than love for natural law.'[43] It served only to provide explanations of natural phenomena which might be attributed to the gods.

Stoicism, which also met Paul at Athens, was contemporaneous in origin with Epicureanism. Its founder was Zeno, but it took its name, not from him, but from the *Stoa* or porch in which he taught,[44] and rightly so for, unlike Epicureanism, which remained static, it did not remain constant but from time to time absorbed teachings other than those with which it began. It was a school rather than a closed system. It was also less Greek. Zeno was born at Citium in Cyprus in 336 B.C. and seems to have had both Phoenician and Greek blood in his veins. As a boy he heard of the conquests of Alexander of Macedon and he was thirteen years old when the news came that the would-be prince of the world was dead.[45] After coming to Athens he picked up Xenophon's account of Socrates in a bookshop and determined to become a philosopher. Thus he entered, but not wholeheartedly, into the tradition of Socrates and Plato. His *Politeia* was both an attack on, and an alternative to, Plato's

Republic. Alexander had tried to create a world state, and had failed. Zeno's perfect state was to embrace the world so that a man would no longer say that he was a citizen of Athens or of Sidon, but 'I am a citizen of the world'. In this ideal state the only laws would be those of nature; there would be no images or temples since these were unworthy of the deity; no law-courts, no statues, no gymnasia; virtue would be the only ornament and time would not be wasted.[46] This, and much else in Zeno, was more suggestive in some ways of Jerusalem than of Athens.

Hasty assertion — a fault of the will rather than the intellect — was the main cause of error. He rejected the Platonic theory of ideas, maintaining that they were not realities but had only a subjective existence in our minds, yet he still held that the world began with the working of mind on unordered matter. There were two beginnings, the *active,* to be identified with the *deity* or *logos,* and the *passive,* to be identified with inert matter or substance without quality. Despite this early tendency to dualism in Zeno, monistic doctrine prevailed among the Stoics. On the other hand, Zeno reversed the Platonic teaching on the opposition between soul and body; they were but aspects of one reality, a microcosm mirroring that of the macrocosm in which the logos pervaded the material universe.[47] God was not separate from body, but was body in its purest form. As divine reason the logos gave shape to the universe through which it ran and was identical with the deity. Also, as divine reason, the logos brought into harmony the parts of philosophy, guided men to true thinking and prescribed law for the state and the individual.[48]

Zeno believed that there was no such thing as chance; all nature was ruled by law; but if the Stoic universe was so, he was intent on preserving the freedom of the human will, and this provided his followers with much room for argument and fine distinctions.[49] All was ruled by providence, which differed from fate since it contained the element of personality.[50] Divine providence had created a cosmos where originally there had been chaos, waste and void, and in the beginning there had been a golden age when men lived according to nature, happy and innocent. Virtue was the supreme good and consequently the wise man must be indifferent to health, circumstances and possessions. While they identified the deity with Zeus, 'the father of gods and men', they explicitly accepted the reality of the lesser gods and of the oracles of popular religion. They were strongly moralistic. 'If all things are determined by fate,' their argument ran,

> 'then the ordering of the universe must be smooth and unhindered; if this is so, there must be an ordered universe; and if so, there must be gods. Now if there are gods, the gods are good; and if they are good, goodness exists; and if goodness exists, so also does wisdom. And goodness and wisdom are the same for gods and men. If this is so, there must be a science of things to be done and to be avoided, that is, of right actions and of sins. But right actions are praiseworthy, and sins blameable. Things praiseworthy deserve reward, and things blameable deserve punishment. Therefore if all things are determined by fate, there must be rewards and punishments.'[51]

Stoicism had drawn, probably from Semitic sources, a religious quality of which men felt the need, but which Greek philosophy had not supplied. Unlike the earlier schemes of thought, it was emotionally narrow and, in a sense, fanatical. It offered moral ideals for an élite minority but little for the masses. It formed no community remotely comparable with the Church and if it has obvious points of contact with the Old Testament it also has fundamental differences.

'Wisdom,' says one of the sacred books of Israel included, not in the Old Testament, but in the Apocrypha,

> 'is the brightness that streams from everlasting light, the flawless mirror of the active power of God and the image of his goodness. ... Age after age she enters into holy souls, and makes them God's friends and prophets, for nothing is acceptable to God but the man who makes his home with wisdom. ... If virtue is the object of a man's affections, the fruits of wisdom's labours are the virtues; temperance and prudence, justice and fortitude, these are her teaching, and in the life of men there is nothing of more value than these.'[52]

Whoever wrote this had read the Stoics. He accepted their four cardinal virtues, to which the Church was to add the three 'theological virtues' of faith, hope and charity, and so obtain the seven virtues to set against the seven deadly sins.

Nor was he the only one of his race to be influenced by the Stoics. *I* and *II Maccabees* tell how the Jews of Palestine were determined to remain free and distinctive, uninfluenced by Hellenistic thought or worship, but their success was not as complete as they had hoped and in the *diaspora*, and especially in the large Jewish community at Athens, this was even more so. Very largely, the result was creative, providing a terrain intellectually congenial to the Christian faith. However much they absorbed, the Jews retained their traditional faith intact, but in Alexandria, Greek philosophy was deliberately and systematically recast in a Hebrew mould. This was the work of Philo, a somewhat older contemporary of Jesus. Occasional autobiographical passages in his writings show that he was no recluse but took an active part in Alexandrian life, attending dinner parties and theatres, watching wrestling and chariot racing.[53] Like most Alexandrian Jews of the time he had little knowledge, if any, of Hebrew and his Bible was the Septuagint. But though he had assimilated both the language and the culture of Greece he remained a loyal and devout Jew, whose twofold aim was to expound the Mosaic Law to his own people in terms of Greek culture and to convince the Gentiles of the truth and superiority of Israel's faith. He was its best-known spokesman, and so chosen, when he was an old man, to lead the Jewish embassy sent to Rome in A.D. 40 to dissuade Caligula from inflaming Jewish fury by erecting his statue in the temple.[54]

Philo's life work was to reconcile the Old Testament faith with Greek philosophy. He taught the existence and unity of God, his providence, his creation of the universe and the unity of creation. God was immutable and did not vary, whatever the language of the Old Testament might suggest. Man held a high place in his creation, but God's providence was universal and the cosmos did not exist for man's sake alone. He had been made to contribute his part to the whole. God's activity was seen, not in miraculous interference with the order of nature, but in that very order. His redemptive purpose and demands were made known in the Law of Moses which possessed, not a temporary, but an eternal validity.[55] Philo worshipped no philosophical abstraction but the God of Abraham, Isaac and Jacob,[56] a personal God of love and judgement, the God of the whole earth who had chosen

Israel for a special destiny, the God whose thoughts are higher than our thoughts and on whose will all things depend. All that had been rightly taught by the philosophers could be in Moses. As Scripture was inspired by God, it could never mean anything unworthy of God or useless to man,[57] nothing impossible or absurd; and this he justified by an allegorical interpretation which set him free from restraint to the literal meaning of the text. Thus, commenting on the story of how the world was created in six days, he wrote, 'It is quite foolish to think that the world was created in six days or in a space of time at all . . . since the number of six means not a quantity of days but a perfect number.'[58]

Philo was committed to the Old Testament faith but to no single guide in philosophy. Like most of his generation, he was eclectic, selecting what suited his mind and purpose. Jewish monotheism found much that was congenial in the Stoic conception of the immanent divine power pervading the universe, but it was to Plato, above all, that he turned for the concept of a transcendent God supreme above the created universe. He set out to unite the personalist language of the Old Testament with the impersonal language of Greek philosophy. God, for him, is the One or Monad, 'the ultimate ground of being beyond all multiplicity'.[59] He is immutable, infinite, self-sufficient, and not needing the world. His will is pure goodness. He brought all into being from nothing and the material world which he created is not eternal like himself but created and dependent. From Plato he took the concept of the ideas, but with him these are efficient causes which are the media of God's activity in the world.[60] He is the earliest witness to the doctrine that the ideas are the thoughts of God. Although God had always been an intellectual problem for the Greeks but a continuing presence for the Hebrews, Philo accepted the God of the philosophers as the equivalent in philosophical terms of the God of Israel.[61] While seeking the concept of a God who was infinite fullness the philosophers might have seemed to the Old Testament prophets — had they known them — to have reached an abstract result, little more than infinite emptiness. Seeking the ultimate and the real, they had thought of God in negative ways, as self-sufficient, passionless, in need of nothing. How far could this be reconciled with the faith of the Old Testament?

Thus far Philo's thought relates to the Gentile world and his own Jewish inheritance, but his use of the concept of the logos has relevance for Christian thought. He found the logos described in Stoicism as the active principle permeating material things, as the mind permeates the body. It was variously described as God, providence, nature, or the soul of the universe, and from this came the Stoic view of man as a portion, or emanation, of the divine logos. Philo so stressed the transcendence of God that he had to find some means of relating God to his creatures. 'It was not right for the wise and blessed to come into contact with indeterminate and mixed matter; but he used the incorporeal powers, whose real name is *ideas,* that the fitting form might take possession of each genus.' At the head of these was the logos, the mind, reason, rational principle, or law of God, the intelligible image after which the visible universe is framed, and even the workshop in which the ideas are fashioned, the divine agent in creation. Man has been formed in the image of God and consequently, 'if we have not become fit to be considered children of God, at least we are children of his eternal image, the most sacred logos.' He could speak of the logos as the first begotten Son of the uncreated Father, the pattern and mediator of creation, the archetype of human reason, and 'the man of God'. The logos is God immanent, the vital power holding together the hierarchy of being, who as God's viceroy mediates revelation to the created order so that he stands midway on the frontier between Creator and created.[62] Those who could not yet see God mentally perceived his image, the logos, as himself, just as those who are unable to gaze on the sun look on the reflected rays as the sun. Thus the logos was seen by Philo both as an objective and a subjective activity, the intermediary between God and the universe and also the means by which the human mind apprehended the invisible God.[63]

Here is the background not merely to the explicit description in *St John* of Jesus as the logos or word of God, but also to words like those of Paul in *Colossians* 1.

> [Christ] who is the image of the invisible God, the firstborn of every creature; For by him were all things created, that are in heaven, and that are in earth, visible and invisible, whether they be thrones, or dominions, or principalities, or powers; all things

were created by him, and for him; And he is before
all things and by him all things consist. And he is the
head of the body, the Church; who is the beginning,
the firstborn from the dead; that in all things he
might have the pre-eminence. For it pleased the
Father that in him should all fullness dwell.

These might be the words of Philo but for the fact that they
refer to an event of which he had not heard. It is not that John
or Paul consciously borrowed from Philo so much as that they
moved in the same world of thought.[64] And they had received
other thoughts which Philo did not share. In particular, in the
passage quoted, Paul passed on to speak of the reconciliation
made between God and men at the cross. Philo had so entered a
Greek world that the thought of the Messiah, if present in his
mind, was no more than residual and not integral, a legacy from
the history of his people and therefore not discarded. He did not
think of identifying the logos with the Messiah.

Yet grace, another concept of vital importance to Christians,
was a subject on which he had much to say. His was a pioneer
attempt to deal with the paradox which Stoicism never faced, the
failure in the last resort of earnest moralism to achieve its own
end. As the soul toils upwards in search of perfection it discovers
that it must cease from toil and that everything that is good
comes as a gift from God.

When Abraham most knew himself, at this point did
he most despair of himself, that he might attain to an
exact knowledge of him who truly is. And this is the
fact of the matter; the man who has wholly compre-
hended himself utterly despairs of himself through
having first discovered the absolute nothingness of
created being. It is the man who has despaired of
himself who comes to know him who is.[65]

Philo, after his death, was more famous than read. Eusebius
had heard a report that he met with Peter on his visit to Rome
and supposed that his description of the Essenes applied to
early Christians, but he was wrong on both points.[66] In a way this
was a recognition of the affinity between Philo and Christian
faith. Judaism survived in the second and third centuries as
shaped by the the rabbis. Philo's influence was discarded.

Probably, if we knew more, we would find that Jews who read him attentively found their way into the Church.[67]

Greek thought penetrated more deeply into the Roman mind than into exclusive Judaism but never, though most Romans shared Cicero's smug assurance that his own people did most things better than the Greeks, with comparable result. Philo had taken from Plato and the Stoics only what he believed could be reconciled with Israel's faith, but Rome admitted all schools of Greek thought indiscriminately. When Carneades arrived in Rome in 156 B.C. as an ambassador he took the opportunity to shock a new audience with his scepticism in a series of lectures. Never before had his hearers known such mental agility. He was too clever to be good, or so it seemed to Cato, an exponent of a stern puritanism like that which has left such unpleasant memories in Scotland and New England.

Cato practised hard work, simple living and strict economy. Like Henry Ford, he did not love money, but just made it. He was known for early rising and spartan habits. As censor he removed a man from the senate because his wife had been seen kissing him in daylight, a thing which his own wife never did unless when it thundered. He made sure that his slaves worked until they lay down to sleep, and when they grew too old to work he sold them. For the vices of Rome under the emperors the modern reader can go to Suetonius or Petronius, but for the flavour of strict Roman morals before they were corrupted he can go to Plutarch's life of Cato.

Cato demanded in the senate that Carneades should be sent home. If their elders permitted, the youth of Athens might be corrupted by him, but it must not be so with the children of Rome.[68] But, like most defenders of the *status quo*, Cato fought a losing battle. His own great-grandson, another Cato, was as bad-tempered and dogmatic as his famous ancestor, but he accepted Stoicism, at least so far as morals were concerned, for he had no love of man and no hope in providence. At the crisis of his life, when Caesar was fighting for control of the Roman state, the younger Cato followed one of the Stoic precepts by committing suicide in 46 B.C.[69]

It was a Roman, Lucretius, who gave the world the most eloquent expression of the philosophy of Epicurus.[70] Born about 100 B.C., he died about 50 B.C., and this is almost all that can be said of him, for we know almost as little of his life as of that

of Homer. When the writer read Virgil as a schoolboy it seemed
to him that Virgil was no more than a second-rate echo of
Homer, but that Lucretius was a great voice from the past
consistent with what was taught in the science classes of Allan
Glen's School. This was a schoolboy's error. Any resemblance
was more apparent than real. But it was a pardonable error, for
there were late Victorians who saw Lucretius as a prototype of
that agnosticism which nineteenth-century science created in
them.

He wrote against the brutal background of the civil wars
preceding the fall of the Roman republic, the luxury, vice and
unscrupulousness of the rich and powerful, and the bread and
circuses offered to the masses, and his opening lines are an
invocation to Venus to end these and bring peace. His great
poem appears to be unique in that it is a reasoned system of
philosophy written in verse. Superstition and ignorance had
produced the disorder of his world and he turned for guidance to
Epicurus whose courageous mind had destroyed the power of
superstition.[71] All knowledge is derived from the senses and an
explanation can be found for all phenomena. This universe
consists of atoms, tiny particles forming matter, acting — for
the most part — under law, though occasionally capable of
diversion and empty space. Lucretius took it for granted that the
gods existed, but nature owed nothing to them and ran itself
without their aid or control.[72] Mind and spirit in man were parts
of his body and would die with it.[73] Death is a release and in no
way to be dreaded since all that superstition tells of torment in
an afterlife is false.[74] Our senses, our dreams, sex and
procreation are all open to physical explanation, and this is
equally true of animal and vegetable life. Human society is a
natural development and so are disturbing phenomena of the
world such as volcanoes and floods. Unpredictable and possibly
malevolent spirits have nothing to do with the matter. Epicurus
had delivered man from superstition; he had seen that man was
the source of his own ills and could set himself free by
knowledge of the truth.[75]

But Lucretius was not representative of Roman thought.
More characteristic is the conformity, the less dogmatic
scepticism, and the tentative belief of Cicero, his great
contemporary. In his treatise *On the Nature of the Gods* three
speakers set forth contrasting views. Velleius first states the

scepticism of Epicurus. God is aloof and inactive in the world and in the affairs of men and the knowledge of this sets a man free from superstitious fears.[76] Cotta then refutes what he has heard for, he says, it is easier to disprove a thing than to demonstrate the truth. Epicurus, he says, did not believe in the gods at all but gave them a place in his speculations only to allay popular resentment.[77] Balbus then speaks for the Stoics, arguing from such grounds as the general consent of mankind and the examples of divination. His outlook, at bottom, is a form of pantheism in which God is identified with the universe. Any names given to the gods, he says, in fact are no more than the personification of natural forces.[78] Yet he is anxious to disclaim an atheistic position. Even this, limited as it is, brings down the violent criticism of Cotta, not so much to refute the case as to make plain its obscurity. On this melancholy and uncertain note the contestants part, to meet and fight again another day.

Cicero evinces some sympathy for the outlook that the world is divinely guided, but leaves his readers to make up their minds for themselves; or not to do so.[79] He is not committed, either intellectually or emotionally. A similar agnosticism appears in his treatise *On Old Age*. He speaks warmly and hopefully of a life beyond the grave where old friends will meet again, but there is never a hint that their delight will be in God and, as the discussion tails off, there comes the sad comment that if, after all, nothing more remains, then he will not be aware of it.[80]

Moralism rather than intense conviction, the Stoic frame of mind and the temper of Cicero, marked the most upright men of a Roman republic that was dying even as it conquered the Mediterranean world, and it reappears in the men who knew the empire in the age of Augustus and his successors. But scepticism was confined to a limited circle and the power of the temple cults in Roman life must not be underestimated. After the great fire of Rome which led to Nero's persecution of the Christians the sibylline books were consulted and sacrifices made to Vulcan, Ceres, Proserpine and Juno. Some very primitive rites were practised.[81] Philosophy, which purported to supply morals without religion, was not always respected. 'He was a man', says Tacitus of one of Nero's freedmen, 'with Greek philosophy fluent in his mouth, and not one virtue in his heart.'[82] Yet it was Stoicism which, together with conventional respect for the gods of the state, provided the working religion of many in high life.

Seneca was born in Cordova in Spain, possibly in the same year as Jesus. He was launched on a political career in the reign of Caligula, banished to Corsica for a time after Caligula's death in 41 and then recalled by Claudius to act as tutor to Nero. Despite this, he wrote a vitriolic satire on the death of Claudius. It was he who wrote Nero's speeches.[83] For a time he held the reins of power until he, too, fell under suspicion and was told to commit suicide. It was a course which he had always commended and as he did so he poured a libation 'to Jupiter the deliverer'.[84] He was a voluminous writer, and a moralist with a religious tone which gave rise to the legend that he had been in correspondence with St Paul.[85]

A more attractive character is Epictetus, a man of warm feelings and a clear head. His dates are unknown, but he probably was born about the middle of the first century. Originally he was a slave and lame, it is said, as a consequence of ill-treatment, and so his circumstances contrast forcibly with those of Seneca, of whom an opponent said, 'By what system of ethics, and by what rules of philosophy, has this professor wriggled into the favour of the emperor and, in less than four years, amassed three hundred millions of sesterces?'[86] A hardness and want of sympathy, which reveals the Stoic origin, still remains in his ethics, but the pantheism of the Stoics is less in evidence and is replaced by a deeper reverence. 'When you have shut the doors and have made all dark within,' he says in a passage which recalls the words of Jesus on prayer,

> 'remember never to say that you are alone, for you are not; but God is within and so is your angel (daimon); and what need of light have these to see what you do? To this God alone you ought always to swear allegiance, as soldiers do to Caesar.'[87]

For Seneca suicide was an escape from an evil world, to which the wise man was always entitled; but while Epictetus was much concerned with death his intention was to accept it with indifference when it came. A man was not entitled to abandon life irrationally but only when God gave the signal that his time had come.[88] He had some knowledge of Christians. 'Is it possible,' he wrote,

'that a man may be so disposed under these
circumstances from madness, or from habit like the
Galileans, and can no one learn by reason and
demonstration that God has made all things which
are in the world?'[89]

Once again rumour suggested, but without foundation, that
Epictetus had been a Christian. While he could not defend the
claim, J.B. Lightfoot, a great Victorian scholar, obviously
found much in Epictetus that was akin to the Christian faith.
Cleanthes, a Stoic of the third century B.C. was the author of
the hymn to Zeus which Paul quoted at Athens.

Supreme of gods, by titles manifold
Invoked, O thou who over all dost hold
    Eternal dominance, Nature's Author, Zeus,
Guiding a universe by law controlled;

Hail! For 'tis meet that men should call on thee
Whose seed we are; and ours the destiny
    Alone of all that lives and moves on earth,
A mirror of thy deity to be.

Therefore I hymn thee and thy power I praise
For at thy word, on their appointed ways
    The orbs of heaven in circuit round the earth
Move, and submissive each thy rule obeys.[90]

A scepticism as melancholy as that of Cicero is found in the
famous lines of the dying emperor Hadrian to his soul.

Little, winsome, wandering thing,
Bosom friend and guest today,
Whither now, my soul, away,
Wan, and cold, and unattended,
All our former frolics ended?[91]

And it is found again on a wider scale in the *Meditations* of
Marcus Aurelius, first begun as an exercise in his tent when
campaigning on the German frontier where Rome had suffered a
terrible defeat and was never to know final victory. His was an
austere creed which offered no consolation save that of doing
one's duty with neither pleasure nor hope. Historians have
always honoured him as the noblest, if not of all the Romans, at
least of the emperors, but the Roman population had been

attracted more by the early days of Nero, who at least sinned colourfully, and had dreamed of his return.

A Stoic and a pantheist, he had learned from his adoptive father, Antoninus Pius, 'not to worship the gods to superstition',[92] yet, like the other Stoics, he paid the appointed dues at their shrines.

> To those that ask me the reason of my being so earnest in religious worship; did I ever see any of the gods? Or which way am I convinced of the certainty of their existence? In the first place, I answer, that the gods are not invisible. [This, it seems, means that he regards the sun, moon, and stars as manifestations of the divine beings.] But, granted they were, the objection would signify nothing, for I never had a sight of my own soul, and yet I place a great value on it, because it is discoverable from its operations. And thus by my constant experience of the power of the gods I have a proof of their being, and a reason for my veneration.[93]

In typical Stoic fashion he could speak of God as 'the soul of the universe' and as 'the deity within himself'.[94] Resignation and that stern self-control which he himself practised were therefore the only courses open to the wise man as he passed through this life. Less violent and more passionate men should be regarded with patience and tolerance. For the philosophic mind the one consolation in this life was that, being transient, it would pass. 'What is death?' he asks. 'It is a resting from sensation and desire; a stop to the rambling of thought, and a release from the drudgery about your carcase.'[95] His stress on duty appealed greatly to many Victorians who found in him morals without a creed. He had a great reputation for wisdom. Yet he was the only man in Rome who did not know that his wife Faustina regularly slept with gladiators and seamen,[96] and he broke the rule of adoption to leave the empire to his son who, at the age of twelve, when the bathwater was not hot enough, ordered the bathmaster to be put in the furnace.[97] He has enjoyed an honoured name, but the *Meditations* can also be seen as the saddest of all books.

Marcus Aurelius, like most of his contemporaries, had turned his back on the greatest thinker of the ancient world, for the intuitions of Plato had been found too vague and unsubstantial for the practical Roman mind, just as the subtle analyses of Aristotle were too hard and cold to satisfy the natural craving of men for some guidance on how they should live and die.[98] Stoicism provided the ethos of most educated people in these years when the Church was a negligible minority fighting not merely for a hearing but for its life.

In the middle of the third century when the numbers of the Church were increasing, Platonism, which had never disappeared, assumed new vitality in the hands of Plotinus. Not much can be told of his early days, for he chose to tell very little to his biographer. Evidently he was born in 204 or 205, but in 232, when he was about twenty-eight, he came to study at Alexandria under a teacher named Ammonius Saccas who may at one time have been a Christian but by this time was an exponent of Plato. Eleven years later Plotinus left Alexandria to accompany the Emperor Gordian III on his expedition against Persia in the hope of learning Persian and Indian philosophy.[99]

When Plotinus lived and wrote the empire was passing through disastrous years. From Nerva onwards emperors had been succeeded by their adopted sons, chosen for their character and ability, but Marcus Aurelius passed on the rule of the empire to his own son, Commodus. What followed was a strange comment on the father's great reputation. While Commodus reigned, his acts of folly and brutality terrorised Roman society until, on the last night of 192, Pertinax, the Prefect of Rome, was wakened from sleep by knocking on the door. He opened, expecting that his last hour had come, but instead was told Commodus had been strangled by a wrestler and that he was being offered the throne.[100] Pertinax, an old associate of Marcus Aurelius, set out to give the state a better character, but after a reign of only eighty-six days he in turn was murdered by the Praetorian Guard who then degraded the throne by putting it up for auction.[101] Civil war broke out, and when Severus emerged in control he signalised his victory by the execution of forty-one senators, their wives, families and dependents.[102] Till now the Guard had mainly been recruited from Italy, but Severus filled its ranks with men from the remoter provinces and increased its numbers fourfold. It became a great and unpredictable power and as disorder increased the Praetorian Prefect, once no more than a military man, came to control much of the machinery of the state. When Severus died in 211 he left the empire to his two sons, Geta and Caracalla. A year later Geta was murdered by his brother who, in turn, was murdered in 217. And so it went on. While Rome fell into disorder the Goths made inroads in Europe and the Persian monarchy recovered strength on the eastern frontier. Gordian III had reached Mesopotamia in 244 when he, too, was murdered. Plotinus escaped with difficulty, first to Antioch and then to Rome, and the safer employment of lecturing on philosophy till his death in 270.

So far as the writings of Plotinus show, none of these things might have happened. Instead he turned from the bloodshed and degradation around him to contemplate the mysteries of an eternal world of goodness and beauty. He lived in a dream world. It is said that Dean Inge, who was tone deaf, used to read Plotinus as he sat in his stall while the choir of St Paul's was singing. There have always been some who shared this enthusiasm, but they must be few. 'In point of style,' A.W. Benn wrote, 'Plotinus is much the most difficult of the ancient philosophers, and in this respect is only surpassed by a very few of the moderns.'[103] He never spoke a truer word. It was in the pages of Dean Inge that the writer first made acquaintance with Plotinus. For the most part Dean Inge can be understood, but there are many passages in Plotinus where a reader of normal intelligence will find it hard to know what he is talking about. Nevertheless his constant repetition makes plain the outlines of his system of thought. Plato, though in a changed guise, was his master, of unquestioned authority if only because the more ancient a doctrine, the more likely it was to be true. Deeply religious, Plotinus was not so much hostile as totally indifferent to the cults around him, and of all religious sects only the Gnostics roused his wrath because they fraudulently claimed the support of sages even older than Plato.[104] Religion for him was what a man did with his solitariness, purely individual and with no social relevance, the lonely journey of the thoughtful mind upward to the unknown God.

Plotinus began with a trinity consisting of the One, Spirit or *Nous*, and Soul, but these three were not equal for the One is supreme, Spirit comes next, and Soul last. As opposed to the many, the One is the primeval being, the source of all, and the only real existence. It is the good, to which all ought to return.

In so far as they draw their being from this source, all things are divine, and the One — God — is all in all. But the further off from its source derived being becomes, the less is its reality. Spirit, or *Nous*, contains an intellectual element and is the image of the One, at once being and thought.[105] Soul is the image and product of the motionless Spirit, standing between it and the world of phenomena in which unity and harmony are replaced by strife and discord. Bodies in this world rest on a substratum of matter and, when the hour strikes, Soul descends into them to give them an individual being.[106] When it leaves this body, if it has been sinful, it must enter another until it is able to make the ascent again. All memory of earthly things will be lost. Friends and loved ones will be forgotten until, being unaware of itself, soul is lost in the eternal being. While the Christian Gospel told of a Saviour who had come to seek those who were lost, Plotinus told of the search for God. He had no need for a community or church, no help for a troubled world, no interest in science. He had intellect, but no love.

According to Plotinus human identity is spent on the borderline between two worlds, reflecting the divine but inhabiting corporeal matter. Though bound to material life while on this earth, man's true nature is spiritual, thus, as his disciple and biographer, Porphyry, said, 'Plotinus seemed to be ashamed to be in a body.' From this involvement the soul of man can escape to spiritual being by the road of contemplation which led, not to vision, since this implied distinction, but to union with the One. 'He will be that which he sees. There is nothing between; they are no longer two, but one.'[107]

Nowhere in his writings does Plotinus specifically mention Christians and there is no evidence that he had had contact with any. His speculations have recurrently shown an unexpected attractiveness to men; they have much in common with Christian thinking, and in time much of them came to be absorbed into Christian mysticism through the so-called Dionysius the Areopagite and to be transmitted to the west through Erigena. There was never any possibility that Neoplatonism would become a living religion, partly because of the limitations of its founder, partly because it could not tell how the state of blessedness would become permanent or more than fleeting, and most of all because it could attract none save those with an abnormal speculative faculty.

Augustine was deeply indebted to Plotinus for release from the fanaticism of the Manichees.[108]

> You brought in my way because of a certain man — an incredibly conceited man — some books of the Platonists translated from Greek into Latin. In them I found, though not in the very words, yet the thing itself and proved by all sorts of reasons: that *in the beginning was the Word and the Word was with God and the Word was God.*[109]

But Augustine realised how good the things of earth were, even if capable of corruption and, more important for him, that there was no release or salvation in an ideal until he embraced the *Mediator between God and man, the man Christ Jesus.*

> Now that I had read the books of the Platonists and had been set by them towards the search for a truth that is incorporeal, I came to see your *invisible things which are understood by the things that are made.* I was at a standstill, yet I *felt* that through the darkness of my mind I was not able actually to see: I was certain that you are and that you are infinite, but not as being diffused through space whether finite or infinite; that you truly are and are ever the same, not in any part or by any motion different or otherwise; and I knew that all other things are from you from the simple fact that they are at all. ... I talked away as if I knew a great deal; but if I had not sought the way to you in Christ our Saviour, I would have come not to instruction but to destruction. ... Where was that charity which builds us up upon the foundation of humility, which is Christ Jesus? Or when would those books have taught me that? Yet I think it was your will that I should come upon these books before I had made study of the Scriptures. ... If I had been first formed by your Holy Scriptures so that you had grown sweet to me through their familiar use, and had come later upon those books of the Platonists, they might have swept me away.

'The philosophy of Plotinus,' says Bertrand Russell,

'has the defect of encouraging men to look within
rather than to look without: when we look within we
see *nous,* which is divine, while when we look
without we see the imperfections of the sensible
world.'[110]

This subjectivity at first was only doctrinal, not
temperamental; but it was to end the cultivation of science.
From the earliest days of Greek thought until Plotinus there had
been men who knew that the temple cults were, at best, no more
than shadows of the truth and, at worst, gross corruptions. They
had sought for that eternal reality from which all comes. Both in
its destructive effect on popular cults and in this search for God,
philosophy had been a preparation for the faith, as Augustine
tells.

However, there is another side. God as he was known in Israel
was utterly unknown in the religious world of the Near East. He
was wholly other than the natural experience of man, not to be
found within him by his searching, nor in the world of nature as
were the Baals of the Canaanites. He stood above man and the
world, Creator of both, sovereign and transcendent, but never
indifferent or inaccessible. On the contrary, he spoke to his
people and made himself known to them in the historical events
of their communal life; his word to men was, first and foremost,
an overpowering ethical demand. It stood in sharp opposition to
any form of mysticism which identified God with the depths of
consciousness.

If the opening verses of *St John* and the identification of the
incarnate Christ with the logos recall the language of Plato and
Philo, 'the remainder of the Gospel is more concerned with
other questions that are oddly nearer to Kierkegaard than to
Plato, who cannot be said to be more than a remote
influence.'[111] In *Romans* St Paul utilised Stoic concepts of
natural theology and ethics, but otherwise the gap is very wide.
Seneca commended suicide and if he speaks grimly of human
depravity he lacks the concept of God's grace as found in St
Paul. Stoic ideals of universal brotherhood fall short of the
active charity of the early Church. Nothing existed in Greek
thought to be set beside God, the Creator, who had founded his
Kingdom in the coming of his Son, who had called a people out
of the world to await the final consummation of his purpose of

love and power. So if this varied world of philosophy confronted the early Church, there was still a wide gulf to be crossed. Plotinus was still dominated by the Greek ideal of salvation for the wise man through reason, while the world went its own way. 'The wise man,' he said, 'will attach no importance to the loss of his position or even to the ruin of his fatherland.' As he said this, the whole fabric of the empire was on the verge of collapse but, in Dean Inge's words, Plotinus 'ignored the chaos which surrounded his peaceful lecture room'. This fact is enough to indicate that, with him, classical philosophy had reached the end of the road.[112] Plato had dreamed of a revitalised community; his disciple turned his back on the hard realities of the third century. But this was the world in which the Church was growing as never before.

Notes to Chapter 3

1. Arrian, *The Campaigns of Alexander*, V, xxv-xxix.
2. *ibid*. III, ii, iii.
3. *ibid*. III, xxvii; IV, ii.
4. Rostovtseff, p.236.
5. *ibid*. p.258.
6. *ibid*. pp.93, 147. *cf*. Eusebius, *Ecclesiastical History*, V, x. *CEHE*, II, pp.36, 50.
7. *Acts* 6:9. Jaeger, *ECGP*, pp.6ff., 108ff.
8. Sandmel, p.15.
9. Prestige, *Fathers and Heretics*, p.180.
   A. Richardson, *A Theological Word Book of the Bible*, pp.133ff.
10. W. Jaeger, *The Theology of the Early Greek Philosophies*, p.131.
11. *ibid*. p.42.
12. *ibid*. p.48.
13. Plato, *Republic*, II, lxxvii, lxxviii.
14. Augustine, *Civitas Dei*, VIII, iii.
15. *ibid*. VIII, iv.
16. *ibid*. VIII, ix.
17. *ibid*. VIII, xi, xii.
18. Pascal, *Pensées*, 555.
19. van der Meer and Mohrmann, p.128.
20. A.W. Benn, *The Greek Philosophers*, II, pp.165ff.
21. G. Lowes Dickinson, *The Greek View of Life*, pp.76-82.
22. Karl Popper, *The Open Society and its Enemies*, I, p.88.
23. Aristotle, *Politics*, ii, 9 (1269B-1270A).
    Plutarch, *Lycurgus*.
24. 'Plato's philosophy is the most savage and most profound attack upon liberal ideas which history can show.' R.H.S. Crossman, *Plato Today*, p.132.
25. Russell, p.122.
26. Dickinson, pp.138-147, 201-203.
27. Jane E. Harrison, *Prolegomena to the Study of Greek Religion*, p.vii.
28. Plato, *Republic*, X, 614-621.
29. Tertullian, *De Praescriptione Haereticorum*, VII.
30. A.N. Whitehead, *Adventures of Ideas*, p.104.

31. Cicero, *De Divinatione,* I, ii.
32. Horace, *Odes,* I, xi.
33. Russell, p.221.
34. *ibid.* p.226.
35. W.C. Dampier, *A History of Science,* pp.40-48.
36. M.L.W. Laistner, *Christianity and Pagan Culture in the Later Roman Empire,* p.17.
37. Collingwood, *IH,* pp.28-31.
38. H. Butterfield, *The Origins of Modern Science,* p.163.
39. Benn, II, pp.58ff.
40. *ibid.* II, pp.61-63.
41. *ibid.* II, p.72.
42. *ibid.* II, pp.85ff.
43. *ibid.* II, p.87.
44. *ibid.* II, p.8.
45. Vernon Arnold, *Roman Stoicism,* p.64.
46. *ibid.* p.66. *cf.* Origen, *Against Celsus,* I, v.
    J.M. Rist, *Stoic Philosophy,* pp.64-66.
47. Rist, pp.258ff.
48. Arnold, p.7.
49. Rist, pp.116-132.
50. Arnold, p.203.
51. *ibid.* pp.214ff.
52. *Wisdom of Solomon,* VII, xxvi-xxviii; VIII, vii.
53. *Cambridge History of Later Greek and Early Mediaeval Philosophy,* (*CHLGEMP*), p.137.
54. Josephus, *Antiquities,* XVIII, viii. Eusebius, *Ecclesiastical History,* II, v.
55. H.A. Wolfson, *Philo,* I, pp.164ff.
56. Wilson, p.36.
57. Daniélou, p.179.
58. Wolfson, I, p.120.
59. *CHLGEMP,* pp.141ff.
60. Wolfson, I, pp.217-226.
61. C. Bigg, *The Christian Platonists of Alexandria,* p.49.
62. *CHLGEMP,* p.144.
63. Bigg, pp.40-46.
64. Sandmel, pp.20ff.
65. *CHLGEMP,* p.150.
66. Eusebius, *Ecclesiastical History,* II, xvii.
67. Sandmel, pp.135ff.
68. Plutarch, *Cato Major,* XXIII.
69. Rist, pp.233-255.
70. Benn, II, pp.100-114.
71. Lucretius, *De Rerum Natura,* 1, 63-80.

72. *ibid.* II, 1089-1098.
73. *ibid.* III, 446-459.
74. *ibid.* III, 985-1036.
75. *ibid.* VI, 1-33. In his doctoral thesis Marx depicted Epicurus as the first materialist. (E.H. Carr, *Karl Marx*, p.13.)
76. Cicero, *De Natura Deorum*, I, xix; I, xx.
77. *ibid.* I, xliv.
78. *ibid.* II, xxiii. Arnold, pp.108ff.
79. *ibid.* I, ii; II, vi.
80. Cicero, *De Senectute*, xxiii.
81. Tacitus, *Annals*, XV, xliv.
82. *ibid.* XV, xiv.
83. *ibid.* XIII, iii.
84. Rist, pp.246-250.
85. J.B. Lightfoot, *Philippians*, pp.270-333.
86. Tacitus, *Annals*, XIII, xlii.
87. Epictetus, *Moral Discourses*, I, xiv.
88. *ibid.* I, ix.
89. *ibid.* IV, vii.
90. *Acts* 17:28. Arnold, pp.84-87.
91. Spartianus, *Hadrian*, XXV.
92. Marcus Aurelius, *Meditations*, I, xvi.
93. *ibid.* XII, xxviii.
94. *ibid.* V, xxx; III, iv.
95. *ibid.* VI, xxviii.
96. Julius Capitolinus, *Marcus*, XIX.
97. Aelius Lampridius, *Commodus*, I.
98. J.B. Lightfoot, p.272.
99. *CHLGEMP*, pp.195-201.
100. Lampridius, XVII. *cf.* Tertullian, *Apology*, XXV.
101. Julius Capitolinus, *Pertinax*, XI.
102. Spartianus, *Severus*, XI.
103. Benn, II, p.282.
104. *CHLGEMP*, p.206.
105. *ibid.* pp.236ff.
106. *ibid.* pp.250-256.
107. M. Grant, *The Climax of Rome*, pp.139-159.
108. Peter Brown, *Augustine of Hippo*, pp.95-98, 122, 168, 307.
109. Augustine, *Confessions*, VII, viii-xx.
110. Russell, p.300.
111. *CHLGEMP*, pp.158ff.
112. C.N. Cochrane, *Christianity and Classical Culture*, pp.172ff.

Chapter 4

The Bible in the Church

4

Though we have in the New Testament letters from two of his brothers, Jesus left nothing in writing. He committed himself, not to a booklet, but to a community. Few Marxists have been actively concerned with the rise of the Church but those, like Kautsky, who have been, have had their own insights. While almost all western interpreters of the life of Jesus have shared the assumption that society is normally acceptable and stable, Marxists have seen it as so intrinsically unjust that its overthrow is both desirable and inevitable. Otherwise perverse, they have understood that the Church began as the alternative society and that it, rather than a set of documents, is the key to what is for them rather a mystery. Yet the Church inherited a normative literature and promptly made an even more authoritative addition to it.

When Jesus spoke of the Scripture he spoke of the Old Testament; and the same is true of the Church of the first century. But the Old Testament then had a somewhat different form. *I* and *II Samuel* were reckoned as one book; so were *I* and *II Kings, Ezra* and *Nehemiah, I* and *II Chronicles,* and the twelve minor prophets. *Ruth* was included in *Judges,* and *Lamentations* in *Jeremiah.* So while the Old Testament today is printed in thirty-nine books Josephus could speak of it as consisting of twenty-two. 'All the Jews,' he wrote,

> 'from their very childhood, have it implanted and sown in their minds to believe that these are the precepts of God, to stand by them at all times and for their sake, if occasion requires, to sustain death with a willing mind. . . . Tell me, who of the Greeks would suffer such usage if all the things their historians have written were at stake and on the point of destruction?'[1]

There were also other books known to Josephus, 'not so authentic or carrying such authority', and to these books, known as Apocrypha, a limited recognition was given. Thus *I Esdras, Judith, Tobit* and *I* and *II Maccabees* came to be included in the historical books, the *Song of the Three Holy Children, Bel and the Dragon* and the *History of Susanna* were added to the book of *Daniel,* and *Ecclesiasticus,* the *Wisdom of Solomon* and the *Prayer of Manasses* to the Wisdom Literature.[2]

Further, in the synagogues of the *diaspora* the understanding of Hebrew had largely been lost and the Old Testament was read in the Greek translation made at Alexandria in the reign of Ptolemy II in the third century B.C., by the supposed seventy translators and so known as the *Septuagint.* This was the version used in the early Church both in worship and controversy and its importance as a doctrinal norm can scarcely be exaggerated.[3] The Church saw the Old Testament as the word of God, appropriated it and read it in the light of Christ,[4] the supreme evidence for the Church as the true Israel against the Jews who had repudiated the Covenant which God once had made with their forefathers.[5]

Among the Apostolic Fathers, Clement and Barnabas make most use of the Old Testament, but it is the second writer, not to be identified with Paul's companion, who turns it against the Jews. He quotes *Isaiah, Jeremiah* and *Zechariah* to demonstrate that God has no use for the sacrificial system of the temple. [6] *Isaiah* 58 is evidence for him that the prophet foresaw a day when,

> a people prepared in the beloved should hold the faith in its perfect purity; He made all these things clear beforehand for us, so that we should not be wrecked on the reefs of adherence to the Law.[7]

The Covenant which God made with Moses applies to Christians, for the Jews had barely received it when they repudiated it. 'Moses, Moses,' Barnabas read in *Exodus* 34.28, 'make haste and get down, for the people you brought out of Egypt have broken my Law.'[8] 'Let us see,' he wrote,

> 'whether the Covenant is meant for them or for us.
> . . . It was, to be sure, given to them; but their sins
> disqualified them for the possession of it.'

Here he quotes *Exodus* 24 and 31 on how Moses received the tables of the Law only to smash them when he found Israel given to idolatry.

Mark, now, how it came to belong to us. Moses was given it as a servant; but it was the Lord himself who conferred it on us, making us the people of the inheritance by his sufferings on our behalf. Though the purpose of the incarnation was partly to allow them to put the final seal on their sins, it was also that we might receive the Covenant of the Lord Jesus from its rightful heir.

All this goes back to the Old Testament thought of the faithful remnant, through the speech of Stephen before his judges, and the terrible words of Jesus,

I send you therefore prophets, sages, and teachers; some of them you will kill and crucify, others you will flog in your synagogues and hound from city to city. And so, on you will fall the guilt of all the innocent blood spilt on the ground, from innocent Abel to Zechariah, son of Barachiah, whom you murdered between the sanctuary and the altar.[9]

It is a curious fact that many passages in the Septuagint lend themselves better to a Christian interpretation than did the original Hebrew. Nor is this to be explained away by the obvious argument that the Christian message was itself adapted to the existing Septuagint, for Christians read their faith into the Old Testament, often without any justification and sometimes when the occasion was quite accidental and even, as in more than one instance in *Barnabas,* muddled and trivial.[10] So completely was this done as to cause a Jewish reaction against the Septuagint, which the Jews abandoned to the Church. Early in the second century they felt that they could no longer regard it as their own. 'The Jews everywhere,' says Justin, 'have the Old Testament, but though they read it, they do not understand what it says, but consider us their enemies and opponents.'[11]

Modern readers, who see the Old Testament in the light of the New and tend to undervalue it, scarcely guess how great an asset it was to the Christian evangelist. In writings meant for Jewish readers, such as the *Dialogue with Trypho,* abundant use is made of it, but even when Justin wrote for a predominantly Gentile circle of readers, as in the *Apology,* where no less than twenty-four out of a total of sixty-eight paragraphs are devoted to the Old Testament, it is plain that he not merely found it weighty evidence for his own mind but knew that it also would be for his readers. What impressed was not only the age of the Old Testament writings. In all classical literature, despite its great achievements, there was nothing comparable. Some of the questions asked by Job can be heard among the Greek tragedians, but philosophy returned no single authoritative answer. The Old Testament, however, set before men the faith in one God, beyond time or space, the creator, source and ruler of all, whose providence ruled both the history of mankind and the lives of each of his children for his own supreme purpose; and it provided men with a comprehensive and authoritative system of ethics. Beside this the mythology and worship of classical paganism was a collection of outworn superstitions as the opponents of the faith, both learned and simple, well knew.

Early Christians used the *Psalms* very frequently, presumably in part because continual liturgical use of them brought the words readily to mind, but apart from this the books most frequently quoted are *Genesis* and *Exodus, Isaiah* and *Jeremiah*. Other books, such as *Deuteronomy* and *Job* are used to a lesser degree, and some small books, such as *Ruth* and *Nahum,* hardly at all. This literature, consistent in its faith over so many different writers and ages, had already brought a host of Gentile enquirers to the synagogues, but the Church presented it to a wider audience and stripped it of some features which were repellent to Gentiles. The argument from prophecy has largely been discredited by trivial and naive employment, but its basic concept is that of one divine purpose running through all things and rightly to be read, in the light of Christ, even where the original writers were unaware of the full import of their words. Accordingly the early Church reinterpreted the Old Testament,[12] not merely because Christ himself had set a precedent for doing so, but because his incarnate life had made explicit what had been implicit before.

But the Church was soon to set her own Scriptures beside those she had inherited. The literature of the classical world of the first century was the product and property of the élite but the New Testament was addressed to the masses and rose out of their ranks. Its background is that of the proletariat, and this makes doubly remarkable the fact that in half a century or so this small and embattled community produced writings which,

The Bible in the Church 143

for relevance to men of all races and every range of intellect, stand alone. The New Testament is unique. First in time came the epistles of Paul, the one outstanding man of education in the circle of early converts. These are written to churches already in existence and deal with a Gospel already known. Such information regarding the life of Christ as they provide appears incidentally, since their character, for the most part, is that of *didache*, or teaching on the content of the Christian faith and life for those already converted. Next came the four Gospels, dealing with the words and acts of Christ and, above all, concerned with the mystery of the person of the one who proclaimed the coming of the Kingdom of God; these are predominantly *kerygmatic,* concerned with the declaration of the Christian message to the unconverted. As copies of these were circulated they were read in the worship of the local churches after the Old Testament, more or less in order of appearance. Thus originated the liturgical sequence of Old Testament, Epistle and Gospel.

Occasionally there survives in the Gospel text a brief word or phrase in the Aramaic spoken by Jesus himself;[13] behind all lies constant allusion to the Old Testament and a world of Hebrew thought; and there was a tradition that a Hebrew or Aramaic original lay behind *St Matthew*;[14] but otherwise all these writings were in Hellenistic Greek, as contemporary as the columns of the daily press today. Like all other writings of the time, the New Testament documents are undated. More important is the fact that while the epistles, with the exception of *Hebrews* and the Johannine letters, carry the names of their writers, the four Gospels are anonymous.

Yet from early times names were attached to them and these attributions go back at least as far as Papias, Bishop of Hierapolis in southern Asia Minor who, sometime before 150, wrote a book, now lost, entitled *Explanations of Sayings of the Lord.* Papias placed a higher value on oral tradition than on writings; what he had heard directly from one who had personally known the Lord counted for more than anything written in a book. But the Church was passing into a time when these personal links were becoming too few and too tenuous to be reliable, and was turning instead to those writings which she recognised as authentic and authoritative. She was beginning to recognise a *canon,* or list of New Testament books of such a nature that they could be set alongside the Old Testament. By subjecting all further tradition to this norm the Church demonstrated her understanding of the need to subordinate the oral tradition to the written word, from a certain point onwards.[15] Plainly the Church was continuing when the apostles were long dead, and by thus fixing the apostolic witness that Christ had come in the flesh, the Church remained true to the original evaluation of the apostolate as a unique function.[16] No longer were there men who could tell how they had once seen Christ in Galilee and relate the words that they had heard him speak. Instead the New Testament was to perpetuate the witness of those who had seen and believed him. Thus a unity of essential witness was assured, while making possible a multiplicity of interpretation within the Church comparable to the multiplicity of the New Testament writings.[17] As the New Testament made room for such diverse witness to Christ as the *Gospel of St John* and the *Epistle of St James,* so the Church could contain widely differing men with one basic faith, that which they confessed in baptism and which was to take shape in the Apostles' Creed; she was to be the household of faith and also, for the time being at least, of liberty.

Papias had some knowledge of how the books of the New Testament had come to be written. 'Whenever anyone came,' he wrote,

> 'who had been a follower of the presbyters, I enquired into the words of the presbyters, what Andrew or Peter had said, or Philip or Thomas, or James, or Matthew, or any other disciples of the Lord were still saying; for I did not imagine that things out of books would help me as much as the utterances of a living and abiding voice.'[18]

But he went on to add,

> 'This, too, the presbyter used to say, "Mark, who had been Peter's interpreter, wrote down carefully but not in order all that he remembered of the Lord's sayings and doings. For he had not heard the Lord or been one of his followers but later, as I said, one of Peter's. Peter used to adapt his teaching to the occasion, without making a systematic arrangement

of the Lord's sayings, so that Mark was quite justified in writing down some things just as he remembered them. For he had one purpose only — to leave out nothing that he had heard, and to make no misstatement about it."'

As for Matthew, Papias wrote that he 'compiled the *Sayings* in the Aramaic language, and everyone translated them as well as he could.'

Aware of what Papias had written, later writers added a few more details. In the second half of the century Irenaeus told that Matthew wrote while Peter and Paul were at Rome, that Luke, 'the follower of Paul, set down in a book the Gospel preached by him,' and that 'lastly, John, the disciple of the Lord, who had leaned on his breast at supper, once more set forth the Gospel while residing at Ephesus in Asia.'[19] Clement of Alexandria wrote that 'last of all, John, perceiving that the external facts had been made plain in the Gospels, being urged by his friends and inspired by the Spirit, composed a spiritual Gospel.'[20] Origen adds that Mark, because of his short hands, was called 'stumpy fingered', and that Luke was a Syrian of Antioch.[21]

But this human tendency to attach the name of one writer to each book is misleading. It is apparent to every reader that the first three Gospels have an intimate and complex relationship. An older generation of Biblical critics[22] concluded that Matthew and Luke had each made extensive use of *Mark* as a source and of another document, long since lost, which dealt with the teaching of Jesus, his relationship with John the Baptist, his temptation, the calling of the disciples and controversies.[23] More recently *form criticism* has described within these documents the employment of various categories such as parable, miracle and gnomic saying, which reflect the use of different types of the tradition employed in the preaching of the Church.[24] Consequently the Gospels can be seen to be the testimony, not alone of the men whose names they bear, but of the community committed to faith in Christ. 'Our Gospels are not biographies, not "memoirs of the apostles" as Justin wrongly calls them, but just testimonies to the faith, all of which originated in one and the same oral tradition of the early Church seen from different points of view.'[25] Widely varying estimates of the authorship and dating of the books of the New Testament have been made in modern times; but the original writers had no interest in telling us anything about themselves; they wrote only to tell about Christ and the Gospel.

The early Church produced a surprising amount of literature, partly because of the precedent of the Old Testament, partly because of the impression made by the New, and partly because the written page gave an outlet for Christians anxious to communicate their faith but frustrated by persecution and lesser restrictions. Some of this might be described as improving fiction. An example is found in the *Acts of Paul,* composed, Tertullian tells us, shortly before his own time and probably about 160, by a presbyter of Asia, who was convicted of the imposture and removed from his office.[26] Other writings are more tendentious. Writing to pagans, the Apologists did so under their own names; but there was also a minor flood of writings from outside the main stream of Christian doctrine.[27] Coming into the Church from an environment teeming with every possible variety of religious thought and mythology[28] converts could not always be expected to shed their old habits of thought completely. Deviations appeared. Writings intended to influence the Church in such directions were likely to be better received if they bore an honoured name. This was therefore attached. Standards differed from those of a later day and no dishonesty was intended, for it was considered legitimate to use the name of a greater man who, it was held, would not have dissociated himself from the contents.

So it became necessary for the Church to make up its mind as to what writings were authoritative or, in other words, to recognise a canon. The word *canon*[29] is an etymologist's delight. The root from which it first derived meant a reed and hence came to mean anything used as a standard of correctness, a measuring rod, a plumb line, or a builder's spirit level. From these beginnings it found its way into all sorts of places, from the music room to the artillery and the billiard saloon; but in the early Church it came to be used for a clear decision. As such it was not applied to the Scriptures until 363, but the concept was very much older and was taken over, like so much else, from the older Israel. In the synagogues of Palestine the canon of the Old Testament was traditionally divided into the Law, the Prophets and the Writings, but in the large Jewish community of Alexandria the Greek-speaking members were more lax and admitted the Apocrypha. As the New Testament writings came to be accepted by the Church as equal to the Old and so received canonical status a distinction became necessary; sometimes the older and newer books were distinguished as the Old Law and the New Law; more commonly a word was used which in ordinary Greek meant a last will and testament, but in the Septuagint and Christian usage meant a covenant. Unfortunately it is the former which came into the English language, for it is the second which gives the true meaning. The Old Testament tells of the Covenant once made at Sinai, the New Testament of the New Covenant in the blood of Christ.

What gave the books of the New Testament an immediate place in the Church was their faithful account of Christ and his Gospel. As they were publicly read in Christian worship they were heard with the reverence due to the Lord himself. It was the consensus of opinion which formed the canon, but in a deeper sense the New Testament books formed the canon by the impression they made on the Church. Anyone can experience this for himself by reading *Barnabas, Hermas,* or some such. The best answer to the question why the apocryphal Gospels and Acts were not included in the New Testament, says their translator,

> has always been, and is now, to produce the writings and let them tell their own story. It will quickly be seen that there is no question of any one's having excluded them from the New Testament; they have done that for themselves.[30]

The Church did not create the character of the canonical books; she merely recognised it. Books which were apocryphal were not necessarily spurious but, as the word implied, were for private reading only; canonical books were for common worship.

There could be no such thing at first as a formal decision on which books comprised the New Testament; instead there came the emergence of a general recognition, and while the result is plain, our knowledge of the process is far from complete. The Gospels created the nucleus of the New Testament canon and apostolic authorship or association was the first criterion. Signs of this recognition may be found as early writers start to quote them as authoritative. Clement of Rome in the last decade of the first century quotes briefly from *Romans, I Corinthians* and *Philippians*. His quotations of words of Jesus may have come from some collection of the Lord's sayings, but it is more likely that, as many of us do, he confused passages from *St Matthew* and *St Luke*.[31] Ignatius and the *Didache* refer incidentally to 'the Gospel' and evidently mean one or more of the written Gospels.[32] When Tatian composed his *Diatessaron* — an account of our Lord's life and ministry — about 170, he used the four Gospels and no other. The second-century sermon known as *II Clement* quotes *St Matthew* as Scripture and Irenaeus justified the standing of the four Gospels by arguments so bad as to show that they were beyond question.[33]

Beside the Gospels stood the Epistles, which were already being circulated and read in worship in the life-time of St Paul.[34] The earliest collection was of the nine epistles to churches together with *Philemon*. To this the Pastoral Epistles were added and, probably about the middle of the second century, *Hebrews* came to be regarded as Pauline and was included. It was the small epistles, such as *II* and *III John,* and *Jude* which, understandably, were the last of the epistles to be recognised.

What forced the matter upon the mind of the Church was the coming of Marcion to Rome about 140 and his assault not merely on the Old Testament but on those New Testament books which did not conform to his scheme of thought. If a specifically Christian canon of Scripture was already well rooted in the Church's convictions and practice, Marcion's challenge played an important part in its definition.[35] The influence of Montanism worked in the same direction. Our earliest surviving list of New Testament books is the so-called Muratorian canon of late second century date.[36] It begins with some words evidently referring to St Mark, and then tells how the third Gospel was composed on Paul's authority by Luke the physician. The fourth, it says, was written by John, one of the disciples, and rather a fantastic story is told of how he did so after fasting for inspiration. The *Acts of the Apostles,* it says, was written by St Luke to tell of events at which he had been present. Among the Pauline epistles *Romans, I* and *II Corinthians, Galatians, Ephesians, Philippians, Colossians, I* and *II Thessalonians* and *Titus* are listed. Then comes a borderline group.

There is in circulation also one to the Laodiceans, another to the Alexandrians, both forged in Paul's name to suit the heresy of Marcion, and several others which cannot be received into the Catholic Church; for it is not fitting that gall be mixed with honey. The Epistle of *Jude* no doubt, and the couple bearing the name of John, are accepted in the Catholic Church; and the *Wisdom* written by the friends of Solomon in his honour. The *Apocalypse* also of John, and of Peter also we receive, which some of our friends will not have read in church. But the *Shepherd* was written quite lately in our times in the city of Rome by Hermas while his brother, Pius, the bishop, was sitting in the chair of the church of the city of Rome; and therefore indeed it ought to be read, but it cannot to the end of time be publicly read in the church to the people, either among the prophets, who are complete in number, or among the Apostles. But of Arsinous, called also Valentinus, or of Miltiades we receive nothing at all; those who have also composed a new book of Psalms for Marcion, together with Basilides and the Asian founder[37] of the Cataphrygians are rejected.

Here is a list of Scriptures recognised as apostolic, a shorter list regarded with some hesitation, and a third group rejected as Gnostic and heretical.

These books circulated, not in one volume as in modern times, but in separate copies; and it is easy to understand how brief leaflets like *II Peter, II* and *III John* and *Jude* were little used and long in being accepted. But the more notable books on the margin of the canon were the anonymous *Hebrews* and *Revelation*. Tertullian[38] attributed *Hebrews* to Barnabas, the companion of Paul. Origen had heard it attributed to Clement of Rome or to St Luke; his critical mind accepted its doctrine but questioned its authorship:

In the epistle entitled *To the Hebrews* the diction does not exhibit the characteristic roughness of speech or phraseology admitted by the apostle himself; the construction of the sentence is closer to Greek usage, as anyone capable of recognising

differences of style would agree. On the other hand
the matter of the epistle is wonderful, and quite equal
to the apostle's acknowledged writings; the truth of
this would be admitted by anyone who has read the
apostle carefully. ... If I were asked my personal
opinion, I would say that the matter is the apostle's
but the phraseology and construction are those of
someone who remembered the apostle's teaching and
wrote his own interpretation of what his master had
said. So if any church regards this epistle as Paul's, it
should be commended for so doing, for the primitive
Church had every justification for handing it down
as his. Who wrote the epistle is known to God alone;
the accounts that have reached us suggest that it was
either Clement, who became Bishop of Rome, or
Luke, who wrote the Gospel and the Acts.[39]

A similar critical interest, but with a different conclusion, is
found in the discussion of *Revelation* by Origen's contemporary,
Dionysius, Bishop of Alexandria. Dionysius was puzzled by the
apocalyptic framework which its writer had taken over from
Jewish sources and disturbed by its millenarianism. 'Some of
our predecessors,' he wrote,

'rejected the book and pulled it entirely to pieces,
criticising it chapter by chapter, pronouncing it
unintelligible and illogical and the title false. They
say it is not John's and is not a revelation at all, since
it is heavily veiled by a thick curtain of incomprehen-
sibility; so far from being by one of the apostles, the
author of the book was not even one of the saints, or
a member of the Church but Cerinthus, the founder
of the sect called Cerinthians after him. ... This,
they say, was the doctrine he taught — that Christ's
kingdom would be on earth. ... But I myself would
never dare to reject the book, of which many good
Christians have a very high opinion, but realising
that my mental powers are inadequate to judge it
properly, I take the view that the interpretation of the
various sections is largely a mystery, something too
wonderful for our comprehension. I do not understand it, but I suspect that some deeper meaning is

concealed in the words; I do not measure and judge these things by my own reason, but put more reliance on faith, and so I have concluded that they are too high to be grasped by me; I do not condemn as valueless what I have not taken in at a glance, but rather am puzzled that I have not taken it in. . . . That the writer was John he himself states, and we must believe him. But which John? He does not say here, as so often in the Gospel, that he was the disciple loved by the Lord, the one who leaned back on his breast, the brother of James, the eyewitness and earwitness of the Lord. He would surely have used one of these descriptions had he wished to reveal his identity. But he uses none of them. . . . I think there was another John among the Christians of Asia. . . . From the ideas, too, and from the words used and the way they are put together, we shall readily conclude that this writer was different from the other. There is complete harmony between the Gospel and the Epistle . . . but there is no resemblance or similarity whatever between them and the *Revelation*. . . . By the phraseology also we can measure the difference. The first two are written not only without blunders in the use of Greek, but with remarkable skill . . . the other uses barbarous idioms, and is sometimes guilty of solecisms.[40]

Thus the Church received the Bible, more or less as we have it today. As to the points of difference, the Church of the first two centuries accepted the Old Testament Apocrypha without hesitation until controversy with Jews and the Christian habit of finding New Testament doctrine in Old Testament texts made the Church aware that the Jews valued their Apocrypha but did not set it on the same level as Scripture.[41] Accordingly in the course of the fourth century the writers of the Church in the eastern empire relegated the Apocrypha to a subordinate position outside of the Old Testament canon. Less in contact with Jewish controversy, the Church in the west accepted the Apocrypha up to a point; its books were ecclesiastical but not canonical, to be read by Christians but not advanced as grounds for doctrine. *Revelation* had been accepted at an earlier date and in the course of the fourth century *Hebrews* and the brief epistles which had been questioned became generally received as canonical.[42] It was the influence of the *Vulgate*, St Jerome's great Latin version of the Scriptures, the Bible as known in western Europe throughout the Dark and Middle Ages, when critical minds like those of Origen and Dionysius were scarce, which placed these books beyond question by its inclusion of them.

For the Church as for the older Israel, the Scriptures were the word of God. 'The sacred writings,' wrote St Paul,

> 'have power to make you wise and lead you to salvation through faith in Christ Jesus. Every inspired Scripture has its use for teaching the truth and refuting error.'[43]

Written about the Old Testament, this was cordially applied by the Church to the New. She received the New Testament, not merely because it was a permanent testimony to the words and acts of Jesus, but because it was divinely inspired. Near the end of the first century Clement of Rome quotes the Old Testament as the words of the Holy Spirit.[44] In the early years of the next Ignatius speaks of the prophets as 'inspired by the grace of Christ Jesus'.[45] Midway through the century Justin wrote, 'when you hear the words of the prophets spoken as in a particular character, do not think of them as spoken by the inspired men themselves, but by the divine Word that moved them,'[46] and shortly afterwards Athenagoras wrote of Moses and the prophets that 'under the influence of the divine Spirit and raised above their own thoughts, they proclaimed the things with which they were inspired. For the Spirit used them just as a flute player blows on a flute.'[47] As soon as the New Testament took shape the Church assigned to it exactly the same origin and inspiration as she had attributed to the Old. 'The Holy Spirit,' says Irenaeus, 'foreseeing the corrupters and guarding against their deception, says through Matthew . . .'[48]

No modern fundamentalist ever stated the doctrine of verbal inspiration more unequivocally. It followed that one divine message ran through every part of Scripture. Unfortunately there were also many obscurities since men had little to draw with and the well was deep. To quote Irenaeus again:

> The entire Scriptures, the prophets and the Gospels,
> can be clearly, unambiguously, and harmoniously
> understood by all. . . . However, we cannot discover
> explanations of all things in Scripture . . . inasmuch
> as we are inferior to, and later in existence than, the
> Word of God and his Spirit, and on that very account
> are destitute of the knowledge of his mysteries. . . .
> The migration of birds is beyond our understanding.
> So, if there are some things even in creation, the
> knowledge of which belongs only to God, what
> ground for complaint is there if we are able by the
> grace of God to explain some things in Scripture,
> while we must leave others in the hand of God?[49]

Obscurities in Scriptures which were held to contain one
divine message called for explanation. So commentaries came to
be written. Origen was not the first in this field but he was the
first to develop the principles which exposition was to follow
and to apply them on the widest scale.[50] About 215 he was
requested by the Bishop of Caesarea to expound the Scriptures
publicly. This gave offence to his own bishop, who recalled him.
Back in Alexandria Origen met a Gnostic named Ambrose
whom he brought into the faith of the Church.[51] Full of gratitude
Ambrose, who was a wealthy man, provided Origen with all he
needed for intensive Bible study, including seven shorthand
writers, copyists and secretaries. Origen was thus enabled to
launch out on a vast scheme of scriptural commentaries. Among
the first problems awaiting him was that of textual variants,
which he constantly recorded, even if he had little or nothing to
contribute to solving the question of which might be the best
text. As part of this work he produced a vast edition of the Old
Testament in six columns — the *Hexapla* — one containing the
Septuagint, another the best-known Hebrew text and others the
alternative translations.

> He hunted them out in their hiding places and
> brought them to light. These were wrapped in
> mystery, and he had no idea who wrote them . . . in
> the case of one, he has added a note that it was found
> at Jericho in a jar during the reign of Antoninus, the
> son of Severus. All these he combined in one volume,
> breaking them up into clauses and setting them side

> by side in parallel columns, along with the original
> Hebrew text. [52]

Nothing like this had been done before.

Origen knew perfectly well that the Scriptures had been
written by men, but he was certain that they were divinely
inspired.

> He who reads the words of the prophets with care
> and attention, feeling by the very perusal the traces
> of the divinity that is in them, will be led by his own
> emotions to believe that these words which have been
> deemed to be the words of God are not the
> compositions of men. [53]

Scripture must therefore be interpreted by Scripture and an
isolated text should not be allowed to lead to a heretical
conclusion. Where there was obscurity, confusion, or ground
for scandal one must look for the spiritual meaning, for men
could scarcely expect to identify the oracles of God with the
obvious and superficial.

> If the usefulness of the legislation and the sequence
> and beauty of the history were universally evident of
> itself, we should not believe that any other things
> could be understood in the Scriptures save what was
> obvious. [54]

Similarly, though the narrative is fundamentally historical there
are passages which no one can be expected to take literally.

> Who is so foolish as to suppose that God, after the
> manner of a husbandman, planted a paradise in
> Eden, towards the east . . . and again, that one was a
> partaker of good and evil by masticating what was
> taken from that tree? [55]

Or did anyone actually suppose that in the temptation, Satan led
Christ up a mountain in Palestine so high that he could see
Russia and India? [56] Here and in multitudes of other passages the
meaning must be sought for with care. There was, in fact, a
threefold interpretation of Scripture; literal, moral and
spiritual, [57] and this was not surprising but inevitable if the
wonder of the ineffable God was to be revealed to limited men.

This method of interpretation, much misunderstood and even more often abused, finds few admirers in the twentieth century and had its critics in Origen's own. 'In their eagerness to find, not a way to reject the depravity of the Jewish Scriptures,' wrote the pagan Porphyry,

> 'but a means of explaining it away, the Christians resort to interpretations which cannot be reconciled or harmonised with these Scriptures, and which provide not so much a defence of the original authors as a fulsome advertisement for the interpreters. This absurd method must be attributed to a man whom I met while I was still quite young, who enjoyed a great reputation and thanks to the works he has left behind him, enjoys it still. I refer to Origen ...'[58]

There was a strong element of truth in the Neoplatonist's charge, but this is not the whole of the matter. Origen made it possible for intelligent Christians who inevitably lacked any historical approach for centuries to come to read the Bible with reverence and reward.

Variants of this method became familiar in the Church and are still used even when unrecognised. When Augustine was twenty-eight years old and outside the fold of the Church,

> a message came from Milan to Rome ... asking for a professor of Rhetoric for that city. ... I applied for the post. ... So I came to Milan, to the bishop and devout servant of God, Ambrose, famed among the best men of the whole world, whose eloquence did then most powerfully minister to *Thy people the fatness of Thy wheat and the joy of Thy oil and the sober intoxication of Thy wine.* All unknowing I was brought by God to him. ... That man of God received me as a father and as a bishop welcomed my coming. I came to love him, not at first as a teacher of the truth, which I had utterly despaired of finding in Your Church, but for His kindness towards me. ... His words I listened to with the greatest care; his matter I held quite unworthy of attention. ... Yet along with the words, which I admired, there also came into my mind the subject matter ... especially

after I had heard explained figuratively several
passages of the Old Testament which had been a
cause of death for me when taken literally. Many
passages of these books were expounded in a spiritual
sense . . . [59]

'You know well,' Augustine wrote to a former student friend,

'that the Manichees by their censures of the Catholic
Faith, and chiefly by their destructive criticism of the
Old Testament affect the unlearned. . . . Listen, I pray
you, to the considerations which influence me. . . .
The whole Old Testament Scripture, to those who
diligently desire to know it, is handed down with a
fourfold sense.' [60]

These he names as the historical sense, the aetiological, the
analogical and the allegorical, with an apology for the
clumsiness of the names. The first is the explicit meaning of
what is written, while the second deals with the reason why
something was done or said. Thus, when Christ forbade divorce
he told his hearers that Moses had permitted it 'on account of
the hardness of your hearts'. [61] In other words, the Old
Testament Law had been adapted to the circumstances of the
time, but the analogical sense shows that the Old and New
Testaments, properly understood, do not conflict. Thus our
Lord used the analogy of the eating of the shewbread by David
and his men as an indication that his own disciples were not
breaking the Sabbath. [62] To vindicate the allegorical — obviously
the most questionable use — Augustine turned to our Lord's
saying that, 'as Jonas was in the belly of the whale three days
and three nights, so shall the Son of Man be three days and three
nights in the heart of the earth.' [63] Whatever the modern reader
may think of these methods, they enabled those of an earlier day
to put aside small things and to listen to the full message of the
Bible. More than those who spoke the prophetic words had ever
dreamed, their words pointed to the Lord in whom all was
fulfilled.

I call God who dwells in pure souls to witness, that I
am convinced there is nothing more wise, more
chaste, more religious than those Scriptures which the

Catholic Church accepts under the name of the Old Testament.[64]

It was left to a later age to contrast the authority of the Bible with that of the Church, but the Christians of an early day made no distinction. Any consideration of the place of the Bible in the early Church is naturally drawn to the acceptance of the Old Testament by the Church and the formation of the canon of the New Testament, but the central fact is the acceptance by the Church of the whole Bible as the Word of God. She was not prepared to allow its transmission, as early folk epics were passed down in simple societies with each narrator using his own words, but to preserve it exactly, word for word. By the time of Diocletian even the pagans understood this. They set out not only to persecute Christians, but to destroy every copy of the Scriptures, and the reaction of the Church is seen in its hostility to those — the *traditores* — who surrendered even a spare copy.

Notes to Chapter 4

1. Josephus, *Against Apion*, I, viii.
2. Sandmel, pp.28-33. Daniélou, p.137.
3. J.N.D. Kelly, *Early Christian Doctrine*, p.32.
4. W.D. Davies, p.104.
5. Minucius Felix, *Octavius*, XXXIII.
6. *Barnabas*, II.
7. *ibid*. III.
8. *ibid*. XIV.
9. *St Matthew* 23:34-35.
10. *Barnabas*, IX.
11. *Apology*, I, xxi.
12. Cyprian, *Ad Quirinum*, I, iv-v.
13. *e.g. St Mark* 5:41; 14:36.
14. Eusebius, *Ecclesiastical History*, III, xxiv, xxxix; V, viii.
15. Cullman, *Christ and Time*, p. 170.
16. *ibid*. p.172.
17. Bultmann, *Theology of the New Testament*, II, pp.141ff.
18. Eusebius, *Ecclesiastical History*, III, xxxix.
19. *ibid*. V, viii. Irenaeus, III, i.
20. Eusebius, *Ecclesiastical History*, VI, xiv.
21. *ibid*. VI, xxv.
22. Hoskyns and Davey, *The Riddle of the New Testament*, pp.76-79.
23. F.C. Grant, *The Gospels*, pp.59ff.
24. *ibid*. pp.55ff.
25. Cullman, *Christ and Time*, pp.53ff.
26. James, pp.270-299.
27. *ibid*. pp.504-521. Duchesne, I, pp.370-373.
28. Nock, pp.33-137.
29. C.R. Gregory, *Canon and Text of the New Testament*, pp.15-20.
30. James, pp.xiff.
31. Clement, XIII, xlvi.
32. Ignatius, *Philadelphians*, VIII. *Didache*, VIII.
33. *Adversus Haereses*, III, xi, 4.
34. *Colossians* 4:16.
35. A. Soutar, *Text and Canon of the New Testament*, pp.165ff.
    Kelly, *ECD*, p.58.

36. Souter, pp.208ff.
   Stevenson, pp.143-146.
37. *i.e.* Montanus.
38. Tertullian, *De Pudicitia,* XX.
39. Eusebius, *Ecclesiastical History,* VI, xxv.
40. *ibid.* VII, xxv.
41. Kelly, *ECD,* pp.54-56.
42. B.F. Westcott, *The Canon of the New Testament,* pp.319-364.
43. *II Timothy* 3:15-16.
44. Clement, XIII, i.
45. Ignatius, *Magnesians,* VIII.
46. Justin, *Apology,* XXXVI.
47. Athenagoras, *Apology,* IX.
48. *Adversus Haereses*, III, xvi.
49. *ibid.* II, xxvii, xxviii.
50. Prestige, *FH,* p.43.
51. Eusebius, *Ecclesiastical History,* VI, xviii, xxiii.
   Jerome, *Epistle,* XLIII.
52. Eusebius, *Ecclesiastical History,* VI, xvi. Daniélou, pp.133-136.
53. Origen, *De Principiis,* IV, vi.
54. *ibid.* IV, xv.
55. *ibid.* IV, xix.
56. *ibid.* IV, xvi.
57. *ibid.* IV, xi-xiii.
58. Eusebius, *Ecclesiastical History,* VI, xix.
59. Augustine, *Confessions,* V, xiii.
60. Augustine, *De Utilitate Credendi,* II, iv.
61. *St Matthew* 19:8.
62. *St Matthew* 12:3-4.
63. *St Matthew* 12:39-40.
64. Augustine, *De Utilitate Credendi,* VI, xiii.

Chapter 5

In Defence of the Church

5

We do not know the level of literacy in Roman times, but it must have been considerably lower than that of an age when printing and cheap writing materials have made it general; and there is reason to think that the Church drew most of her members from those ranks of society which were anything but bookish. Probably therefore it is misleading if we interpret the early Church too much, as we are almost forced to do, from the contents of her literature other than the New Testament and the liturgy. Yet if those of her people who wrote in the early days were no more representative than are those who write today, some of them at least were closer to the average man than any others of the time.

It has already been noted that Greek literature was at a low ebb in the first Christian century.[1] Tacitus and Juvenal are the great names in Latin literature in the opening years of the second century. Political considerations and the readership for which they wrote imposed restraint on each, but neither conceals his fierce indignation against the abuses of the society to which he belonged. If we had more literature surviving from less privileged sections of Roman life, there can be no question but that we should find a still deeper resentment. Yet Rome never produced a Tom Paine or William Cobbett. If we ask why the late republic and early empire never knew a social revolution, part of the answer must be that the minds of men were dominated by two philosophies, one of which counselled resignation and a stiff-lipped acceptance of fate, and the other recommended men to eat, drink and be merry since tomorrow we die. Only the Church offered an alternative society, and while her Apologists were men of classical culture her literature, for the most part, sprang from a sub-culture. Until Augustine the educated read it with distaste.

Although it was written in Greek, *Revelation,* the most obvious instance of this in the New Testament, was as puzzling to Greeks of the first century as to most readers today. It was written in an apocalyptic framework familiar to Jews since the second century B.C. so that Christians who knew the conventions, and only they, would have the key to its contents. Whoever the writer was, he was far removed from the mind of Jesus in his pitiless lack of love for his enemies, but otherwise no book of the New Testament is so close to the Gospels in its preoccupation with the Kingdom of God at war with the kingdoms of this world. After an introduction containing the letters to the seven Churches of Asia the apocalyptic vision begins with an account of the book with seven seals which only the Lamb, 'the Lion of the tribe of Judah and the Root of David,' can open.

> And they sung a new song, saying, Thou art worthy to take the book, and to open the seals thereof; for Thou wast slain, and hast redeemed us to God by Thy blood out of every kindred, and tongue, and people, and nation: and hast made us unto our God kings and priests: and we shall reign on the earth.[2]

As each seal is opened a new plague comes upon the earth to herald the great day of the wrath of the Lamb. Judgement begins with the fall and ruin of Jerusalem.[3] Unfortunately the writer has been all too successful in concealing his meaning, not merely from the non-Christian, but from later Christians who do not have the clues, so that it has been possible to debate whether he wrote when the fall of Jerusalem was impending or whether it was in the past.

Next comes a vision of the Church delivered from her ordeal.

> I heard a loud voice in heaven saying, Now is come salvation, and strength, and the kingdom of our God, and the power of his Christ; for the accuser of our brethren is cast down, which accused them before God day and night. And they overcame him by the blood of the Lamb, and by the word of their testimony: and they loved not their lives unto the death.[4]

There follows a vision of the beast with seven heads and ten horns, an image of the Roman state under its seventh emperor, and another of it as 'the woman drunken with the blood of the saints, and with the blood of the martyrs of Jesus'.[5] Then her fall is foretold.

> And the kings of the earth ... when they shall see the smoke of her burning, standing afar off for the fear of her torment, saying, Alas, alas, that great city, Babylon, that mighty city! for in one hour is thy judgment come. ... And the merchants of the earth shall weep and mourn over her; for no man buyeth their merchandise any more ... and every shipmaster, and all the company in ships, and sailors, and as many as trade by sea, stood afar off, and cried when they saw the smoke of her burning, saying, What city is like unto this great city?[6]

Its place is taken by the heavenly city, whose King has destroyed the earthly city. 'And he hath on his vesture and on his thigh a name written, KING OF KINGS, AND LORD OF LORDS.'

Once removed from the impact of the immediate presence of Jesus, Christian literature immediately loses his clarity and acuteness. The doctrinal lucidity of Paul and John, and the violent contrast in *Revelation* is first concealed and, in time, lost. What we find is a collection of little books of no literary merit and of limited thinking, the productions of a simple but earnest community unaccustomed to authorship. Yet it is remarkable how soon the Church, largely drawn from the lower levels of society and under constant threat of persecution, ventured to present her faith in writing to the reading public of the age. If Paul had confined himself to the people of Lycaonia and the like he would not have had to face this problem, but when he came to Athens or any other great city he had to participate in the debates of the Hellenistic world. Far from being confined to the classrooms, they percolated down through almost every class to the arguments at the street corner. Apart from the New Testament, which reflects this more than casual reading might suggest, the earliest Christian writers are those known as the Apostolic Fathers, but only one of them — the author of *The Epistle to Diognetus* — wrote for the outsider.

Probably the earliest is *The Epistle of Clement to the Corinthians.* Eusebius, probably wrongly, identified its author with the companion of St Paul[7] and, more reliably, recorded that after Linus and Anacletus he was the third successor of St Peter

as Bishop of Rome from A.D. 91 to 100.[8] There had been
dissension in the Church at Corinth and Clement wrote to
commend unity, peace and respect for those set in charge of the
congregation by apostolic authority.[9] Unfortunately his letter is
diffuse and rambling[10] and overloaded with quotations from
Paul, *Hebrews,* Peter and James and, above all, from the Old
Testament.

What is worse, his understanding of the New Testament is
limited. Much that Christ said was not as new as is sometimes
thought. He had not come to destroy the Law or the prophets.
Yet the Gospels and Epistles also contain so much that is
startlingly new and original that it would be strange indeed if
they were not misunderstood by some who thought they had
accepted them. Old habits of thought are not easily shed. 'Have
ye understood all these things?' said Jesus[11] to the disciples. They
answered, 'Yea, Lord', but their confidence was unfounded.
'Have I been so long time with you, and yet hast thou not known
me, Philip?' he said at the last supper.[12] Paul found that the
Galatians, like many since, had not understood what he said
about the Law.[13] His converts at Corinth were still, as he put it,
carnally minded, and he had to treat them gently, giving them
the milk of the word rather than strong meat.[14] When he did
venture on a profound statement of his theology he addressed it,
not to any of those whose limitations he knew by experience, but
to a congregation still known to him only by repute, the Church
at Rome.

It is surprising, then, that when F.C. Baur in the nineteenth
century dated the New Testament documents as late as he did, he
failed to observe the marked contrast between their calibre and
that of Clement and his contemporaries, mediocre and third-rate
literature as it is. It survived, not because of its merits, but for its
interest as a survival from the early Church.

Clement thinks of God in Old Testament terms and seldom
calls him Father. 'My brothers,' he says, echoing words of Paul
when he had used the language of Stoicism, 'our Master is one to
whom need of any sort is unknown.'[15] Distinctively Christian
thoughts of God are in short supply. Christ's death is cited as an
example of obedience and humility. When he speaks of Christ in
the language of *Hebrews* as 'our great high priest', it is not
because he offered himself as a sacrifice for us, but because
'through him the eyes of our hearts are opened'.[16] Paul would

have been surprised to find that Clement spoke of faith, not as the trust in which men commit themselves to Christ, but as that belief which enables the Christian to exhibit the conduct which is pleasing to God and by which in turn he is justified. More than he knew, Clement was still restricted by his upbringing and environment. His letter, which seems to the modern reader to be meandering and repetitive, follows instead the order of classical rhetoric[17] and its contents, as well as its order, are equally indebted to classical rather than Christian precedents.[18] Much that is in it might have come from the average Stoic.

Clement wrote in the last years of the first century. A decade later when Ignatius, the Bishop of Antioch, was on his way to Rome to be martyred he wrote a series of letters to churches and in these we find a faith closer to the New Testament than that of Clement. Apart from the warmth of his goodwill towards his correspondents his letters have three main themes. Firstly, he was alarmed at the teaching of Docetism, a form of heresy which denied the reality of the body and physical experiences of Christ and treated them as no more than appearances. He insists that Christ was, in sober fact, the child of Mary, that he was born, that he ate and drank, was crucified and raised from the dead.[19] Secondly, he protests against the Jewish demand for the observance of the Law.[20] His third theme follows from these two. Heresies divided the Church, whose unity was essential, but in the absence as yet of formal statements of Christian orthodoxy how was unity to be maintained and orthodoxy upheld? At this point he relied on the office of bishop, whose succession from apostolic days guaranteed the authenticity of his teaching. This was the bond of unity and truth for Christians and through all his letters runs the warning that no Christian must separate himself from the divine society thus defined.[21]

Clement and Ignatius wrote in response to events, but the *Didache*, or *The Teaching of the Twelve Apostles*, is a little tract meant as a handbook for some small and isolated congregation. Its first part has taken over an ancient Jewish comparison of the Two Ways, the Way of Life and the Way of Death, and made it the basis of teaching on Christian morals for catechumens. In the second part are instructions for baptism, fast days and prayer, the Eucharist, the treatment of teachers, prophets and clergy, and a warning to be ready for the Judgement. It contains nothing original and has been put together from various sources.

There has been much speculation about its date, but apart from the fact that it is early no conclusion can safely be drawn.

Barnabas, on the other hand, is mainly a polemic against the Jews. It has nothing to do with the companion of Paul whose name it bears, but wås written after the fall of Jerusalem in A.D. 70 and presumably before the revolt of Bar Kochba, which its writer might have been expected to mention. He had failed to grasp the arguments of Paul and *Hebrews* on the Law and the Covenant. So far as he was concerned all Jewish history was a misunderstanding and he bases this on an allegorical interpretation of the Old Testament much of which is merely ridiculous.[22]

Barnabas is a warning against idealisation of the early Church and so is *The Shepherd* of Hermas. As we have seen, it was excluded from the canon of the New Testament, and with good reason, but was kept for private reading. Its author[23] lived in the first half of the second century and his book shows him to have been 'a timid, fussy, kindly, incompetent, middle-aged freedman, delightfully naive, just a little vain of his prophetic gift, and with a wife and children decidedly out of hand.'[24] He was, says Duchesne, 'a simple soul, of limited culture'.[25] Evidently his book was meant to be light reading of a fictional character for Christians, but the only human touch it contains is the story of how he saw a girl washing in the Tiber, wished he had chosen her as his wife, and then had a bad conscience.[26] Hermas divided his book into three parts, telling of visions, commands and parables, and reveals a Church proud of its martyrs but also with many unsatisfactory Christians, some ready to deny their Lord under persecution, and others none too steadfast in morality. So he was concerned with problems of repentance and forgiveness for post-baptismal sins.[27] It is a complacent, pretentious and dull little book but of interest as a sample of Christian literature from a section of society which normally did not write.

By comparison, when we come to those Christian writers who wrote for the outsider, and especially for those of some education, we meet with work of a much higher standard. These are known as the Apologists. The name is that used by Peter when telling Christians to be ready to give a defence for the hope that is in them;[28] and far from being apologetic in the modern sense they were aggressive defenders, ready not merely to refute slanders but to state the faith in terms of the culture around them. After his conversion Justin Martyr still wore his philosopher's cloak and taught publicly in the Mediterranean cities until he took up residence at Rome 'above the baths of Timothy';[29] but in a dangerous age writing offered a wider and a safer outlet than public disputation. Josephus had set the pattern for this when writing *Against Apion*.

Eusebius tells us that the earliest of such apologies was written by Quadratus in the time of Hadrian. Copies were extant in his own time, and he possessed one himself from which he quoted a passage which tells how close in time Quadratus came to the apostles. Those who had not merely witnessed but experienced the miracles of Jesus had long survived him, some of them into the lifetime of Quadratus himself.[30] This document has been supposed to be lost, but it is possible that the greater part of the *Epistle to Diognetus* is a fragment of it.[31] Significantly, the passage quoted by Eusebius would fit comfortably into it at a point where there is a gap in the manuscript. Whoever wrote the *Epistle to Diognetus* expected a reader who, far from being hostile, had some friendly interest in the subject and wished, in particular, to understand the Christian faith in God and the secret of their common life. Christians, he was told, are not to be distinguished by country, language, or customs. They do not live apart; yet they give daily proof,

of the remarkable and admittedly extraordinary constitution of their own commonwealth. ... They busy themselves on earth, but their citizenship is in heaven. They obey the established laws, but in their own lives they go far beyond what the laws require. They love all men, and by all men are persecuted. They are unknown, and still are condemned; they are put to death, and yet they are brought to life. They are poor, and yet they make many rich. ... When they do good, they are punished as evildoers; undergoing punishment, they rejoice because they are brought to life. ... To put it simply; what the soul is in the body, the Christians are in the world. The soul is dispersed through all the members of the body, and Christians are scattered through all the cities of the world. ... The soul, when faring badly

> as to food and drink, grows better; so too Christians,
> when punished, day by day increase more and more.
> It is no less a post that God has ordered them, and
> they must not try to evade it.

This Christian faith, says the writer, is no human invention,
but a revelation made by God. He did not make it through some
lesser creature but rather,

> he sent the Designer and Maker of the universe itself,
> by whom he created the heavens and confined the sea
> within its bounds, him whose hidden purposes all the
> elements of the world faithfully carry out, him from
> whom the sun has received the measure of the daily
> rounds it must keep. . . . God sent him to men. Now,
> did he send him, as a human mind might assume, to
> rule by tyranny, fear, and terror? Far from it! He
> sent him out of kindliness and gentleness, like a king
> sending his son who is himself a king. He sent him as
> God; he sent him as Man to men. He willed to save
> man by persuasion, not by compulsion, for
> compulsion is not God's way of working. In sending
> him, God called men but did not pursue them; he
> sent him in love, not in judgment. Yet he will indeed
> send him one day as our Judge, and who shall stand
> when he appears?[33]

At this point comes the gap where the quotation given by
Eusebius might properly fit, for it would seem that the writer
went on to tell of the acts of Christ's life on earth. In Christ, he
resumes, God has made himself known to men; but he has done
more, for when we could not deliver ourselves God gave his Son
as a ransom for us and brought us into the Kingdom of God.

Because of its early date this fragmentary document has been
classed among the Apostolic Fathers; but whether by Quadratus
or not, it sets a pattern for later apologies and does so with
brevity and not without a certain graciousness. A second
apology, long lost, but more recently rediscovered, is that of
Aristeides of Athens and this, too, is largely concerned with the
knowledge of God and the Church's life. A book by Fronto, the
teacher of Marcus Aurelius, had listed the legal and moral
charges against the Christians and sometime later came Celsus'

True Word which had to wait two generations before it received a massive refutation from Origen. Several Apologists, though not all of them, saw the need to defend Christians against scandals, but for the most part they saw their task in a positive light. And here they were hindered by the fact that the Church did not choose to tell all her rites and doctrines to outsiders. Celsus objected that non-Christians were excluded from the Eucharist and that Christian doctrine was a secret system of belief, and Origen could only reply that while the main points of Christian faith were common knowledge in the Church, as elsewhere, there were other matters of doctrine and practice reserved for those who had been initiated.[34]

One other subject on which Christians were obliged to be careful was the charge of disloyalty. 'When you hear that we look for a kingdom,' Justin wrote,

> 'you rashly suppose that we mean something merely human. But we speak of a kingdom with God, as is clear from our confessing Christ when you bring us to trial, though we know that death is the penalty for this confession. For if we looked for a human kingdom we would deny it in order to save our lives, and would try to remain in hiding places in order to obtain the things we look for. But since we do not place our hopes on the present (order), we are not troubled by being put to death, since we will have to die somehow in any case.'[35]

He then goes on to tell, with less than complete relevance, how law-abiding Christians are.

Of all the Apologists Justin is the most representative. He had the mind of a convert, and knew it, for like all the second century Apologists he had been born a pagan and so wrote out of personal experience. Born of Gentile parents near Sichem[36] in Palestine about 114, he was cosmopolitan. It chanced one day as he was walking on the Aegean shore near Ephesus that he fell into conversation with an elderly stranger who introduced him to the Christian faith. 'Straightway,' he wrote,

> 'a flame was kindled in my soul, and a love of the prophets and of those who are the friends of Christ possessed me: and whilst revolving his words in my

mind I found this philosophy alone to be safe and
profitable.'[37]

Justin had been trained as a philosopher. In student days he
had listened to the Stoics, and to the followers of Aristotle,
Pythagoras and Plato, but it was Plato above all who had given
him most and whom he never forgot. His conversion and
baptism provided Justin with the answer where previously he
had known only the quest, but he gladly and consciously carried
into the Church his inheritance of Hellenistic thought. There
was no repudiation of his past culture, and it now became for
him the medium of communication with the non-Christians.[38]
He was deeply committed to the Johannine understanding of
Christ as the Logos, the Word of God. God had initiated and
fulfilled his purpose for men in Israel and in the incarnate Lord,
but Christ, as the eternal Word, had not confined himself to
Israel. All that was rational and true in the thoughts of men was
his work.

> He is the Word, of whom every race of men are
> partakers; and those who live according to the Word
> are Christians even though they have been thought
> atheists.[39]

Socrates and Heraclitus were inspired by the Word, and those
who killed Socrates did so out of enmity to the Word.
Ultimately, through the will of God the Father, the eternal Word
'was born of a virgin as a man, and was named Jesus, and was
crucified, and died, and rose again, and ascended into heaven.'
Up to a point what Justin had said would find many listeners,
but when he came to the last sentence he knew that he had
reached the crux of the argument and had to commence
demonstration. To do this he employed the argument from
prophecy, so little used today.
Whatever had rightly been spoken by any of the philosophers
might therefore be appropriated by Christians. It could not be
said that the writings of Plato were fundamentally alien to the
words of Christ, but only that they were different in some
respects. One passage in the *Timaeus*, Justin claims, was
borrowed by Plato from *Numbers* 21.[40] What was true of Plato
was also true of Stoics, poets, and historians.

> For each man spoke in proportion of the share that
> he had of the spermatic Word. ... Those who
> contradict themselves on the more important points
> appear not to have possessed the heavenly wisdom
> and the knowledge which cannot be spoken against.
> Whatever things are rightly said among all men are
> the property of us Christians.

Quite distinct from this was the presence of Christ, the living
Word, and the grace which came through him.[41] From this grace
came Christian love for one's enemies, patience, chastity,
truthfulness and fortitude in death. Justin provided a classic
precedent for the use of non-Christian thought to commend the
faith to the outsider and provided a warrant, if any was needed,
for the assimilation of Hellenistic culture. It would have been
hard, indeed, for Christians to resist the continual intellectual
pressure of their environment, but where the reader is left with
the impression that Hermas' grasp of the Gospel was far from
complete, Justin's apprehension, however he had to limit it for
unbelievers, was full and deep.

He addressed his *Apology* to the Emperor Antoninus Pius and
to his adopted son, the future Marcus Aurelius, by his boyhood
name of Verissimus, to the senate, and people of Rome. One
may ask what chance there was that his work would be read by
the emperor and his son. In the opening of his *Meditations*
Marcus Aurelius thanked those who had instructed him in
boyhood and among them Rusticus.

> Of the same master I learned to read an author
> carefully; not to take up with a superficial view, or
> resign to every noisy impertinent, but to look
> through the argument, and go to the bottom of the
> matter.[42]

Shortly after the accession of Marcus Aurelius in 161 Justin was
arrested with six other Christians and put on trial before
Rusticus, now Prefect of Rome. He regarded Justin as an
educated man while the others, it seems, were not.

> The prefect Rusticus said: 'Let us now come to the
> pressing matter in hand. Agree together and sacrifice
> with one accord to the gods.'

Justin said: 'No one who is rightly minded turns from true belief to false.'

The prefect Rusticus said: 'If you do not obey, you shall be punished without mercy.'

Justin said: 'If we are punished for the sake of our Lord Jesus Christ we hope to be saved, for this shall be our salvation and confidence before the more terrible judgment seat of our Lord and Saviour which shall judge the whole world.' So also said the other martyrs: 'Do what you will. For we are Christians and offer no sacrifice to idols.'

Rusticus the prefect gave sentence: 'Let those who will not sacrifice to the gods and yield to the command of the emperor be scourged and led away to be beheaded in accordance with the laws.'

The holy martyrs went out glorifying God to the customary place and were beheaded, and fulfilled their testimony by the confession of their Saviour. And some of the faithful took their bodies by stealth and laid them in a convenient place, the grace of our Lord Jesus Christ working with them, to whom be glory for ever and ever. Amen.[43]

Here is part, at least, of the answer to our question as to how far Justin's *Apology* was read by those to whom it was addressed. However, there were other readers. In view of the current inclination to minimise the numbers of the martyrs it should be noted, in passing, that we should never have known of the half-dozen illiterate or semi-literate Christians who accompanied him had they not died in the company of this notable man.

A similar *Apology* from Athenagoras of Athens was dedicated to the Emperors Marcus Aurelius and Commodus who reigned jointly from 176 till 180. It was, says the writer, a time when the empire was at peace, and so we learn that it was written in 176 or 177. Like all Apologists he had to refute the charges of vice brought against Christians by the ignorant. Here he had no great difficulty, but on the delicate matter of the refusal to sacrifice to the genius of the emperor, despite many protestations of loyalty, he had to be discreetly silent. More positively, his aim was to set forth the Christian faith in God, and he had less to say about Jesus and the life of the Church. He had much in common with Justin, the doctrine of the Logos, the inspiration of the prophets, and the reality of spirits, good and bad, angels and demons. Unlike Christians, the poets and philosophers had not been classed as atheists because they speculated about God.[44] Plato, Athenagoras said, had regarded God as uncreated and eternal. Aristotle said of God that he was compound, composed of body and soul, his body being the universe and his soul the rational principle by which all moves. According to the Stoics, God is one though names are multiplied for him by the terms used for the varieties of matter, all of which is permeated by him. None had been prepared to learn of God from God himself and therefore their doctrines conflicted; but Christians had listened to God speaking by his Holy Spirit.

There was, said Athenagoras, a rational defence for the concept of the divine unity and a demonstration from the Scripture and the prophets. From this he went on to state the Christian doctrine of the Trinity.

> I have sufficiently shown that we are not atheists since we acknowledge one God, who is uncreated, eternal, invisible, impassible, incomprehensible, illimitable. He is grasped only by mind and intelligence, and surrounded by light, beauty, spirit, and indescribable power. By him the universe was created through his Word, was set in order, and is held together. ... The Son of God is his Word in idea and in actuality; for by him and through him all things were made, the Father and the Son being one. ... The Son came forth from God to give form and actuality to all material things ... the Holy Spirit himself, who inspires those who utter prophecies, is an effluence from God, flowing from him and returning like a ray of the sun.[45]

Academic debates begin and end in the lives of the classroom but the results of Christian teaching are seen in the lives of 'unlettered people, tradesmen and old women'.

A full statement of Christian belief cannot be extracted from Athenagoras, for he had deliberately limited himself to the defence of the one doctrine most likely to appeal to the philosophic reader, monotheism; but it can be seen that he held the full Christian faith as found in the New Testament. Hermas accidentally reveals that his mind was not always orthodox; but this is never so with Athenagoras. He was as hospitable to Greek philosophy as Justin, and this was to be the main stream of Christian thought. Those who came from the west and wrote in Latin were less assured, but it was the writers of the Greek Church who set the main course.

Those who would allow no concordat between the faith and secular culture came from lands less affected by Hellenistic influence. Tatian was an Assyrian who wrote in Greek but came from a land where Greek influence counted less. Yet he had travelled widely in the eastern Roman empire, had been familiar with the cults of the temples, and had been initiated into several of the mystery religions before he made the acquaintance of the Old Testament.[46] This was a new world for him ... one 'too old to be compared with the opinions of the Greeks and too divine to be compared with their errors.' He found himself convinced by its unpretentiousness and simplicity, by its moral character, by the fulfilment of prophecy, and by its teaching that the whole world is ruled by God. At Rome he frequented Justin's school of philosophy and became a Christian convert. Yet he remained an independent thinker and different from his master in two respects, thus foreshadowing the great breach when much of the east refused to be loyal to the Byzantine empire and its Church. Firstly, he deliberately turned his back on Hellenistic thought and culture as a road to truth. Secondly, he withdrew from the Catholic Church because of a growing asceticism. About 172 he returned to the east beyond the Roman frontier and there founded a sect known as the *Encratites,* or abstainers.[47]

Standards of sexual morality in the Roman empire were brutal and coarse from the imperial family downwards. Foundlings exposed at birth, says Justin, if found in time were brought up as prostitutes, 'females and hermaphrodites and doers of unspeakable deeds', and their earnings taxed. 'Some even prostitute their own wives and children, and others are admittedly mutilated for purposes of sodomy, and treat this as part of the mysteries of the mother of the gods.'[48] Tacitus, Juvenal and Petronius confirm that this is, if anything, an understatement. Christians reacted violently, and some went to extremes. Tatian joined those who condemned marriage as no better than adultery, forbade the eating of meat, and were so strictly teetotal that they refused to use wine in the Eucharist. Best known as the writer of the *Diatessaron* in which the four Gospels were combined into a single narrative, Tatian was also the author of an *Apology* far different from that of Justin in spirit and marked by his own rigorist temper.

But a better instance of this is found in Tertullian. Like Tatian he belonged to a land outside the Hellenistic sphere, for he was born in Carthage about 155 and grew up in that land of Semitic traditions which had challenged the might of Rome in the Punic wars. Very early in her history the Church had entered Egypt and Cyrenaica from Palestine. A man of Africa carried Christ's cross and seems to have been known later as a believer. But when the North African coast beyond Libya received the Gospel it was from Rome. Greek had been the original tongue of the Roman Church, for it was the language not only of the most highly educated but of the immigrants in the slums, and the first records of the North African Church are in Greek,[49] but it was here that the Scriptures were first translated into Latin[50] and that Christian Latin literature was born.

Not until the middle of the third century were most villages in the hinterland of Carthage converted to the Christian faith[51] and yet, if the Church in Persia was too intimately associated with minorities, the opposite may have been the case in North Africa. Its version of the Scriptures was so colloquial as to invite the scorn of Augustine.[52] From the first appearance of the Church until the time of deliverance under Constantine a hard and courageous struggle was fought against persecution. From the death of a group of Numidian Christians[53] on 17 July 180 through the writings of Tertullian and Cyprian down to those of Lactantius and Arnobius the record of the African Church is one of suffering. 'If the Almighty cares for you,' asks the opponent of Arnobius, 'why does he let you suffer such persecution, punishment and torture?' And the Apologist answers, 'No hope has been held out to us as regards this life.'[54] It was here that the phrase, 'The blood of the martyrs is the seed of the Church', was coined.[55]

Here, too, the Church found herself involved in fighting deviations from the faith; as in modern Africa, the rise of deviations is a sure sign that the Gospel has successfully rooted itself in a society and culture previously alien. A fighting and passionate note entered her literature, and nowhere more markedly than in Tertullian. He was a lawyer by training, but his temper was that of a prosecuting counsel cross-examining a recalcitrant witness and not that of a judge impartially summing up the evidence for a dim-witted jury. Like Tatian, he had nothing to do with that acceptance of philosophy which is so unqualified in Justin and was to be characteristic of the Greek-speaking Church; but while Tatian left virtually no successors in the orient, Tertullian was only the first of a long succession of writers in the west. Like him, they wrote in Latin and, if they did not so frankly dismiss philosophy, they cared less for it.

Possibly the development of Christian theology might have been different if Augustine and others had been more thoroughly at home in Greek; yet the Latin theologians were the younger pupils of the Greeks. They had all learned from them, even if they had gone out to work in a different kind of world. Since the days of the Pilgrim Fathers there has been a steady flow of emigrants from Europe to America. Many go west, but few return from Chicago or California to settle in Connemara or Poland. It was the same in the ancient world so far as ideas were concerned. There was a constant stream of intellectual stimulus from the east to the west,[56] but little in the opposite direction. And as American life has surpassed that of the homelands in vigour, so the western Church, whatever it had to endure from the barbarian inroads, produced new and potent forms of Christian life and thought in no way inferior to those of the Greeks and more seminal for the future. From the start the western Church had its own approach to the Bible and was less concerned with the metaphysical and speculative obsessions of the Greek mind until, in the fourth century, a more philosophical theology developed in the west, linked with the rediscovery of the Pauline antithesis between faith and law, an aspect scarcely ever considered by the Greek theologians.

What Enoch Powell has been to the Conservative Party in modern Britain, Tertullian was to the Church; its most brilliant advocate with a totally unexpected appeal among its enemies and yet with a fiery uncompromising spirit. Like Powell he was hot blooded, impetuous and reckless. Yet his temper was always under control; the greater his anger, the sharper his logic, the more polished his style, and the more mordant his wit. He is the most fascinating writer from the ancient world.

He did not deny that philosophers at times had said things with which Christians might be in agreement[57] but, like other Apologists, ascribed this to borrowing from the Old Testament. Socrates,[58] whom Justin had revered, for him was 'a corrupter of youth', and he could speak of 'miserable Aristotle'. Only Seneca,[59] whom he admired, at times won a word of praise. Far from offering a preparation for the Gospel, in his eyes, philosophy, when attempts were made to construct a synthesis between it and the faith, was the parent of heresy. Nor was he entirely wrong in this, but while Justin had Plato in mind when he spoke of philosophy, Tertullian thought primarily of later teachers and especially of the Gnostics.

'Philosophy,' he said,

> 'is the material of the world's wisdom, the rash interpreter of nature and the dispensation of God. Indeed, heresies are themselves inspired by philosophy. From this source come "aeons" and I know not what infinite "forms", and the trinity of men in the system of Valentinus; he was a Platonist. From the same source came Marcion's better god with his tranquillity; he came of the Stoics.'

All this must be repudiated and reliance placed on the Christian revelation alone.

> What has Jerusalem to do with Athens? What has the Church to do with the Academy? What have Christians to do with heretics? Our instruction comes from the porch of Solomon [this is a reference to the porch or *stoa* which gave the Stoics their name] who has himself taught that the Lord should be sought in simplicity of heart. Away with all attempts to produce a Stoic, Platonic and dialectic Christianity! We want no curious disputation after possessing Christ Jesus, no search after receiving the Gospel. When we believe we desire no further belief. For this is our first article of faith, that there is nothing which we ought to believe besides.[60]

Like other masterly stylists, he does not translate well. Minucius Felix had been an earlier Apologist in Latin, but whereas he had written in Ciceronian prose which reminds a modern reader of Matthew Arnold, Tertullian's sharp tongue had the vivid and pointed colloquialism of the best of contemporary journalism. Other Apologies had been addressed to emperors who had no intention of reading them. Tertullian's was addressed to the provincial governors in the form of a legal plea which he knew they would not permit to be heard in their courts, and its core is the charge that even the pagans do not believe in their own gods. If the gods existed and vile things told of them were true their place would be, not in heaven, but in hell.[61] Pagans cheat their gods in the sacrifices, for the worshippers get the best cuts of meat while the gods get only the guts ... all they deserve.[62] In the theatres they are mocked. But Christians worship the one omnipotent and invisible God by whom all things were made, and to whom both nature and the soul of man bear testimony.[63] He is made known in the Scriptures, and it is he whom the Jews worship, but with this difference, that Christians know him in Christ whom the Jews have rejected.[64]

> Scattered abroad, wanderers, exiles from their own sky and soil, they roam over the world without either man or God for their king, nor is it permitted to them so much as to set foot upon their native land, not even in the character of strangers. And the same holy oracles, which used to threaten them beforehand with these disasters, were all ever urging the fact that in the last courses of the world God would, out of every nation and people and clime, choose for himself other more faithful worshippers.

Christians pray for the emperor[65] because the calamities of a disturbed empire fall on their shoulders also and because it is only the existence of the empire that prevents terrible woes coming upon the earth. Yet they cannot sacrifice to the emperor, and they cannot call him *Lord,* for that supreme title belongs to Christ alone. By this time even the radical Tertullian has accepted the necessity of the state, but at this point it is the Apologist who speaks; in reality he knew that pagan life, the domain of evil spirits, was a society in the midst of which Christians had to live but into which they could not fully enter.[66] At the back of his mind is 'the old, primitive Christian view of believers as strangers here, and of the necessity of their affliction in this world, and of the all-determining future of God.' He was a formidable controversialist with a distinctive style, but though he was well remembered in the west, the Church as a whole was not inclined to follow him, and this not merely because of his aberrations in old age. As we shall see, before his death he was to join a party of extremists.

Tertullian's less forceful but influential contemporary, Clement of Alexandria, was born about 150, probably at Athens, but became a student at Alexandria and spent most of his life there.[67] Until his time the age had been one of attack and defence, so far as the faith was concerned, but changed days and the growth of the Church had brought the need for an orderly and comprehensive statement of Christian belief. Thus the Apologists became the first theologians of the Church, and their defence was an open one in the sense that it involved constant reference, not merely to the sources of Christian faith, but to secular thought. It is no accident that this took place when the canon of the New Testament was approaching definition, for Christians no longer could write as personal witnesses of the revelation in Christ nor even as those who had received it from the Apostles. They wrote as free men, and yet within a well-defined tradition. Orthodoxy, a slightly different matter, was scarcely defined as yet but was clearly taking shape under the influence of the New Testament canon, of which we have written, and of the authority of the apostolic ministry, of which we have yet to write. In particular, for the ordinary worshipper it was fixed by the weekly hearing of the liturgy.

For generations the Christians of Alexandria attributed the foundation of their Church to St Mark and the patriarchs of the city were elected beside St Mark's tomb among the wharves and granaries of the harbour. Three times in the course of a century Egypt had endured the horrors of unsuccessful rebellion, but the Church of Alexandria had steadily advanced to be wealthy and flourishing. Commonly the execution of Christians in the eastern provinces was a concession to mob violence, but the need to prevent disturbances in the depot from which the corn of Egypt was shipped to Ostia, the port of Rome, ensured a stricter control than was usual elsewhere. At any rate, Christians seem to have escaped lightly and the Church had grown rapidly in every class. Clement speaks of 'coming from church' just as we do, so it would seem that the older house churches had been replaced in Alexandria by great public buildings for worship.

In some of the western Churches such as the Lyons of Irenaeus, the gulf between clergy and people may well have been as wide as that between priests and people in nineteenth-century Donegal or Mayo, but in wealthy and educated Alexandria the relationship was more like that between ministers and strong-minded laymen in American churches today. In particular, the presbyters of the twelve city parishes formed a college which enjoyed the singular privilege not merely of electing, but of consecrating, one of their own number to the episcopal see. When Bishop Julian was on his death bed in 189 he was warned in a dream that the man who brought him a present of grapes next day was to be his successor. This proved to be Demetrius, an unlettered countryman and, which seemed even stranger to later generations, a married man. In obedience to the warning he was installed almost by force in the chair of St Mark and for forty-three years proved a stern and enterprising ruler over this great see.[68] He restricted the powers of the laity and took away the privileges of his clergy.

Alexandria was now the centre, not only of commerce, but of scholarship, so that the Catechetical School of the Christians far exceeded the normal classes for instruction of catechumens. Though it had no buildings of its own it became a great denominational college affiliated to the university with each master teaching students in his own premises, like a *privat-dozent* in Germany, across the whole range of studies until philosophy and theology were reached.[69]

> The truth is that, so far as the Church differed from the rest of society, it differed for the better. Whatever treasures of knowledge belonged to the ancient world lay at its command and were freely enjoyed in its service; and it possessed besides the inestimable advantage of purer morals and a more reasonable creed.[70]

This was written by a great Oxford scholar in the days before the first world war. It is not clear whether he spoke of the Church at large or of the Church in Alexandria; but if he spoke of the latter, not everyone need agree with his judgement.

In this environment a gulf not unlike that between modern Fundamentalists and Liberal Protestants had grown up between conservative Christians and those who expressed their faith in terms more philosophical than scriptural. Although he stood between the two to mediate, it was to the second that Origen himself belonged. He wrote of 'the so-called orthodox' who 'like beasts which work from fear, do good works without knowing what they are doing.'[71] As he saw it, his task was to show that the faith was not obscurantist and that it had a place for the values of philosophy, and so to refute those who despised the Church. At the same time he had to deal with the Gnostics. Gnosticism, of which more must later be said, has been defined as,

> a dark form of the religious syncretism of the Hellenistic age, combining many diverse religious elements within a generally dualistic system to provide a rationale for a morality usually ascetic, though sometimes going to the opposite extreme.[72]

Set in a rapidly-growing community which was losing something of its original intensity as it began to explore the intellectual content of the faith, Clement, though he wrote no formal Apology, was in his own way a defender of the faith, and one who has been greatly honoured by some. His methods and some of his convictions were precisely contrary to those of Tertullian[73] and as the Church has had its reservations about the Carthaginian, so the Church, or at least one wing of Christian opinion, has had reservations about the Alexandrian, and still more about his greater successor.

Clement was greatly indebted to Philo, from whom he took respect for the Scripture, allegorical interpretation of it, and the conviction that philosophy confirmed its message. 'There is one river of Truth but many streams fall into it on this side and on that.'[74] Faith by itself is not to be despised. Mature Christians must be on their guard against pagan ideas incompatible with the faith, but true knowledge will always be compatible with it and therefore necessary.[75] His thought begins with God and ends with God. All things were created by him. Accordingly Clement had to face the problems of the origin of evil and the nature of freedom. He could not accept the Gnostic reply that evil was inherent in matter and hesitated about the idea that the origin of evil lay in the descent of the soul into a material world. Nor could he accept determinism, for goodness implied the freedom of the will. God had not restricted the knowledge of himself to

one nation but had breathed the knowledge of himself into
Adam at the creation.[76] Consequently all men had some
knowledge of God. Before religion was corrupted into
polytheism there had been a primitive monotheism. Philosophy
had been given to the Greeks as the Law had been given to Israel
to be a schoolmaster to bring men to Christ. At the time when he
wrote, the Church stood by the doctrine of the Trinity but had
still to define it. There was much room for speculation.

> God is formless and nameless, though we sometimes
> give him titles, which are not to be taken in their
> proper sense; the One, the Good, Intelligence, or
> Existence, or Father, or God, or Creator, or Lord.

These are but phrases on which our limited minds may lean.
God's Son is Wisdom, and Knowledge, and Truth, the consciousness of God. He is the Word who took flesh and became
Man. He alone is both God and Man, and his soul is our ransom.
It is the Holy Spirit, equally with the Logos, who speaks by the
prophets, and who binds together the whole Church, visible and
invisible.

Even those who respect Clement most are aware of his limitations and deficiencies. In speaking of the Son he had asked not,
'What is Spirit?' but 'What is the simplest thing possible?' and
had emerged with a heathen conception.[77] His Christology has
been regarded as meagre and unsatisfactory.[78] One senses a
strange difference between his language and that of the Gospels.
Coming from a background of Hellenistic scholarship he had
aimed at a systematic pattern of Christian teaching which his
diffuse manner of writing failed to provide, and for which one
must turn to Origen.

> Before the coming of the Lord philosophy was
> necessary to the Greeks to bring them to
> righteousness, but now it is profitable to bring them
> to piety, seeing that it is a sort of training for those
> who are gaining the fruit of faith for themselves. . . .
> For God is the cause of all good things, but of some
> primarily, as of the Old and New Covenants, and of
> others consequentially, as of philosophy. Per-
> adventure also it was given primarily to the Greeks in
> times before the Lord called the Greeks; for

> philosophy educated the Greek world, as the Law did
> the Hebrews, to bring them to Christ. Philosophy
> therefore is a preparation, making ready the way for
> him who is being perfected by Christ.[79]

Before Constantine the name of *Saint* was generally reserved
for a martyr. Because of his later eccentricities the Church did
not canonise Tertullian, but it never occurred to her to canonise
Clement. However honourable his case might be, as a man he
was something of a dilettante; Tertullian's faults were of ruddier
hue, but they were those of a man. Clement's was a noble and
optimistic creed, but the difference between him and Tertullian
has been recurrent in the Church, even if the inclination to relate
the faith to secular thought has usually been uppermost.
Classical religion was always rejected by the early Church. We
know the cults and myths of the classical world chiefly through
generously expurgated versions, but to understand the contempt
and disgust of the Apologists for their brutalities and obscenities
one must read Arnobius.[80] Philosophy, on the other hand, could
be seen as a path to Christ. Before it the Church stood, on the
whole, respectfully prepared to listen, to find common ground,
and perhaps even to learn.

In the west the need for Apologies continued right up to the
conversion of Constantine, but the greater growth of the Church
in the eastern half of the empire is seen in the ending of the
writing of Apologies as such. By the time the Emperor Decius[81]
launched his great persecution in 249 the Church in the eastern
provinces, if not always in the west, had ceased to be a negligible
minority and was a community whose strength was evident to
all. An historical accident, the writing of *Acts* and the Pauline
epistles, misleads us into supposing that the advance of the
Church had been westwards through Greece into Italy, but
Alexandria, the home of a large Jewish community and the centre
of Hellenistic thought, had become the strongest centre of
Church life.

Two facts reveal the increase in the number of Christians;
firstly, the considerable number[82] who apostasised and received
certificates stating that they had offered sacrifice when
instructed, and secondly, the instances of popular sympathy
with Christians. At Alexandria in the time of Decius the
authorities hunted widely for four days for the bishop as it had

not occurred to them that he was waiting patiently at home. When he did go out he was arrested and taken to a village some thirty miles from the city, the kind of place where Christians could not be expected to be numerous. One of his household who had been overlooked met a party of villagers on their way to a wedding. They asked the reason for his hurry. On hearing of the bishop's arrest they collected the rest of the wedding guests, and put the guards to flight. 'At first,' wrote the bishop,

> 'God knows, I thought they were bandits who had come to plunder and steal, so I stayed on the bed. I had nothing on but a linen shirt; my other clothes that were lying near I held out to them. But they told me to get up and make a bolt for it. Then I realised what they had come for, and called out, begging and beseeching them to go away and let us be. . . . They pulled me up by force . . . set me on a donkey bareback, and led me away.'[83]

In this changed atmosphere Origen's reply to Celsus is, in effect, the last as it is also the greatest of the Apologies from the eastern half of the empire, but it lacks the direct popular appeal of the earlier ones. That the Christian Apologies had been effective is to be concluded from the steady succession of those written. Men knew that they brought results. They had three main aims, to refute scandals, to secure toleration from the state and to make a reasoned statement of the faith for the thoughtful enquirer. Conditions imposed restrictions not merely on public speech but on what it was convenient to put down in writings. Hitler made a clean breast of his intentions in *Mein Kampf,* but not all opponents of society have been so uninhibited, and propagandists who practise reserve, if they disarm opponents, also restrict their own supporters' understanding of the cause. On the negative side the Apologists exposed the bankruptcy of classical religion which many of their readers already knew, and whatever their respect for philosophy they urged its deficiencies as compared with the faith. On the positive side it must be noted that they invariably wrote, not on behalf of a religion, nor as individuals, but as spokesmen for a community, the Church, and that they did so against the background of a daily liability to martyrdom.

Origen doubted if Apologies were still needed.[84] This is a sure sign that the climate of opinion had been transformed. Formerly pagans had seen the Church as a menace and had been ready to believe anything bad about her, as the scandals and gossip popularised by men like Lucian reveal. Men no longer credited these bogus scandals — which one might call the peripheral ones — since they saw their Christian neighbours and found them not as different as they once had thought, and since they had some idea of the nature and faith of a Church in which the basic scandal was no longer so evident. 'The Jews require a sign,' said St Paul, 'and the Greeks seek after wisdom: But we preach Christ crucified, unto the Jews a stumbling block, and unto the Greeks foolishness.' His word for *a stumbling block* has given modern English the word *scandal*, and his word for *foolishness* has given us the word *moron*, but the Gospel was ceasing to be a scandal and Christians were not all classed as morons. Not merely had the Church grown by conversions; she had mellowed as she accommodated herself to the secular society in which her people spent their days. We know too little about social conditions in the empire to be confident, but by this time the Church seems to have moved upwards in society and especially in the east the educated and moneyed were increasingly found within her. In the west Tertullian might protest that Christians paid their taxes and were loyal to the state, but any pillar of the establishment who read his fiery prose would have seen him as an opponent, and a dangerous one. Yet was the Church now drawing her membership less from those classes which were alienated from secular society as they knew it? Was she less feared by the authorities because she was less to be feared?

Origen himself had been the son of a Christian family while the Church was still fighting for her life. He was a child when his father Leonidas died as a martyr at Alexandria.[85] Origen wrote a tract on martyrdom:

> The saint asks what he can do for the Lord for all he
> has received from him; and he finds that a man with
> a thankful heart can render to God nothing else
> capable of being — as it were — a counterweight to
> his benefits except a martyr's death.

This was more than rhetoric, for when a period of deceptive security ended and his own time came he did not flinch. During the Decian persecution the aged scholar suffered brutal treatment in 253. 'He endured dreadful cruelties for the word of Christ, chains and bodily torments, agony in iron and the darkness of his cell; for days on end his legs were pulled four paces apart in the torturer's stocks.'[86] His tormentors were exceedingly anxious to obtain a retraction from so notable a prisoner, but equally unwilling to kill outright a man so honoured in the intellectual world. Thus Origen bore the martyr's pains but did not gain the martyr's palm. He was released only to die of ill-treatment.

Gibbon[87] attributed the success of the Church to the inheritance of Jewish zeal, the doctrine of the immortality of the soul, the impression made by supposed miracles, the character of Christians and the effective organisation of the Church. He was oddly insensitive to the courage of the martyrs, whose numbers he minimised and whose example was alien to his temperament. A number of academics have followed him in this, but it is hard for any warm-blooded reader of the records not to think that it counted more than the other factors he listed. Yet it may be of interest to compare his assessment with those subjects which the Apologists thought likely to influence men to become Christians.

Occasionally a reference to miracles is found, as in Arnobius,[88] but this is trifling when compared with the *Apology* as a whole, and it is clear that the writers knew that miracles could be explained away. Celsus regarded the miracles of Jesus as instances of sorcery.[89] Origen replied that the life of Jesus was inconsistent with imposture,[90] and gives an answer which will commend itself to ordinary people today.

> The name of Jesus can still remove distractions from the minds of men, and expel demons, and also take away diseases; it can produce a marvellous meekness of spirit and complete change of character, and a humanity, and goodness, and gentleness in those individuals who do not feign themselves to be Christians for the sake of subsistence or the supply of any mortal wants, but who have honestly accepted the doctrine concerning God and Christ, and the judgment to come.[91]

Bertrand Russell's statement that 'miracles certainly played a very large part in Christian propaganda' is quite baseless and an instance of the capacity for self-deception among even the most logical of men.[92] Far more space is given to the argument from prophecy. Justin Martyr, who in this is representative of the Apologists as a whole, deals largely with it not only in the *Dialogue with Trypho*, where one might expect it, but also in his *Apology*.[93] This argument, to which modern man is unsympathetic, was in fact an appeal to the inner consistency of a revelation made over many centuries and culminating in the fulfilment of an ancient but persistent expectation. 'The God of the Law and the Gospels,' said Origen, 'is one and the same.'[94]

A twentieth-century reader might anticipate that the first weapon of the Apologists would be an appeal to the life and example of Jesus, but this is an expectation derived from late nineteenth-century German theologians such as Ritschl, just as Gibbon's stress on miracles was a reflection of the theologians of his day. Reference to the life of Jesus, it is true, is not lacking in the Apologists, but it takes an unexpectedly small place. While they have much to say on the historical events of his life as contrasted with the myths of paganism, their first concern is with Christ as the Logos, the eternal word of God. Prominent in the great Apologists, this is found in lesser ones like Theophilus of Antioch or Melito of Sardis.[95]

But beyond all this, two elements in their case are most forcefully urged. The first is the true knowledge of God given to men, and the writer has been surprised to find this still the case among first-generation converts from paganism, today. In every Apologist appears the dismissal of the pagan divinities and the assertion that he to whom the mind of man has uncertainly reached out is now revealed as Creator and Lord of the Universe, majestic and loving. They were confident that the knowledge of God in Christ could not fail to move the minds of men.

> The object of our worship is the one God, he who by his commanding Word, his arranging wisdom, his mighty power, brought forth from nothing this entire world ... the Cosmos. The eye cannot see him, though he is spiritually visible. He is incomprehensible though in grace he is manifested. He is beyond our utmost thought, though our human faculties conceive of him. ... He is presented to our

minds in his transcendent greatness, as at once
known and unknown. And this is the crowning guilt
of men, that they will not recognise one, of whom
they cannot possibly be ignorant. ... Would you
have the testimony of the soul itself? Though under
the oppressive bondage of the body, though
enervated by lusts and passions, though in slavery to
false gods; yet, whenever the soul comes to itself ...
it speaks of God. ... O noble testimony of the soul,
by nature Christian.[96]

There was truth in the teaching of Zeno of Citium, the
Apologists were convinced, that a measure of belief in God was
natural to all men.[97] Christ had brought men the knowledge of
him.

With this went the second weapon confidently used by the
Apologists, the undeniable transformation of life in Christian
converts. Cyprian had publicly opposed the Church before his
conversion, but came to see paganism as 'barren, corrupt, and
lacking in inspiration'.[98] But the Church could be seen by the
outsider to have a new way of life. This was the work of the
Holy Spirit, even if the outsider did not know it, but only saw
'love, joy, peace, patience, kindness, goodness, fidelity,
gentleness and self-control'.[99] 'Christians,' said Aristides, and
any other Apologist could be cited to the same effect,

'have the commandments of the Lord Jesus Christ
engraven on their hearts. ... They commit neither
adultery nor fornication; nor do they bear false
witness; they do not deny a deposit nor covet other
men's goods; they honour father and mother, and
love their neighbours; they give right judgment; and
they do not worship idols in the form of men. They
do not unto others that which they would not have
done unto themselves. They comfort such as wrong
them, and make friends of them; they labour to do
good to their enemies; they are meek and gentle. ...
They despise not the widow, and grieve not the
orphan. He that hath distributeth liberally to him
that hath not. For Christ's sake they are ready to lay
down their lives. ... Such is the ordinance of the law
of Christians, O king, and such is their conduct.'[100]

It is easy to dismiss the claim of a new life, but the assurance with which it was unceasingly made, and the conviction that it would bring converts, is evidence that it was found effective because it was true; it was a realistic description of changed lives. Men were not merely told that the Church was the alternative society; they could see that she was.

Three main elements were found in the assertion; firstly, the claim that Christians had conquered the natural fear of death; secondly, that they had subdued the strong urges of sex and lived either in celibacy or in pure marriage; and thirdly, that the very passions and moods of the mind had been controlled. We do not find that the Apologists argue the case for moral standards; they assume that thinking men, at least, are aware of them; but they claim that while philosophy asserts these standards the Gospel creates them. 'Philosophy', said Lecky, 'was admirably fitted to dignify and ennoble, but altogether impotent to regenerate, mankind.'[101] Origen, who lived through it, put the matter otherwise but to the same effect:

> The words of those who at first assumed the office of Christian ambassadors, were accompanied by persuasive power, though not like that found among those who profess the philosophy of Plato, or of any other merely human philosopher, which possesses no other qualities than those of human nature. But the demonstration which followed the words of the apostles of Jesus was given by God, and was accredited by the Spirit and by power. And therefore their word ran swiftly and speedily, or rather the Word of God through their instrumentality transformed numbers of persons who had been sinners both by nature and habit, whom no one could have reformed by punishment, but who were changed by the Word, which moulded and transformed them according to its pleasure.[102]

This change of life, the Apologists tell, was found in all ranks of the community. Christians, said Tertullian, knew their faith and could speak for it:

> The meanest mechanic among the Christians apprehends God and can answer the question, and

> can assign substantial reasons, and very sensibly
> explain himself upon all these disquisitions about the
> divine nature; though Plato affirms it to be so
> difficult...[103]

This, it is notorious, is no longer true of majority Churches, but it remains true of minority ones as anyone who, like the writer, has conducted an argument with a Plymouth Brother at a pithead, can confirm. 'No one trusted Socrates,' Justin Martyr wrote, 'so as to die for his doctrine, but in Christ ... not only philosophers and scholars believed, but also artisans and people entirely uneducated, despising both glory, and fear, and death.'[104] And if Athenagoras was not so confident as Tertullian about the ordinary Christian's capacity for theology he knew that the fruits of the Gospel were to be found where, by pagan standards, they were least to be expected:

> You will find among us unlettered people, tradesmen
> and old women who, though unable to express in
> words the advantages of our teaching, demonstrate
> by acts the value of their principles. For they do not
> rehearse speeches, but display good deeds. When
> struck, they do not strike back; when robbed, they do
> not sue; to those who ask, they give; and they love
> their neighbours as themselves.[105]

No one could say this, on the whole, about the Church in our time, for the result would be counter-productive.

Thus it appears that the Apologists, who must be credited with some knowledge of the world in which they lived, held that the two most powerful factors in making converts were the knowledge of God the Father as revealed in Christ the eternal Word, and the power of the Spirit in changing the lives of believers. A Trinitarian basis, if often unstated, always underlies their thought.[106] In other words, while they had to speak the language of their environment, they knew that the faith could best be commended, not by stating it in sub-Christian categories which must always be inadequate, but by allowing it to speak for itself. In his great debate with Celsus, Origen saw the Church not as a body of doctrines but as a divine force changing men's hearts. Celsus admired the noble words in which Epictetus accepted his broken leg, but Origen replied that,

> those words will not bear comparison with the astounding words that Jesus spoke or with his deeds, of no account though Celsus thinks them. The words that Jesus spoke, he spoke with a divine power, and that power still produces conversions, sometimes among the simple but often, too, among those whose reasoning powers are well developed.[107]

Like Tertullian and Augustine, he knew that men must believe in order to understand.

Yet it must be asked whether, in stating the faith to the Hellenistic mind, the Apologists had not gone some way in accommodating it to a non-Christian framework of thought. Where the New Testament spoke of grace and faith, the Hellenistic world spoke of reason and knowledge. It was from the acts of God in the history of his people Israel that the Church had come, but the philosophical mind looked for a coherent body of teachings rather than the historical realities of Christ and the Church. From this came the development of reckoning a body of beliefs, rather than participation in the divine community, to be the mark of the follower of Christ.

Notes to Chapter 5

1. See p.109.
2. *Revelation* 5:9, 10.
3. *ibid.* 11:1-13.
4. *ibid.* 12:10, 11.
5. *ibid.* 17:5.
6. *ibid.* 18:9, 11, 17, 18.
7. Eusebius, *Ecclesiastical History*, IV, iv.
   Philippians 4:3.
8. Eusebius, *Ecclesiastical History*, IV, xxi, xxiv.
9. Clement, *Epistle*, I, LVI.
10. M. Staniforth, *Early Christian Writings*, p.21.
11. *St Matthew* 13:51.
12. *St John* 14:9.
13. *Galatians* 3:2.
14. *I Corinthians* 3:1-3.
15. Clement, LII.
16. *ibid.* XXXVI.
17. Jaeger, *ECGP*, p.13.
18. *ibid.* pp.15-26.
19. Ignatius, *Trallians*, IX.
20. *Magnesians*, VIII.
21. *Philadelphians*, III.
22. *Barnabas*, X.
23. Soutar, p.210.
24. B.H. Streeter, *The Primitive Church*, p.203.
25. Duchesne, I, p.165.
26. Hermas, *The Shepherd*, II, iii.
27. *ibid.* I, i. J. Lawson, *A Theological and Historical Introduction to the Apostolic Fathers*, pp.219-225.
28. *I Peter* 3:15.
29. *Acts of Justin*, II. Quasten, I, p.197.
30. Eusebius, *Ecclesiastical History*, IV, iii.
31. C.C. Richardson, *Early Christian Fathers*, pp.206-210, 219.
32. *Epistle to Diognetus*, VI.
33. *ibid.* VII.
34. Origen, *Against Celsus*, I, i, vii.

35. Justin Martyr, *Apology*, XI, XII.
36. Justin Martyr, *Trypho*, I; *Apology*, I, i.
37. *Trypho*, II-VIII.
38. Quasten, I, pp.196-219. H. von Campenhausen, *The Fathers of the Greek Church*, pp.5-15.
39. Justin, *Apology*, XLVI.
40. Justin, *Apology*, LX.
41. Justin, *Second Apology*, XIII.
42. Marcus Aurelius, *Meditations*, I, vii.
43. Stevenson, pp.29ff.
44. Athenagoras, *Plea Regarding Christians*, V.
45. *ibid.* X.
46. Eusebius, *Ecclesiastical History*, IV, xvi; V, xiii, xxviii. Quasten, I, pp.220-228.
47. Eusebius, *Ecclesiastical History*, IV, xxix.
48. Justin, *Apology*, XXVII.
49. Quasten, II, p.243.
50. K. Lake, *Text of the New Testament*, pp.30ff. B.F. Westcott, *CNT*, pp.224-239.
51. Frend, *Religion etc.*, XI, p.490.
52. Augustine, *Confessions*, III, v.
53. Quasten, I, pp.178ff.
54. Arnobius, *Adversus Gentes*, II, p.76.
55. Tertullian, *Apology*, L, xiii.
56. von Campenhausen, *The Fathers of the Latin Church*, pp.1ff.
57. Quasten, II, p.321.
58. Tertullian, *Apology*, XLVI.
59. Tertullian, *De Anima*, XX.
60. Tertullian, *De Praescriptione Haereticorum*, VII.
61. Tertullian, *Apology*, XI.
62. *ibid.* XIV.
63. *ibid.* XVII.
64. *ibid.* XXI.
65. *ibid.* XXXII. *Ad Scapulam*, II.
66. von Campenhausen, *The Fathers of the Latin Church*, pp.15-17.
67. Quasten, II, pp.1-36.
68. Bigg, pp.66-70. Eusebius, *Ecclesiastical History*, V, xxii; VI, xxvi.
69. Eusebius, *Ecclesiastical History*, VI, xviii.
70. Bigg, pp.71ff.
71. *CHLGEMP*, p.168n.
72. *ibid.* p.166.
73. Frend, *The Early Church*, p.95.
74. Bigg, p.76.
75. *CHLGEMP*, p.169.

76. *ibid.* p.176.
77. Bigg, p.95.
78. Bigg, p.103.
79. Clement, *Stromateis,* I, 5, 1-3.
     Prestige, *FH,* p.62.
80. Arnobius, *Adversus Gentes,* V, v-vii, xviii-xix.
81. Eusebius, *Ecclesiastical History,* VI, xxxix-xlii.
82. Cyprian, *De Lapsis,* VIII-IX.
83. Eusebius, *Ecclesiastical History,* VI, xl.
84. Origen, *Against Celsus,* I, Preface, i, iv, vi.
85. Prestige, *FH,* p.44.
86. Eusebius, *Ecclesiastical History,* VI, xxxix.
87. Gibbon, xv.
88. Arnobius, *Adversus Gentes,* I, xlii, xlv-lv.
89. Origen, *Against Celsus,* II, xlviii-liii.
90. *ibid.* I, lxviii.
91. *ibid.* I, lxvii.
92. Russell, p.331.
93. Justin, *Apology,* I, xxx-liii.
94. Origen, *De Principiis,* II, iv.
95. Theophilus of Antioch, *Ad Autolycum,* II, xxii.
     Quasten, pp.240, 244. Nock, p.210.
96. Tertullian, *Apology,* XVII. *cf.* Minucius Felix, *Octavius,* XVIII.
97. J. Baillie, *Our Knowledge of God,* pp.40ff.
98. Frend, *DC,* p.95.
99. *Galatians* 5:22.
100. Aristides, *Apology,* XV, iii-xii.
101. W. Lecky, *History of European Morals,* II, p.4.
102. Origen, *Against Celsus,* III, lxviii.
103. Tertullian, *Apology,* XLVI.
104. Justin Martyr, *Second Apology,* X.
105. Athenagoras, *Plea,* XI.
106. Daniélou, p.125.
107. *ibid.* p.103.

Chapter 6

Christian Deviations

6

When Paul preached at Athens he used the same line of attack as that later followed by the Apologists, but from this he went on to the distinctively Christian affirmations of the resurrection, the Second Coming of Christ, and the Judgement.[1] In *I Corinthians*[2] he anticipated that the Second Coming might well take place in the life-time of his readers, but in *Philippians* and *II Timothy* he calmly contemplated his own coming death. This in no way implies, as has been argued, that he adjusted his thought with the passage of time. As history had a beginning, the Church held, sooner or later it would have an ending; but Paul seems to have been taken aback by the excitement of his converts at Thessalonica[3] when they heard of the Second Coming. In an earlier letter he had told them to live as men who had already been called into the Kingdom of God;[4] instead they were looking for the Kingdom to come when 'the Lord himself shall descend from heaven with a shout, with the voice of the archangel, and with the trump of God.'[5] Like some theologians at the start of this century, they seized on the apocalyptic expectation as the key to the mystery; and like the theologians, some of them never recovered from it. Especially on the Jewish fringe there were Christians of the first and second generations who believed that the time was imminent when Christ would appear to establish the Kingdom of God for a thousand years on earth. Known as *Millenarianism* or *Chiliasm,* this belief held a fascination for the dissidents of society and embarrassment for the more sophisticated, and continues to do so to this day. 'With our vastly different view of the evolutionary process,' C.E. Raven wrote in March 1939 before nuclear physics extended our horizons, 'we do not and cannot believe that history will finish at any arbitrary moment.'[6]

Many expected it quite soon. In his rather muddled vision Hermas saw the tower, which represented the Church, incomplete but not far from completion.[7] 'The last times are come upon us,' wrote Ignatius.[8] Barnabas concluded from the book of *Daniel* that, in a phrase once much used by Jehovah's Witnesses, 'Millions now living will never die.' This, he reckoned, would mark the end of six thousand years since the creation. When that time came the Kingdom of God would also come and the just would be glorified in it.[9] By now Christians were less disposed to remember that Christ had declared that the Kingdom had come and also, as time went by, to expect it immediately. They identified it with the resurrection. God created men at first, Justin wrote,[10] when they had no choice in the matter, but now gave them the choice to be born again in the life to come when the joy of God's servants would be crowned by the vision of himself. And that was how most Christians now saw it. Millenarianism survived as a declining force,[11] though it was soon to show that it was far from a spent force. Not so much a heresy, it was more an eccentricity. Meantime the Church was concerned with the resurrection and the life eternal, until as the Dark Ages and mediaeval times drew on the great painting of the Doom in thousands of village churches and in the magnificence of the Sistine Chapel set Christ before men, not as the Redeemer, but as the stern and implacable Judge.

Theology grew out of the need to understand the implications of the Gospel and to state it to Jewish and Hellenistic listeners. Beyond the central facts of the faith — the *Rule of Faith*[12] committed to candidates for baptism, there was scope for wide variations in thought. At many points no single line of doctrine had been laid down, and could not be so long as Christian minds were exploring new fields. Only with time did orthodoxy become associated with precise definitions and rigid uniformity of doctrine as distinct from faith. When that time came the Church thought twice about men like Tertullian on one flank and Clement and Origen on the other. Tertullian might have overstated his case; the Alexandrians might have compromised; or so it seemed.

As early as New Testament times there was anxiety that believers would not stray from the narrow path of truth. Theology arose from the exploration of new frontiers, yet the Church always retained this anxiety about her frontiersmen, the Davy Crocketts of the ecclesiastical world campaigning on the wild frontier, and tended to forget what she owed to them.

Judaism created the first example of Christian deviation among men who looked, not forward or outward, but back. Paul feared that his converts at Colosse[13] might 'be talked into error by specious arguments' until they forgot that they had been set free from the burdens of the Law, and the writer of *Revelation* was troubled by heretical teachers at Ephesus, Pergamum and Smyrna.[14] But more was involved, for Timothy was warned to turn a deaf ear to 'science, falsely so called'.[15] There is no more misleading translation in the Authorised Version than this for *gnosis,* the word used, could not stand in starker opposition to what is meant by science today. In the beginning it meant knowledge in the normal sense, but here it applies to a pretentious type of religiosity which claimed to be superior to faith. It had no more to do with science than the teachings of Mary Baker Eddy.

Here we have a subject offering great attractions to a certain kind of student, for there is a vast amount of esoteric material to be explored even if it is not always worth the exploring. Gnosticism had no foundation in historical events, as had the Christian faith, and none in the analytic methods of the Socratic mind. It was an ageing philosophy tarted up in the colourful rags of mythology and dependent only on the authority of its teachers and the self-consistency of their systems.[16] 'The aeons of Valentinus and others,' said an unsympathetic writer, 'are but the ideas of Plato seen through the fog of an Egyptian or Syrian mind.'[17]

Essentially the Gnostic was one who *knew*. He had not gradually learned. Instead he had been given a hidden knowledge which gave him redemption, not of the body or soul, but of 'the inner, spiritual man'. To the questions of 'who we are and what we have become, where we were or where we have been made to fall; whither we are hastening, whence we are being redeemed; what birth is and rebirth is,' the Gnostic answer was that we were 'spiritual beings who had come to live in souls and bodies; once we had dwelt in the spiritual world above, but had fallen into this world of sense and sin; now, thanks to our self-knowledge, we are hastening back, redeemed from this lower world; we had been born into it, but were now reborn into the spiritual world.'[18] All this had a vaguely Christian sound, like Wordsworth's *Intimations of Immortality*:

Our birth is but a sleep and a forgetting:
The Soul that rises with us, our life's Star,
    Hath had elsewhere its setting,
      And cometh from afar:
Not in entire forgetfulness,
And not in utter nakedness,
But trailing clouds of glory do we come
    From God, who is our home.

Gnosticism clothed its speculations with so much pretentious nonsense that the reader can easily fail to understand that its impact was at times like that of Wordsworth and Coleridge. But while the Christian faith was centred on God, Gnosticism was self centred, obsessed with mythological speculations about the origin of things, but only because they helped the Gnostic to understand himself. Jesus Christ had a place in its systems, but that was all.

Gnosticism was quickly discovered by the Church and just as quickly disliked. When Philip went on his mission to Samaria he met with Simon, a sorcerer, known to his adherents as 'the great power of God'. Simon was baptised, offered the Apostles money to receive power to bestow the Holy Spirit, and was indignantly spurned.[19] Justin Martyr knew of a Simon from Gitta in Samaria who came to Rome in the time of Claudius along with a woman named Helena who had been a prostitute. His followers worshipped him as 'their first god' and Helena as 'the first Concept produced from him'. A statue had been erected to him on a bridge over the Tiber, said Justin, with the inscription *Simoni Deo Sancto* (To Simon, the holy god).[20] Though the identification of the Simon in *Acts* with his namesake in Justin may be questioned, it is likely to be correct, and there is reason to think that this charlatan was an early Gnostic. Gnosticism, Irenaeus[21] says, derived from Menander, a disciple of Simon. Still more is told in Irenaeus about Simon and Helena, and their story is greatly embroidered in the later pseudonymous *Clementine Homilies* and *Recognitions*.[22]

Until a century or so ago our knowledge of the Gnostics depended on the hostile evidence of early Christian writers, but more recently authentic Gnostic writings have been unearthed, a papyrus codex of the fifth century now in the Berlin Museum, and thirteen leather-bound books containing forty-eight Gnostic treatises on more than seven hundred pages, found around 1946 near Nag-Hammadi in upper Egypt.[23] Gnosticism had no single authoritative exponent or definitive form so it is difficult to trace its antecedents precisely, but current opinion looks on it as an outcome of frustrated apocalyptic Judaism. Alexander's conquests had introduced much oriental thought into the Greek world. In addition, the exile of the Jews in Babylon, their dispersion in the east, and their subjection to Persian rule had made them familiar with oriental religions and, above all, with Zoroastrianism, with its dualism, its contrast between goodness and evil, darkness and light, a religion of conflict and not of sovereignty. When Jerusalem lay waste and the temple desolate and desecrated, apocalyptic hopes in divine vindication were shattered. God had not intervened to establish his Kingdom in the city of David. Many thoughtful Jews, it has been argued, must have been obliged to re-examine their faith and restate it.[24] In addition, there was the world of philosophy pressing hard on orthodox Judaism. Most of all, it was impossible for any potential Gnostic seeking salvation in a disastrous world to avoid hearing the claim that Jesus was not merely the hope of Israel but the Saviour of the world.

Usually heresy rose from the attempt to express the faith in alien terms, but Gnosticism was an attempt to absorb Christian elements into an existing system of thought, a synthesis in which the Christian elements were illustrative and incidental rather than formative. It was a species of theosophy, eclectic, fantastic and bizarre. Irenaeus[25] tells that there was a form of Gnostic baptism where the initiates were led into the water and baptised 'into the name of the unknown Father of the universe — into Truth, the mother of all things, into him who descended on Jesus, into Union, and Redemption, and communion with the Powers,' but while Gnostics may have copied some of the rites of the Church and regarded themselves as Christians, and while Gnostic ideas may have been found in the Church, Gnosticism itself was essentially outside. It claimed no apostolic ministry, it had no canon of Scripture, no sacramental tradition, no communal character. It was not a Church; it regarded itself as the way of the élite, and remained a speculative path for the solitary thinker.

If Gnosticism had many teachers certain ideas ran like a thread through all of them. In the first place it was dualistic, seeing an infinite and almost unbridgeable gulf between the spiritual world to which all goodness and life belonged, and the material world of death which was derivative and thoroughly evil. All this was told to impress the listener. According to Valentinus,[26] who taught at Alexandria and later at Rome in the middle decades of the second century and considered himself a Christian, above and beyond the universe dwelt the only true God, the supreme Father.

> In the invisible and ineffable heights above there exists a certain perfect, pre-existent Aeon, whom they call Before-the-beginning, Primal-father, and Abyss. ... He is invisible and incomprehensible, eternal and unbegotten, and he remained through innumerable cycles of ages in profound serenity and quiescence. There existed along with him Thought, whom they also call Grace and Silence. At last this Abyss determined to send forth from himself the beginnings of all things, and deposited this production (which he had resolved to bring forth) in the co-existent Silence, even as seed is deposited in the womb. She then, having received this seed, and becoming pregnant, gave birth to Mind, who was both similar and equal to him who had produced him, and was alone capable of comprehending his father's greatness. This Mind they also call Only-Begotten, and Father, and the Beginning of All Things. Along with him was also produced Truth; and these four constituted the first and first-begotten Pythagorean Tetrad, which they also denominate the root of all things. For there are first Abyss and Silence, and then Mind and Truth.[27]

It is difficult for any modern reader to make his way with patience through the farrago of nonsense to which Gnosticism reduced the Christian faith and ideas, otherwise sensible, collected from elsewhere.[28] They were concerned with the existence of evil, not merely in man, but in nature, and regarded the material world as evil in itself. Consequently they refused to ascribe creation to the direct action of the ultimate God who was, if one may use a contemporary phrase, the ground of our being, since they could not get away from the fact that he was the beginning of all. So the universe had to be explained, not by a fall after creation as in the Christian scheme of things, but by some primeval disorder in the divine hierarchy preceding creation. So a descending order of aeons was described, which together constituted the *Pleroma,* or fullness, of the divine. But the lowest of these gave way to uncontrollable desire and brought forth a monstrous birth which in turn produced the Creator of the material world. Known as the Demiurge, this was identified with the God of the Old Testament.[29] Yet in the humanity which the Demiurge created there remains spiritual vestiges capable of redemption. Jesus Christ came into the world from the *Pleroma* to redeem the men in whom these traces remained.

> Out of gratitude for the great benefit which had been conferred on them, the whole Pleroma of the aeons, with one design and desire, and with the concurrence of Christ and the Holy Spirit, their Father also setting the seal of his approval on their conduct, brought together whatever each one had in himself of greatest beauty and preciousness; and uniting all these contributions so as skilfully to blend the whole, they produced, to the honour and glory of Abyss, a being of most perfect beauty, the very star of the Pleroma, and the perfect fruit, namely Jesus. Him they also speak of under the name of Saviour, and Christ, and patronymically, Word, and Everything, because he was formed from the contributions of all.[30]

But since matter was essentially evil no real incarnation could have taken place, and the Gospel story had to be explained as a transitory union between a divine aeon and a human personality, or else as a simple illusion. Jesus could not have suffered the limitations of humanity:

> Having endured everything he was continent; thus Jesus exercised his divinity. He ate and drank in a peculiar manner, not evacuating his food. So much power of continence was in him that in him food was not corrupted, since he himself had no corruptibility.[31]

Even more important was the need to explain away his physical suffering and death:

> He appeared, then, on earth as a man, to the nations of these powers, and wrought miracles. Wherefore he did not himself suffer death, but a certain Simon of Cyrene, being compelled, bore the cross in his stead; Simon was transfigured by him, that he might be thought to be Jesus, and was crucified, through ignorance and error, while Jesus himself received the form of Simon and, standing by, laughed at them. For since he was an incorporeal power, and the Mind of the unborn Father, he transfigured himself as he pleased and thus ascended to him who had sent him.[32]

This was an idea which, if it had not already appeared in such a discredited quarter, might have commended itself to some of those who have wished, from quite different premises, to explain away the resurrection. Redemption, by Gnostic standards, was a matter of the enlightenment of the mind, resurrection meant that the spirit of man was lost in the eternal God, and ethics might take the form of extreme asceticism in which sex was condemned as inherently evil or, alternatively, of complete licence since the Gnostic was superior and indifferent to these things. Either the flesh must be annihilated by asceticism or the responsibility of the spirit for the excesses of the flesh must be denied.

As a school of thought Gnosticism died, but the ideas it contained recur from time to time. Its explanation of Jesus Christ is much the same as that given by Mary Baker Eddy and, if it is not a discourtesy to name them in such company, poets like William Blake and Robert Bridges have echoed their ideas at times, usually through points of contact with Neoplatonism.

About 140 there came to Rome from the seaport of Sinope on the Black Sea coast a man named Marcion whose father had been a bishop of the Church. A wealthy shipowner with international connections, he was a committed Christian who signalised his arrival at Rome by the tremendous gift of 200,000 sesterces, a gift which the Church first gratefully accepted but later repaid once she had got a clearer idea of the man with whom she had to deal. Business had not absorbed all his mind.

Highly intelligent, he had thought for himself. It may well be that he had not gone through the formal schooling of the Hellenistic world for his character reveals both the strengths and the weaknesses of great ability undisciplined by training. Following the contemporary fashion of tracing the origins of every heresy to some earlier writer, Irenaeus reckoned him a disciple of Cerdon and Simon Magus, early Gnostics, but this is not entirely accurate since Marcion was a man who thought for himself.[33] He asked questions for which the Church had scarcely adequate answers.

In the first place Marcion's mind was dominated by the love of God in Jesus Christ and by that new way of life, flowing from Christ, by which the Old Testament Law was abrogated. Virtually all our information about him comes from opponents and is unfriendly, but no justice can be done to Marcion unless this admission is made at the start. He did not care for the older Israel; and if he saw the Church as the new Israel the accent was very much on the newness. As we have seen, the Church had taken over the Old Testament uncritically, had interpreted much of it by allegory, and quietly turned a blind eye to much of it as she still does. Marcion was too direct to accept this; he was deaf to the prophetic notes of the Old Testament, and as he read it with a frank mind he was repelled. Mere indifference was contrary to his nature; sensitive to the authoritative power of the Old Testament, he could not dismiss it as no more than human and primitive. His action on coming to Rome shows that this rich merchant sympathised with the Gospel indifference to property rather than with the feeling which we find in the Old Testament that prosperity is a sign of God's approval. Like modern Buddhists he was alienated by the brutality of so many Old Testament narratives and the violence which it continually accepts and occasionally commends. How could this be reconciled with the Sermon on the Mount and the standards which the Apologists said could be seen daily in the lives of ordinary Christians?

Old and New Testament alike, said the Church, came from God. Abraham was the father of the faithful, and Christ was to be found in the Old Testament like treasure hidden in a field.[34] Marcion did not believe this. He read *Isaiah* 45:7 which says, 'I make peace, and it is I who send evil. I, the Lord, do these things.' But he also remembered the words of Jesus that every tree is known by its fruits, and concluded that the Old and New Testaments stood in opposition at this point. Their ethics could not be reconciled. Elisha called bears out of the wood to eat naughty children; but Jesus said, 'Suffer the little children to come unto me.' Joshua commanded the sun to stand still while he completed the slaughter of his enemies; some later readers might be troubled by the apparent interference with the solar system and the cosmological implications; Marcion found a greater obstacle in the command of Paul that we should not let the sun go down upon our wrath. This, he thought, was more important. Divorce was authorised in the Old Testament; in the New it was forbidden, unless for adultery. Jehovah who spoke thus, Marcion concluded, could not possibly be the God and Father of our Lord Jesus Christ. Nor could the cruelty of this earth be reconciled with God as seen in Christ. Like William Blake in these respects, Marcion was unlike him in sharing that revulsion against sex[35] which was steadily growing in the second century. There must, he argued, be two Gods, a greater and a lesser: one was the Creator of this cruel earth, identical with that Jehovah of the Old Testament whose law demanded an eye for an eye and a tooth for a tooth, as demanding of blood as the Aztec gods of Mexico; the other was the Father of that Christ who commanded men to love their enemies.[36] Stripped of its verbiage, here was one of the basic ideas of Gnosticism.

Had he not launched out into heresy, Marcion might well have been listened to by the Church on some of these points, but Gnosticism lay only too handy for his use. Jehovah was to be identified with the Demiurge and the God of the New Testament with that otherwise unknown God who was the primal source of all.[37] Other consequences followed. Marcion had begun by throwing the Old Testament out of the window; he now found himself obliged to rip quite a number of pages out of the New. All that confirmed or commended the Old Testament had to go. Almost alone the apostle Paul — and here Marcion went off on precisely the opposite tack to some liberal theologians of the later nineteenth century — had correctly proclaimed the original Gospel. *Galatians,* which meant to him what it later meant to Martin Luther, and which had also the attraction of having been addressed to a countryside not too distant from his own, told that Christ had brought us freedom from the curse of the Law; and in this phrase Marcion found his theology in a nutshell. Any other Gospel was to be rejected.[38] Even some of the apostles had strayed from the true path. Of the four Gospels one alone was reliable and acceptable, that of St Luke, the friend and disciple of Paul; but even this required a little surgical treatment in places. At the start the nativity narratives called for a major amputation, since Marcion could not admit that 'Christ was born of a woman, born under the Law.' Accordingly the Gospel must begin at *St Luke* 3:1, where we read that Jesus came down to Tiberias in the fifteenth year of Tiberius.[39] So far as Marcion was concerned, wrote Tertullian,[40] the shepherds would have been better to have looked after their flocks and the wise men to have spared their legs so long a journey. Thus Marcion, the shipowner from the Black Sea coast, was what came to be known as a *Docetist*. He could not admit that Christ had had a mortal body, while the Church believed that the eternal Word had taken upon himself, not the nature of angels, but the fullness of manhood, body and soul.[41] In Christ's words, 'Who is my mother, and who are my brethren?' Marcion found confirmation that he was not, in anything more than name and appearance, the child of Mary.[42] Similarly he was embarrassed by the sufferings and death of Christ. How could the eternal possibly die? But the Church lived by the faith of the cross, as Tertullian pointed out in his paradoxical manner.

> The Son of God was crucified; I am not ashamed because men must needs be ashamed of it. ... He was buried and rose again; the fact is certain, because it is impossible.[43]

Starting with so much, Marcion had wandered far from the Gospel, yet it is hard for the modern reader not to respect him. If there was anything of value in the Gnostic speculations, Marcion had asked in sensible terms what they had asked in ridiculous ones. When she lost Marcion, the Church lost more than his money. But his contemporaries were not of this opinion. Perhaps he was too brash, too confident in his own ability, to stop and listen to the Church. Polycarp, otherwise a kindly man, dismissed Marcion with brusque rudeness when they accidentally met.[44] One may laugh on discovering that Tertullian's account of the bleak barbarity of the Black Sea coast is a rhetorical device to put Marcion in his proper place,[45] just as Pelagius was said to have his head stuffed with Scots

porridge; but a moment's thought brings regret for its uncharit-
ableness. Christians reserved for heretics a spite which normally
they did not show to their persecutors or to Christians who
lapsed under persecution, and, conscious that it was the mission
of the Church to proclaim Christ to all the world, had forgotten
that this did not mean that they had all the answers.

Marcion was aware that her fellowship was essential to the
Church and a source of her strength. He therefore set out to
constitute a rival body; but it lacked sufficient vigour to survive
its great spokesman as an effective force. Eusebius tells how one
of Marcion's ageing adherents could say no more than that it
was no good to argue about doctrine, and that those who placed
their hope in the Crucified would be saved, so long as they
continued in good works.[46] With the death of Marcion the fire
had gone out of his church; but this did not mean that his
thoughts were never to arise again.

Manicheanism, which originated beyond the eastern frontier
of the empire, also had a dualistic character. Mani, its founder,
had been born near Ctesiphon, the winter residence of the
Parthian kings, about 215,[47] and first preached in the royal
palace there in 242. He regarded himself as the founder of a new
world religion:

> Wisdom and deeds have always from time to time
> been brought to mankind by the messengers of God.
> So in one age they have been brought by the
> messenger called Buddha to India, in another by
> Zarathustra to Persia, in another by Jesus to the
> west. Thereupon this revelation has come down, this
> prophecy in this last age, through me, Mani,
> messenger of the God of truth to Babylonia. ... He
> who has his Church in the west, he and his Church
> have not reached the east; the choice of him who has
> chosen his Church in the east has not come to the
> west. ... But my Hope, mine, will go towards the
> west, and she will also go towards the east. And they
> shall hear the voice of her message in all languages,
> and shall proclaim her in all cities. My Church is
> superior in this first point to previous Churches, for
> these previous Churches were chosen in particular
> countries, and in particular cities. My Church, mine,

shall spread in all cities, and my Gospel shall touch every country.[48]

And spread it did, since it added a fiery and personal element to what had previously been esoteric doctrine for the élite.[49] It appears from Eusebius that its impact was felt by the Church in the empire soon after 260.

> The maniac whose name reflected his demon-inspired heresy was arming himself. ... A barbarian in mode of life, as his speech and manners showed, and by nature demonic and manic, he acted accordingly, and tried to pose as Christ. ... He chose twelve disciples as partners of his crazy ideas. Bringing together false and blasphemous doctrines from the innumerable long extinct blasphemous heresies, he made a patchwork of them, and brought from Persia a deadly poison with which he infected our own world. From him came the unholy name of Manichee...[50]

Mani taught the existence of two kingdoms. In the first reigned the supreme God from whom radiated the virtues. His kingdom had a heaven and earth, both realms of light, but beneath these was a realm of darkness where Satan reigned. Where these realms met, perpetual conflict raged, forever tormenting humanity. Of all the messengers whom God had sent to men, Mani was the greatest, and the last. His disciples were marked with three seals, one on the mouth, one on the hand and one on the breast. By the first, impure words, animal food and wine were forbidden. Vegetables could be eaten, but not killed. Impure contacts were forbidden by the touch on the hand, and all sexual relationships by the third on the breast. Only a small group of the elect could practise this fully.[51]

Mani's religion spread with such speed in the west that it would seem to have battened upon and absorbed, particularly in North Africa, most if not all of what remained of popular Gnosticism. Since Rome was in deadly rivalry with Persia at the time discontented provincials in the east must have looked to Persia hopefully as, in the early stages of Hitler's invasion of Russia, the Balts and Ukrainians saw the Germans as liberators. Adherents of a Persian religion were therefore looked on with extreme suspicion. It was probably in 297 that Diocletian issued

an edict to the proconsul of Africa commanding that leaders of
the Manichees and their books should be burned, and their
followers punished with confiscation, slavery in the mines, and
even death.[52] Despite this, Manicheanism flourished in North
Africa, a land of great potential importance for the Church.
From the middle of the third century the wealth of its provinces
lay less in the Punic- and Latin-speaking districts around the
cities and more in the villages of the interior.[53] Until then their
people had been worshippers of a deity named Saturn, who was
not the figure of Roman mythology but a thinly-disguised
successor of a Berber Baal. From now onwards his shrines
gradually became deserted. In Numidia many villages became
Christian and something similar happened in parts of Egypt. At
this time the religion of Mani also took root in North Africa, a
score or so of years before the first reference to its presence at
Rome.[54] Notwithstanding persecution, first by the pagan
emperors and then by the Christians, it survived until the coming
of Islam.

As every reader of his *Confessions* knows, it fascinated
Augustine in his youth:

> I fell in with a sect of men [the Manicheans] talking
> high-sounding nonsense, carnal and wordy men. The
> snares of the devil were in their mouths, to trap souls
> with an arrangement of the syllables of the names of
> God the Father and of the Lord Jesus Christ and of
> the Paraclete. ... These names were always on their
> lips, but only as sounds and tongue noises; for their
> heart was empty of the true meaning. ... Indeed,
> they spoke falsehood not only of you, who art truly
> Truth, but also of the elements of this world, your
> creatures.[55]

For much of his later life he was in heated controversy with
them. 'I come now to answer the man who says, "What was
God doing before he made heaven and earth?"' For a moment
Augustine was tempted to reply, 'Making hell for people who
ask silly questions,' but he restrained himself. 'To poke fun at a
questioner is not to see the answer. My reply will be different. I
would much rather say, "I don't know", when I don't, than
hold up to ridicule one who has asked a profound question, and
win applause for a worthless answer.'[56] Manicheanism continued

to raise its questions about the origin of evil in the universe, and in the Middle Ages involved the Church in shameless war and persecution in Languedoc.

Many symptoms of the third century told that the classical world was in sad decline. Others may have been more obvious but none was more significant than the contrast between the wild and pretentious ideologies then current and the austere Judaism and placid philosophy of an earlier time. When Augustus came to power the mood was one of expectation akin to that of Renaissance Florence or Elizabethan England. 'Now is come the promised time,' Virgil wrote,

> 'the world's great age begins anew. Now the Virgin returns and the golden age of Saturn. A new generation descends from heaven. Chaste Lucinda, smile on that child about to be born under whom the iron race shall vanish from the earth. Your own Apollo now is king ... a glorious age begins and beneath your rule the mighty months proceed. If anything of our guilt remains it will become void and earth will be set free from fear.'[57]

Mediaeval Christians saw this as a prophecy of Christ, but, whoever the child may have been, Virgil's lines display the confidence of a generation which seemed to stand on the brink of a golden age. Man spoke of Augustus in terms suggesting a secular equivalent for the Kingdom of God. Two and a half centuries later that confidence had fled, for the empire was in a crisis which was the prelude to its long decline.

In 235 Maximin, a ferocious warrior from the backwoods, seized the throne. It was as though Field Marshal Idi Amin had gained control, not of Uganda, but of the Commonwealth. From then on the empire was in progressive decay in morals, military strength, and financial equilibrium, until under Valerian and Gallienus between 253 and 269 anarchy and demoralisation were everywhere. This period had begun with a struggle between the civil and military powers under the Gordians and Philip the Arabian just before the mid-point of the century. In the east the Persian monarchy had again become a menace, in Germany the hostile tribes across the frontier threatened to form a new and complex military alliance and network, and within the empire the ill-used and semi-civilized peasants and the soldiers recruited from among them seemed on the verge of destroying their aristocratic masters. Inflation undermined the economy and shook the foundations of the social system while plague and famine spread.

In spiritual and intellectual life the results were no less deplorable. Men had lost their assurance in the strength of reason. They were acutely aware of the failure of the state and of the evils unleashed upon them against which there seemed no defence. Greek philosophy with its placid and logical temper had always been superficial socially, the possession of a privileged class, with no roots in the lower levels of the community, and in this troubled age it seemed peculiarly irrelevant. Whatever survived from the classical heritage was to be salvaged, not by paganism, but by the Church. Yet, as the last few pages tell, she was in no way free from the passions of the times and the rising power of the oppressed classes. Marcion had been led out of her by speculation but Montanism was the fanaticism of illiterate and passionate Christians. Marcion's departure had been a heresy, but that of the Montanists was a schism. St Augustine explains the difference:

> Heretics and schismatics also call their congregations churches. But heretics do violence to the faith by holding false opinions about God; and schismatics, although they believe as we believe, have broken away from brotherly love by wicked separations. Wherefore heretics do not belong to the Catholic Church which loves God; nor do schismatics, for the Church loves its neighbour.[58]

Any divergence on points of doctrine by Montanism was accidental and unintentional. It arose in Phrygia in the hill country of Asia Minor, a countryside still dominated by the indigenous population, little affected by the Greek life or speech of the cities, and notorious for the neurotic frenzy of its pagan cults. Perhaps something of the schism was in existence as early as 156[59] but its origins are generally traced to the conversion of Montanus about 170. Montanus was convinced that the Holy Spirit had descended on him to enable him to speak both tongues and prophecy. He was a red-hot Pentecostalist. A neighbouring cleric, called in to deal with the situation, thought that the congregation had gone crazy. Montanism was to him what the Salvation Army was to T.H. Huxley, 'Corybantic Christianity'. Montanus,

> raved and began to chatter and talk nonsense, prophesying in a manner that conflicted with the practice of the Church handed down from generation to generation from the beginning. Of those who listened to his sham utterances, some were annoyed, regarding him as possessed, a demoniac in the grip of error, a disturber of the masses. They rebuked him and tried to stop his chatter, remembering the distinction drawn by the Lord, and his warning to guard vigilantly against the coming of false prophets. Others were elated, as if by the Holy Spirit or a prophetic gift ... [60]

Montanus, however, was convinced that he was no more than the passive instrument of the Holy Spirit.

> Behold, a man is as a lyre, and I fly over it as a plectrum. The man sleeps, and I remain awake. Behold it is the Lord that stirs the hearts of men and gives men hearts. [61]

Two women, Priscilla and Maximilla, wealthy and noble according to St Jerome, left their husbands to prophesy with Montanus. 'Hear not me but Christ,' said Maximilla.

> 'After me, there shall be no prophetess any more, but the consummation. ... The Lord sent me to be the party leader, informer, interpreter of this task, profession, and covenant, constrained, willy-nilly, to learn the knowledge of God.'

Montanus laid down rules for regular fasting and gathered agents to raise funds for his movement. [62] Montanus and his adherents, said those who had grown staid and less heated in the faith, were indifferent to some moral issues; but this may be no more than ecclesiastical scandal. They were, says Eusebius, an ignorant people, and their utterances were lunatic. Obviously the leadership of the local churches was far from sympathetic. 'I am driven as a wolf from the sheep,' said a Montanist. 'I am not a wolf. I am word, and spirit, and power.'

Coming from a simple people in contact with Judaism [63]

Montanus may perhaps have caught the infection of some
lingering elements of first-century Christian life to which the
bishops of his own time were averse. If so, he gave it an odd
twist. He looked for the Second Coming, and he looked for it
immediately. One of his womenfolk had a vision of Christ,
who was said to have informed her that the New Jerusalem was
about to descend upon her local village of Pepuza.

At their worst the Montanists were only a foolish people,
harmless unless when their unmeasured zeal brought down the
strong hand of officialdom upon a Church always under the
threat of persecution. They may have had their own merits. First
reports about them in the west were not unfavourable and the
long-suffering congregations in Gaul hoped for a little that they
might be a new generation of prophetic Christians.[64] Irenaeus,
zealous for orthodoxy, scarcely classed them with Gnosticism as
a substantial challenge to the Church, but was inclined to
dismiss them as fanatics who did not understand the true gift of
the Spirit to the Church.[65]

Had it not been for one important convert they might have
disappeared from the record. At Rome the bishop welcomed
first reports about them until Praxeas, a messenger from the
Church in Asia Minor, arrived to tell the other side of the story.
Something similar happened at Carthage, but there the
Montanists won and retained the formidable Tertullian. When
the rest of the Church had become too reconciled to the
kingdom of this world and distressed at the disorder into which
it was sinking, Tertullian retained the old conviction that there
was no common ground between the Church of Christ and the
state. 'The kingdom of Caesar,' he said, 'is the kingdom of
Satan (*Regnum Caesaris regnum Diaboli*).' He had read the
apocryphal account of Pilate which portrayed him as something
of a Christian believer who ordered the crucifixion against his
will. Christ had rejected an earthly kingdom and this should tell
men that all secular power was not merely alien from, but hostile
to, God. Augustus had repudiated the title of Lord.[66] But law-
abiding as Christians must be, they had a higher loyalty: 'I am
Caesar's free-born subject, and we have but one Lord, the
Almighty and eternal God, who is his Lord as well as mine.'[67] A
Christian Caesar was a contradiction in terms. Christians could
never be Caesars.[68] It was ridiculous to think that a Christian
could accept public office and enforce the law, sending men to

prison or to death.[69] Nor could a Christian be a soldier.

> There is no compatibility between the oath to serve
> God (i.e. *sacramentum*) and the oath to serve man,
> between the standard of Christ and the standard of
> the devil, the camp of light and the camp of
> darkness. One life cannot be owed to two masters,
> God and Caesar.[70]

Perhaps, as we may suspect with Harnack, Tertullian's
sympathy with Montanus would have been less had his
acquaintance been closer but now, to use his own phrase, 'he
withdrew from the carnally minded on acknowledgement of the
Paraclete.'[71] In other words, he joined an exclusive sect.
Intransigent and uncompromising, he was happy among
extremists and in the heated atmosphere of their gatherings he
suspended the use of that critical faculty with which, otherwise,
he was only too well endowed. One Sunday after service a
Montanist sister told him of a vision in which she had seen a
soul. She told him what it looked like. Tertullian, impressed,
wrote it down and published the account.[72]

But there was more at stake than idiosyncrasies or even strong
principles, for as she grew in numbers the Church was beginning
to erase the clearly-marked frontier between her membership
and a secular world. Once it had been as sharply defined as the
Berlin wall but now there was a coming and going across the
frontier and a measure of mellowing. Not all received this
favourably. As Tertullian grew older his originally rigorous and
puritanical temperament was intensified. In his earlier years he
had written that marriage was blessed by God and therefore
good, but that celibacy was better;[73] but after he became a
Montanist he denounced second marriages, which he had
originally permitted with some regret, as no better than
adultery.[74]

This same spirit was seen in a second field. Transformation of
life produced by conversion had been a testimony to the outsider
and a confirmation to those within the fellowship. But did the
converted never lapse into open sin? As Gilbert and Sullivan say,
'What, never? Well, hardly ever.' What then was to happen to a
Christian who fell from grace? His sins had been washed away in
his repentance in baptism, once and for all.[75] But the Church had
made a place in her discipline for Christians who fell into grave

sin. Open confession was made by the guilty man, first, it would seem, to the bishop, but also in certain public cases, it would seem, to the whole congregation. Having shown his penitence he was then formally classed as a penitent. He put on the plainest of dress and restricted his diet. Fasting and prayers were enjoined. He was obliged to prostrate himself and seek the prayers of the church on his behalf.[76] Men shrank from such a public ordeal, but it was a concession to human weakness, made once and once only and never to be repeated. At its close, the penitent was solemnly restored to the membership of the Church, but subject to ascetic discipline for the rest of his life. He could not marry or be ordained. Such a discipline was possible only so long as the Church was a militant minority of burning conviction in the midst of an alien society. Even so, there were three classes of sin to which no absolution might be extended at all, apostasy, murder and adultery.

By the opening of the third century, however, the Church had so grown that she was ceasing to be a beleaguered fortress and becoming a far-flung army with many weaker souls among her ranks, men who were more familiar with grappling with temptation than with trampling Satan under their feet. Now Callistus,[77] the Bishop of Rome and a man involved in much controversy,[78] had a record which may have taught him sympathy and certainly made him vulnerable. He had been the slave of a Christian freedman at Rome who charged him with embezzlement. Callistus fled, was captured, and sent to the treadmill. He was released, tried to recover some money from Jewish debtors, and was denounced by them as a Christian. His former employer denied this, but Callistus was condemned and sent to the Sardinian mines. After five years he was released, and if he had not been a Christian before, the Church now received him so gladly that he was ordained and in time became Bishop of Rome. Callistus permitted the remarriage of widowed clergy, as Tertullian himself once had done. Worse than that in Tertullian's eyes was the fact that, no doubt with the assent of the greater part of the Roman Church, he modified the penitential system so far as to admit adulterers and adultresses and fornicators, once and once only, to public penance.

Tertullian had been a prosecuting counsel at the bar and did not care to see one who had been a prisoner in the dock administering penance as a bishop of the Church. If Callistus may seem to the modern historian[79] to be a moderate and sympathetic shepherd of souls, to Tertullian he was a reprobate,[80] and this was said in no measured language. Callistus' edict, he wrote with venom, should be posted up in brothels. Between the two men was a wide difference in their understanding of the Church. Callistus quoted the parable of the wheat and the tares, if not quite in the original sense. He

> thought of the Church as the home and school of sinners, not a gathered congregation of saints, if saints is to mean those who have reached a high degree of sanctification.[81]

But to Tertullian the Church was the company of those who had been washed from their sins in the blood of the Lamb and were sanctified. So, when he joined the Montanists, Tertullian had not become a heretic like Marcion; instead he had associated himself with a view of the Church's nature which had frequently appeared and was not without reasonable grounds, but was now passing out of favour. A passionate nature led him to state the difference in needlessly provocative words.

It may be taken for granted that Callistus also saw the Church in terms of her apostolic inheritance. Tertullian once had done so also. Like Irenaeus, he had seen apostolic succession not through the predecessor by whom a bishop had been consecrated but through the one whom he had succeeded in the bishop's chair, and more in terms of the authenticity of the faith taught than of any question of sacramental validity, but to him the Church had been the divine community marked out by descent from the apostles.

> Our Lord Jesus Christ ... declared all this either openly to the people or privately to the disciples. One of them was struck off. The remaining eleven he ordered to go and teach the nations. ... At once, therefore, the apostles (whose name means *sent*) cast lots and added a twelfth, Matthias, in the place of Judas, on the authority of the prophecy in the psalm of David; and having obtained the promised power of the Holy Spirit to work miracles and speak boldly, they set out through Judaea first, bearing witness to their faith in Jesus Christ and founding Churches,

and then out into the world, proclaiming the same
doctrine of the same faith to the nations. Again they
set up Churches in every city, from which the other
Churches afterwards borrowed the transmission of
the faith and the seeds of doctrine and continue to
borrow them every day, in order to become
Churches. Things of every kind may be classed
according to their origin. These Churches, then,
numerous as they are, are identical with the one
primitive apostolic Church from which they all are
come. All are primitive and all are apostolic. Their
common unity is proved by fellowship in
communion, by the name of brother, and the mutual
pledge of hospitality — rights which are governed by
no other principle than the single tradition of a
common creed. [82]

By this he meant the Rule of Faith.

Once he had become a Montanist, Tertullian no longer saw
the Church in this way; she was a closed group, the gathering of
the spiritually-minded. In his rigorous view of church discipline
and penance he had a great deal of support from earlier
Christians, but this was forfeited when he dropped all thought of
the continuity of the Church and saw her as a body which
cropped up here and there whenever groups of *real Christians*
might emerge. It was this spiritual Church, he held, which alone
could exercise the apostolic power to bind the loose, the function
of forgiveness.

The Church is properly and fundamentally spirit, in
which is the Trinity of the one Divinity, Father, Son,
and Holy Spirit. It is the Spirit who gathers together
the Church which the Lord made to consist in the
three. From that beginning the whole number of
those who agree in this faith takes its being as the
Church from its Founder and Consecrator. Therefore the Church will indeed pardon sins, but the
Church which is spirit, through a spiritual man, not
the Church which is a collection of bishops. [83]

It would seem that he and other Montanists may have gone
one step further and anticipated later mediaeval heretics who
associated Father, Son and Holy Spirit with three ages of

history, the Father with Old Testament times, the Son with New Testament times, and the Holy Spirit with the time of their own illumination. 'Hardness of heart reigned till Christ came, weakness of the flesh reigned till the Paraclete came,' said Tertullian,[84] and the last words refer, not to Pentecost, but to the new age of Montanus and his followers. Having failed to accomplish the salvation of the world in the two earlier stages of revelation, God had come down in the Holy Spirit upon the Montanists to inaugurate the new age.[85] Had the Montanists confined themselves to their ecstasy and their prophesying and not advanced to such speculations, they would not have been condemned by the Church. As it was, it was they who shook from their feet the dust of a Church reckoned unworthy of their presence; the Church had not ejected them.

Apart from Montanism, there were some speculations which were tacitly accepted in the Church if only, at first, at a popular level. Since the coming of the mass media reading has declined in the west, but even in the heyday of reading in Victorian times when compulsory primary education had been enforced, only a minority regularly read. This must have been even more so in Roman times. Yet for the most part we must interpret the life of the Church from what was written by her literate, and therefore not altogether representative, spokesmen. Essentially the Church was a movement of the masses, motivated by what they heard and saw in worship and among their fellow believers. To this day a priest or minister can make no impression unless he shares a great deal with the mind of his congregation. Each influences the other more than is thought. As we have already said, if the dramatists are excluded, classical writers belonged almost exclusively to an élite culture; but the Church began to create a literature of the masses.

Leaving the New Testament aside, the best early examples of this popular literature after the Apostolic Fathers and Apologists are the *passiones*, or accounts of the sufferings of the martyrs, written by fellow Christians who had witnessed their heroism. Reading these, one suddenly becomes aware that the Church lived by the impression made by the resurrection of Christ and in the hope of life eternal. Love and faith, rather than a mere desire for the perpetuation of existence, fired the Christian hope of resurrection in the heavenly life. When Christ had spoken of resurrection and the life eternal it had been with a measure of reserve; but human curiosity inevitably wished to explore further and there began to appear the popular belief that, apart from the martyrs, God's people would pass through a period of purging and preparation before they came to the full vision of God. In other words, as the Church had begun to obscure the great divide between the Kingdom of God and the kingdoms of this world, so she had also begun to forget that those who had been incorporated in Christ in baptism had entered not merely into the fellowship of his sufferings but into all that he, without their aid, had won for men.

A moving instance of this is found in the record of a young girl martyred about 202 in North Africa, and probably at Carthage.[86] Perpetua, a member of a group of catechumens, was a young mother of twenty-two who was baptised in her prison cell. Though she looked forward without fear to death in the arena she was frightened by the darkness of her dungeon. One day, as she prayed, the name of Dinocrates suddenly came into her mind. This was her brother who had died at the age of seven from a cancer on his face. That night she dreamed that she saw him with others, pallid, dirty, and thirsty, with the cancer showing on his face. There was a wide space between them so that she could not reach him, but she prayed earnestly for him. In her dream she saw him come to a fountain and try to raise himself up to get a drink; but it was so high that he could not reach the water, and at this point she wakened in distress. 'I knew that my brother was in suffering, but I trusted that my prayer would bring help to his suffering.' So she prayed regularly for him until she dreamed again. This time she saw him in the same place, but surrounded by light instead of gloom. He was clean, well dressed, and only a mark on his face told where the cancer had been. By now the fountain was no higher than his waist and on it was a chalice. Dinocrates came to the fountain, drank till he thirsted no more, and then ran off to join the other children at their play. 'I awoke. Then I understood that he was translated from the place of punishment.'

Out of the thought thus popularly expressed was to grow the doctrine of purgatory. At a theological level something of it may be found in Tertullian and Origen.[87] While the Church of the late second and early third centuries spoke of Christ as the eternal Word, the Lord of life, and the Light of the world, she had given less thought to what his death had done for men; she was more concerned with the incarnation than with the atonement.

Notes to Chapter 6

1. *Acts* 17:22-32.
2. *I Corinthians* 15:51. *II Timothy* 4:6-8.
3. *II Thessalonians* 2:1-12.
4. *I Thessalonians* 2:12.
5. *I Thessalonians* 3:16.
6. C.E. Raven, *The Gospel and the Church*, p.47.
7. Hermas, I, iii-v.
8. Ignatius, *Ephesians*, XI.
9. *Barnabas*, IV, XVI, XXI.
10. *Apology*, X.
11. Kelly, *ECD*, pp.474-476.
12. Irenaeus, I, x. Tertullian, *De Praescriptione Haereticorum*, XIII.
13. *Colossians* 2:4.
14. *Revelation* 2:6, 14-15, 20.
15. *I Timothy* 6:20, 21.
16. F.C. Burkitt, *Church and Gnosis*, p.5.
17. Bigg, p.53.
18. R.M. Grant, *Gnosticism and Early Christianity*, pp.7ff. Stevenson, p.75.
19. *Acts* 8:9-24. R. McL. Wilson, pp.99-101.
20. Justin, *Apology*, XXVI. Eusebius, *Ecclesiastical History*, II, i; II, xiii-xv.
    The Apologist's honesty, if not his reliability, was confirmed by the discovery in 1574 of a dedication on the island in the Tiber *Semoni Sanco Deo* (to Semo Sancus, a [Sabine] god).
21. Irenaeus, III, iv. Eusebius, *Ecclesiastical History*, III, xxvi.
22. R.M. Grant, *GEC*, pp.70-96.
23. *ibid*. pp.4ff. Frend, *EC*, pp.62-64.
24. R.M. Grant, *GEC*, pp.32-35.
25. Stevenson, p.132.
26. Kelly, *ECD*, pp.23ff.
27. Stevenson, p.85.
28. Kelly, *ECD*, pp.22-28. Wilson, pp.123-136.
29. Tertullian, *Against the Valentinians*, XVIII-XXXII.
30. Stevenson, pp.88ff.
31. *ibid*. p.91.

32. *ibid.* pp.81ff.
33. Irenaeus, I, xxvii.
34. *ibid.* IV, viii-xii, xxvi.
35. Hippolytus, *Refutation,* VII, xviii.
36. Irenaeus, III, xxv. Hippolytus, *R,* VII, xvii.
    Lietzmann, I, pp.252ff.
37. Tertullian, *Against Marcion,* I, ii, ix.
38. *ibid.* IV, iii. *Galatians* 3:10, 13; 1:6-9.
39. Tertullian, *Against Marcion,* IV, vii.
40. Tertullian, *De Carne Christi,* II.
41. Tertullian, *Against Marcion,* III, viii.
42. *St Luke* 8:20, 21. Tertullian, *De Carne Christi,* VII.
43. Tertullian, *De Carne Christi,* V.
44. Irenaeus, III, iv.
45. Tertullian, *Against Marcion,* I, ii.
46. Eusebius, *Ecclesiastical History,* V, xiii.
47. Duchesne, I, pp.404ff.
48. Stevenson, pp.281ff.
49. G. Widengren, *Mani and Manichaeism,* pp.117-134, 155-157.
50. Eusebius, *Ecclesiastical History,* VII, xxi.
51. Widengren, pp.43-74; 95-98.
52. Stevenson, pp.245-247.
53. Frend, *Religion etc.,* XI, pp.489ff.
54. *ibid.* XII, p.16.
55. Augustine, *Confessions,* III, vi.
56. *ibid.* XI, xii.
57. Virgil, *Fourth Eclogue,* 5-15.
58. Augustine, *De Fide et Symbolo,* XXI.
59. Lietzmann, II, p.194. R.A. Knox, *Enthusiasm,* pp.25-49.
60. Eusebius, *Ecclesiastical History,* V, xvi.
61. Stevenson, p.113.
62. Eusebius, *Ecclesiastical History,* V, xviii. Tertullian, *On Fasting,* I.
63. Frend, *EC,* p.80.
64. Eusebius, *Ecclesiastical History,* V, iii. Hippolytus, *R,* VIII, xii.
65. Irenaeus, III, xi.
66. Suetonius, *Augustus,* LIII.
67. Tertullian, *Apology,* XXXIV.
68. *ibid.* XXI.
69. Tertullian, *De Idolatria,* XVII.
70. *ibid.* XIX.
71. Tertullian, *Against Praxeas,* I.
72. Tertullian, *De Anima,* IX.
73. Tertullian, *Ad Uxorem,* III.
74. Tertullian, *De Monogamia,* XV.

75. Tertullian, *De Paenitentia,* VI.
76. *ibid.* IX-XI.
77. Prestige, *FH,* pp.23-25.
78. Hippolytus, *R,* IX, vii.
79. Lietzmann, II, p.247.
80. Tertullian, *De Pudicitia,* I.
81. S.L. Greenslade, *Schism in the Early Church,* p.112.
82. Tertullian, *De Praescriptione Haereticorum,* XX.
83. Tertullian, *De Pudicitia,* XXI.
84. Tertullian, *De Monogamia,* XIV.
85. St Jerome, *Epistle,* XLI, P.L. 22, col.476.
86. *Passion of the Holy Martyrs Perpetua and Felicitas.*
    Frend, *DC,* pp.116-118.
87. Tertullian, *De Anima,* LV-LVIII.
    Origen, *De Principiis,* II, x.

Chapter 7

Christian Initiation

7

Orthodoxy and unity went together. Orthodoxy was defined and unity secured by the authoritative place of the Scriptures in the Church, the living tradition of the liturgy, and the apostolic ministry. Centuries of sectarianism have made it possible for historians of repute to take it as axiomatic that the Church was divided from the beginning. 'It was badly divided,' says K.S. Latourette of the Corinthian Church. 'Even in the first generation of its existence the Church was torn by dissensions.'[1]

But in *Ephesians* Paul depicts the universal Church as one, holy, catholic and apostolic. In her all Christians are united to one another through union with their Lord who is immanent in his Church. She is therefore the new humanity, called out of the world to bring men to God. Half a century or so later the unity of the Church is a central theme in the letters of Ignatius. 'As children of the light,' he wrote to the Church at Philadelphia,

> 'see that you hold aloof from all disunion and misguided teaching; and where your bishop is, there follow him like sheep. There are plausible wolves in plenty seeking to entrap the runners in God's race with their perilous allurements; but so long as there is solidarity among you, they will find no room for themselves. . . . Where disunion and bad blood exist, God can never be dwelling.'[2]

To the Church at Smyrna he wrote,

> look at the men who have these perverted notions about the grace of Jesus Christ which has come down to us, and see how contrary to the mind of God they are. They have no care for love, no thought for the widow and orphan, none at all for the afflicted, the captive, the hungry, or the thirsty. They even absent themselves from the eucharist and the public prayers,

> because they will not admit that the eucharist is the
> self-same body of our Saviour Jesus Christ which
> suffered for our sins, and which the Father in his
> goodness afterwards raised up again. ... Have no
> dealings whatever with men of that kind. ... The
> sole eucharist you should consider valid is one that is
> celebrated by the bishop himself, or by some person
> authorised by him. Where the bishop is to be seen,
> there let all his people be; just as wherever Jesus
> Christ is present, we have the world-wide Church.[3]

All was not sweetness and light. If all had been harmony
Ignatius would have had no need to commend it. No one can
pretend that the early Church was free of the weakness of
human nature; yet it is less than honest to identify this with the
modern acceptance of sectarianism.

Even these instances of dissent at Corinth and elsewhere
confirm that Paul and Ignatius were obsessed with the essential
unity of the Church; and not merely the Fathers who followed
them, but most early heretics and schismatics were equally so.
They were not dissenters from the Church but the true Church
set free from unworthy members, or so they claimed. When the
Fathers spoke of the Church they meant the empirical, visible
community. If they also thought of her as invisible, it was
because she had existed from the beginning of time.[4] She was the
body of Christ. None thought of the invisible Church in the
modern fashion as comprehending a variety of sects.

> It was held on Biblical grounds not simply that the
> Church ought to be one, but that she is one, and
> cannot but be one. This unity was predicated of the
> visible Church, and the visible Church was thought
> of organically as one structure, one communion. To
> their minds division, breaches of communion, were
> not embraced and overcome by a spiritual and
> invisible unity, nor could a number of denomi-
> nations aggregate into one Church. There was but
> one visible Church in one communion; bodies
> separated from that communion were outside the
> Church.[5]

She held one faith. 'From Libya to the Rhineland, from
Palestine to Spain,' Irenaeus wrote, 'in many languages the

scattered Church speaks this faith to the world as if she were one household. ... The tradition is always one and the same.'[6] By tradition he meant not so much an account handed down from one generation to another, as in modern usage, but a revelation made to men by God in Christ.[7]

An allegory of the Church as the one household of faith was commonly found in the story of the spies sent to Jericho. Rahab concealed them from their pursuers and in return they promised that her household would escape death when the city fell; a scarlet thread was hung from a window to mark the house; the promise was kept, and she was saved alive. A Christian interpretation of this story goes back through Clement of Rome to New Testament times.[8] 'If anyone wishes to be saved,' Origen wrote, 'let him come to this house where the blood of Christ is for a sign of redemption. ... Outside this house, that is, outside of the Church, no one is saved.'[9] Best known in a Latin form, this last phrase was repeated by Cyprian and Augustine and became famous.[10] Allegory does not attract the modern reader, but it is important to see what those who used it meant. Three thoughts were in their minds here; the death of Christ, salvation, and the unity of the Church as the household of faith; and it was the bond between Christ and the believer which created the unity of Christ's people. 'God spared not his own Son, but delivered him up for us all.' Paul's words tell what Christ meant to the first believers and what drew them together.[11]

Thus the unity of the Church began in her faith in Christ, was seen in her worship, and expressed in her fellowship, witness, and doctrine. But here the problems began to rise since liberty of opinion might pass into open division. None too clearly, there was a recognised distinction between faith, which was common to all, and doctrine, which might not be. Origen distinguished three main points of the faith; belief in God the Father, Maker of all things, in Christ the eternal Word and in the Holy Spirit.[12] He then went on to a subject which was later to involve the Church in prolonged debate — the nature of Christ — and acknowledged our limitations here as many theologians who followed him failed to do. The earthly life of Christ had been fully human and yet one with the life of God himself.

It is beyond the power of mortal frailness to understand how that mighty power of divine majesty, that

> very Word of the Father, and that very Wisdom of
> God, in which were created all things, visible and
> invisible, can be believed to have existed within the
> limits of that man who appeared in Judaea. ... We
> see in him some things so human that they appear to
> differ in no respect from the common frailty of
> mortals, and some things so divine that they can
> appropriately belong to nothing else than to the
> primal and ineffable nature of deity. ... If we think
> of a God, we see a mortal; if we think of a man, we
> behold him returning from the grave after
> overthrowing the empire of death ... and therefore
> the spectacle is to be contemplated with all reverence
> and fear. ... To utter these things far surpasses the
> powers of our intellect and language. I think that it
> surpassed the power even of the holy apostles.[13]

But Origen made plain that at many points where faith passed
into doctrine there was ground for debate. What, for example,
was the origin of evil? Here, and at many other points, were
matters on which Scripture had not spoken with such clarity that
a straightforward decision could be made.

It seems a paradox that the Church, with the propagation of
the faith as one of her primary ends, maintained a measure of
reserve in stating her faith publicly. It was declared in preaching
at the gatherings of the faithful, in the instruction of
catechumens, and in liturgical worship, but she held back from
the outside world the detailed knowledge of what Christians
believed. Public preaching of the kind seen in *Acts* soon became
impossible with the coming of official disapproval and
persecution; more, however, was involved. An act of faith is
prior to the acceptance of any system of belief. 'Understanding is
the reward of faith,' wrote Augustine, 'therefore do not seek to
understand so that you may believe, but believe that you may
understand; since, if you had not believed, you would not have
understood.'[14] This was based on the text found in *Isaiah* 7:9 in
the Old Latin version of the Bible which was used in North
Africa and which read, *'Nisi credideris, non intelligeretis* (Unless
you believe, you will not understand).'[15] On this was based the
famous mediaeval principle, *'Crede ut intelligas* (Believe that
you may understand).' 'I do not seek to understand in order to

believe,' wrote St Anselm, 'but I believe in order to understand.'[16]

'A glance at the history of philosophy,' Alan Richardson wrote,

> 'is sufficient to show that there is no key of universal understanding which is, or can be made, evident to all rational beings. The history of philosophy rather proves that it is only by the creatively imaginative act of boldly grasping a faith-principle as a key of understanding that a great and noble system of philosophy can be built. All the great philosophers have done this. *Credo ut intelligas* is as true of Plato, Descartes, Spinoza, Hegel or Marx as it is of Augustine or Anselm. But the advantage enjoyed by Augustine and Anselm was that they were aware of this truth. Compared with the self-knowledge of St Augustine and St Anselm the others were working in the dark, with tools which they but imperfectly understood.'[17]

Accordingly the Church for long issued no formal creed and the writings of the Apologists maintain a strong measure of reserve, not only about her teachings, but about the liturgical acts in which her faith was expressed. Baptism and the Eucharist were new, strange and moving experiences for the convert, and it was only as numbers grew that the Church began to talk openly about the details of her faith and worship. Justin tells no more about baptism and the Eucharist than is necessary for his purpose and Arnobius, who wrote his apology before baptism, shows surprising ignorance of Scripture, liturgy, and doctrine. But if an outsider was moved by admiration and desire for the Christian way of life, he could be admitted to instruction upon an undertaking to submit himself.[18] He then became a catechumen or learner. His first instruction concerned Christian conduct and prayer and he was now permitted to attend the opening half of the liturgy, the *Missa Catechumenorum* or Liturgy of the Word, in the outer hall, leaving as the deacons announced that the *Missa Fidelium* or Liturgy of the Upper Room was about to commence. Credal instruction followed only when the catechumen had proved himself fit for admission to the Church.

Yet if the Church did not have, or did not publicise, a formal creed, she had no doubt about the content of her message. In the apostolic age and the next century the main theme of the Church's faith and worship concerned belief in God the Father, his redemption of the world in Christ, and the gift of the Holy Spirit. At an early date this began to settle down into a formulary which was almost, but not entirely, fixed. Traces may be found in Clement, Ignatius and Justin,[19] and it became known as the *Regula Fidei* or Rule of Faith. As time went by and Christians multiplied, the Rule of Faith came to be stated more openly, as in Irenaeus and Tertullian.[20] Origen speaks of it as 'the preaching of the Church'[21] and by this he meant the faith as taught in the Church of his time and as it had been handed down from the apostles.[22] His use of the phrase tells that the *Regula Fidei* was, in fact, more or less identical with the apostolic preaching, the *kerygma*. Owing to its place in baptism, it was also the mould of the Apostles' Creed.

As a candidate went down into the water to be baptised he was interrogated on the doctrines he had been taught and from this, as it was done in the Roman Church, came the beginnings of the Creed.[23] In the third century the influx of many converts and the threat of heresy caused a tightening of the baptismal instruction and there was introduced the custom of teaching the candidate a creed in which the earlier answers were combined and which he in turn would repeat to the bishop. The so-called Apostles' Creed is based upon the creed so used at Rome, a form which can be traced to the closing decades of the second century, but with the addition of some material which had become popular in the western Church.[24] As the name indicates, a legend grew up that this creed was the work of the twelve apostles:

> On the tenth day after the Ascension when the disciples were gathered together for fear of the Jews, the Lord sent the promised Paraclete upon them. At his coming they were inflamed like red-hot iron and, being filled with the knowledge of all languages, they composed the creed. Peter said, 'I believe in God, the Father Almighty, Maker of heaven and earth ...' Andrew said, 'And in Jesus Christ his Son ... our only Lord ...' James said, 'Who was conceived by the Holy Spirit, born from the Virgin Mary ...'[25]

This fiction did not go unchallenged. In 1438 a spokesman of the Greek Church observed, 'We do not possess and have not seen this creed of the apostles. If it had ever existed, the book of *Acts* would have spoken of it.'[26]

If the New Testament provides examples of baptism immediately following conversion while the faith was still being openly declared, the Church very early insisted upon a lengthy period of preparation. Probably this commenced as soon as there were established congregations with which enquirers could be associated. Those desiring baptism were to pray, fast, keep vigil, and show evident signs of repentance in a change of life, while they received exorcism and instruction. No early specimen of catechumens' instructions survives, but those of Cyril of Jerusalem, delivered in 350, are strongly conservative in character and must reflect a practice which is considerably earlier. Delivered extempore and known from notes taken down by a listener, they have an intimate and homely touch at times. Some catechumens, says Cyril, may have come for the wrong reason; men to meet a girl, or vice versa. If so, they should pay double heed: 'God knows your hearts, and can tell who is genuine and who but feigns, is able to keep the former steadfast and bring the latter to a state of faith.'[27] He exhorts to repentance and then speaks of the sacrament of baptism:

> That to which you draw near is of great import, my brethren, and you must approach it with careful preparation. Each one of you is to be presented before God in the presence of myriad hosts of angels. The Holy Spirit is going to seal your souls. You are about to be enrolled as soldiers of the great King.[28]

The baptism of Jesus has hallowed baptism for his servants. To them it brings forgiveness, grace in their need, and resurrection to eternal life.[29] Cyril then expounds the Apostles' Creed, which by now was available, so far as the clause on the Holy Spirit, when he broke off to speak on human nature. 'I know', he apologised, 'that I am giving a long lecture, and that it is getting late, but what ought we to think about so much as salvation?'[30] He then spoke on the Scriptures and the nature of faith, presumably on another evening, and returned once again to speak on God and the nature of Christ. In his last lecture he dealt with the last clauses of the Creed, the Holy Catholic

Church, the resurrection of the body, and the life everlasting. Here he paused in his lecturing while he asked each present to repeat the Creed which they had been learning by heart, and in closing he called on them to rejoice as they entered the fellowship of the Church.

Baptism, according to the New Testament, was to be in water and in the name of the Father, the Son, and the Holy Spirit (although there are traces of baptism in the name of the Lord Jesus). Its Jewish antecedents lay in the custom of baptising proselytes who, as adults, could scarcely be expected to care for circumcision, and it was the surprising act of John the Baptist in applying baptism to the penitent sons of Abraham which made his critics ask if he claimed to be the Messiah.[31] While Jesus did not baptise, his disciples did.

The command of the risen Christ to baptise among all nations has been questioned on *a priori* grounds. '*Matthew* 28:19-20,' says a great German scholar, as he presents a deduction in the guise of a fact, 'is a theological explanation, added at a later date.'[32] But apart from the question of whether early baptisms may have been in the name of the Lord Jesus and not in the threefold name, there is no evidence for this either in the textual criticism of the New Testament or in patristic usage. All the early writings on baptism, however, associate the practice of it with Christ's own acceptance of the rite, and it is worth noting that all four Gospels relate the descent of the Holy Spirit in this context. In *Acts* and the Epistles baptism is not merely for forgiveness, it is the rite of initiation into the body of Christ and the receiving of the Holy Spirit is essential to it. St Paul speaks of baptism as a symbolic participation in Christ's death and resurrection and in terms which suggest that this was already familiar to his readers, and in a church which he had never visited.[33] Without this, Christian baptism would have been no different from that of John.[34] 'In the *Acts of the Apostles* the Holy Spirit was given by the imposition of the apostles' hands in baptism,' wrote Origen, and 'For this reason was the grace and revelation of the Holy Spirit bestowed by the imposition of the apostles' hands after baptism.'[35]

All early forms of the rite reflect the fact that baptism in the New Testament was for adults; it was addressed to converts and not to infants and led to immediate reception of the Eucharist. It has been argued that reference to the baptism of households implies that children and infants were baptised, but the evidence is such as to carry no conviction to those of a different mind.[36] On the other hand, the early Church lacked the extreme individualism of modern life; she thought in terms of the covenant and of the household of God, and had warrant for infant baptism in the Old Testament precedent of circumcision,[37] meaningless for the Christian of today but entirely authoritative for the Church of the first three centuries. The brief accounts of baptism in the *Didache* and Justin add little except that prayer and fasting preceded it and that, if possible, it took place in running water.[38]

No reliable evidence for infant baptism is available until the end of the second century, but no conclusion can be drawn from this, not so much because new members were predominantly converts as because of the extreme scarcity of information about baptism at all. About 197 Tertullian made it plain that infant baptism was common and that he did not care for it.[39] Had it been an innovation he would gladly have said so, for he had sympathy with the growing custom of delaying baptism of adult Christians till old age or the imminence of death. Infant baptism endangered the sponsors, he argued, because they might die before they could fulfil their vows, or because the child might grow up with a bad disposition. If baptism was for the remission of sins, why need an innocent babe receive it? He blamed Marcion[40] for baptising only the celibate and deferring baptism till death or divorce, but he himself held that baptism should be deferred till marriage put men beyond the reach of some strong temptations.

Writing about 215 Hippolytus took it for granted that children were baptised.[41] If too young to answer for themselves, he wrote, parents or kinsfolk should answer for them. Origen ascribed the custom of infant baptism to the apostles.[42] Conservative in practice if not in thought, he knew no other way in Christian tradition. What was novel was the growing postponement of baptism, ostensibly from the desire to avoid postbaptismal sin, but an abuse which released men from the discipline of the Church and from the obligation to take part in the weekly Eucharist.[43] This indifference to the sacramental life of the Church, even though cloaked by pretensions, is the first of the ominous signs telling that growing numbers brought lower standards.

Tertullian tells that baptisms took place, if possible, at Easter, that they were preceded by an all-night vigil, and usually were at the hands of the bishop.[44] As the candidate entered the water he confessed his faith in the words of the Rule of Faith, renouncing the devil, his angels and pomps.[45] He then received threefold immersion as the divine names were spoken. There were times when immersion was complete but often it was no more than partial.[46] The baptistry in the house church at Dura Europos, dating from the middle of the third century, though large, is quite incapable of immersing an adult, and there were times when only affusion, the pouring of water on the head, was possible.[47] As the candidate came up from the font he was anointed with chrism, or unction.[48] The bishop laid hands on him that he might receive the Holy Spirit. He received a drink of milk sweetened with honey, often in a silver spoon engraved with his name and a brief prayer, and for a week did not bathe. There is a strong tendency to assume that these details were late additions to underline the meaning of the sacrament, and this has even found its way into the New English Bible by the substitution of the word *initiation* for *chrism* in the Greek text; but the tendency has little more support than presumption.

A fuller account is given by Hippolytus.[49] Candidates and their sponsors were to be interrogated. After three years of catechumenate came their baptism. They were to fast from the Friday morning. On the Saturday they received exorcism and kept vigil through the following night. At cockcrow they came to the water and stripped. Children were baptised first, their parents answering for them, if need be. Men were baptised next, and women after. A deacon led the men down into the font, and a deaconess the women, and it would seem there was some degree of privacy.[50] One deacon carried an oil for exorcism, and another an oil for thanksgiving. The presbyter took the hand of the candidate, called on him to renounce Satan, and exorcised him. As he was led down into the font the candidate was asked, first, if he believed in God the Father, secondly, if he believed in 'Christ Jesus, the Son of God, who was born of the Holy Spirit and the Virgin Mary, who was crucified in the days of Pontius Pilate, and died, and rose the third day living from the dead and ascended into the heavens, and sat down at the right hand of the Father, and will come to judge the quick and the dead,' and thirdly, if he believed 'in the Holy Spirit, in the Holy Church and the resurrection of the flesh.' At each stage he replied, 'I believe', and was immersed. As he came up from the font he was to be anointed with the oil of thanksgiving, and after drying himself he put on his clothes and went to be received by the congregation in their nearby place of worship, for baptism was celebrated in a place apart, as the separate baptistries of the oldest surviving churches still show, and those of modern churches such as Coventry Cathedral recall.

The magnificent baptistry of St John Lateran at Rome, built by Sixtus III between 432 and 440, carried a Latin inscription which tells of the new birth in baptism to life eternal.

> A heaven-destined race is quickened here from holy seed; Begotten by the Spirit that upon the waters moved.
>
> Plunge sinner then, who would be pure, into the sacred streams; whom the flood old receives, return to life renewed.
>
> No difference divides the newly born, united by one source, one Spirit, and a common faith.
>
> What children of God's Spirit she receives as a virgin progeny does Mother Church bear here from out this stream.
>
> Would'st thou be sinless? Cleanse thyself beneath the show'ring flood, by thine own sins or by the father's guilt oppressed.
>
> Here springs the fount of life by which th'entire earth is laved since from Christ's wound it takes its origin and source.
>
> Await the heavenly kingdom, who are reborn in this font; eternal life does not accept those who are but once.
>
> Though his sins be many or grievous, let none draw back afraid; reborn from out this stream, a Christian he shall be.

The bishop laid his hand on each new Christian and prayed,

> O Lord God, who didst count these worthy of deserving the forgiveness of sins by the laver of regeneration, make them worthy to be filled with thy Holy Spirit and send upon them thy grace, that they may serve thee according to thy will; to thee is the

glory, to the Father, and to the Son, and to the Holy
Spirit in the holy Church, both now and ever and
world without end, Amen.

He poured the consecrated oil, and laid his hand on the head of
each, saying, 'The Lord be with you,' while they responded,
'And with thy spirit.' All prayed together, and the kiss of peace
was given. From this they immediately proceeded to the
Eucharist, receiving the bread first, then a cup of water, a
mixture of milk and honey and, finally the eucharistic cup.
Paulinus of Nola describes how the new Christians, robed in
white, follow the bishop into the congregation.

> Then fatherlike the bishop leads himself his children
>   forth from the baptismal house, pure white in
>   body, heart and robe,
> And, round the festal altar herding still the timid
>   lambs, he feeds them, fasting, with the Bread of
>   Life.
> Then does the older host approve the younger with its
>   cries, and 'Alleluia' bleats the flock among the
>   new-formed choir.[51]

Obviously this ritual contains much more than the words of
the New Testament tell. Had additions been made in the years
between and especially since the days of Justin? To this it may be
replied that the *Didache* is a very limited document and that
Justin used great reserve, telling no more than he need, while
there are New Testament references, not proving these practices
but capable of being interpreted as relating to anointing and
sealing on the forehead.[52] There has been a strong tendency to
assume that the rites of the early Church were simple in the
extreme until they were complicated and adorned in later
practice. While there is a degree of truth in this, taken on the
whole it is no more than the reading back of a modern prejudice
into earlier times. Word and action in the rite alike told the new
Christian of the baptism of Christ, the forgiveness of sins, the
gift of the Spirit, and the entry into the new life of the Church.[53]
Long afterwards St Thomas Aquinas wrote that

> the perfection of spiritual strength consists in a
> man's daring to confess the faith of Christ in the
> presence of anyone at all, and in a man's not being

withdrawn therefrom either by confusion or terror, for strength drives out inordinate terror. Therefore the sacrament by which spiritual strength is conferred on the one born again makes him in some sense a front-line fighter for the faith of Christ. And because fighters under a prince carry his insignia, they who receive the sacrament of confirmation are signed with the sign of the cross by which he fought and conquered. This sign they receive on the forehead as a sign that without a blush they publicly confess the faith of Christ. This signing takes place with a mixture of oil and balm which is called chrism. ... The oil designates the power of the Holy Spirit ... and by the balm, through its fragrance, good repute is indicated ... brought forth from the hidden recesses of the Church onto the field of battle.[54]

This is what the symbolism of baptism meant for those who received it in the early Church, and what is described here was the general practice in the first quarter of the third century while membership was still comparatively restricted and the threat of persecution periodically imminent.

While normally it was the bishop who baptised, in case of need any cleric or layman could so do,[55] and on simpler lines than has been described here; but it was taken for granted that whoever baptised must himself be a member of the Catholic Church. Probably it was the Marcionites whom Tertullian had in mind when he refused to recognise the baptism of heretics,[56] and in the disputes which arose in North Africa regarding the rebaptism of schismatics and the lapsed this outlook reappeared. When systematic persecution was ordered in 250 widespread apostasy took place in North Africa,[57] many clergy fled or lapsed, and one bishop, Repostus of Suturnica, reverted to paganism with most of his people.[58] Cyprian, whose later conduct showed that he was not ruled by fear, also fled the city, but as soon as the first blast of persecution was over he returned. Acute questions of discipline now arose. Many of those who had technically lapsed, often by bribing officials, now appealed for readmission to the Church. A group of 'confessors', those who had faced persecution and survived, were prepared to admit them, but Cyprian intended to enforce his episcopal authority against groups of enthusiasts. He was prepared to admit the lapsed when they appealed to him, but not to accept their restoration at the hands of any group.[59] Only thus could the unity of the Church be maintained.

> If you abandon the Church ... you are cut off from the promises of the Church. ... You cannot have God for your Father unless you have the Church for your mother. ... To break the peace and concord of Christ is to go against Christ. To gather somewhere outside the Church is to scatter Christ's Church.[60]

At Rome, where the bishop had been martyred, a similar dispute arose and there was a party which refused any consideration to the lapsed.[61] So in the two great cities of the west there was a division within the Church until resumed persecution put an end to it in 257 for the time being. When some who had been baptised among the schismatics desired to be readmitted to the Catholic Church, as many did, the African Church required that they be, in effect, rebaptised. 'The Church,' Cyprian wrote,

> 'alone possesses the water of life and the power to baptise and purify. ... One who has not been ordained in the Church can by no means possess or govern the Church. ... The sacred bond of unity is indissoluble and those who cause a schism desert their bishop and set up a pseudo-bishop for themselves outside the Church. ... It is useless for any schismatic to contend that anyone can be baptised and sanctified with a saving baptism where it is agreed that the minister of the baptism has not authority to baptise.'[62]

But Stephen, the Bishop of Rome, took a somewhat different view.[63] He did not require that baptismal immersion should be repeated but only that the second part, the laying on of the hands of the bishop, be repeated. 'It is a small matter,' Cyprian replied,

> 'to lay hands on them that they may receive the Holy Spirit, unless they also receive the baptism of the Church. For then finally can they be fully sanctified and be sons of God, if they are born of each

> sacrament; since it is written, ''Except a man be born
> again of water and the Spirit, he cannot enter the
> kingdom of God.'' '[64]

In other words, until this time the Church had recognised three
parts, immersion, unction and the laying on of hands, in the one
sacrament of baptism; this was now divided and the gift of the
Holy Spirit was, quite mechanically, associated with the one
part. Cyprian is inconsistent on the point. In one letter he says
that the apostles supplied by the laying on of hands that which
was lacking in immersion, the gift of the Spirit; but in another he
contradicts this.[65] The western Church followed the example of
his opponent and at the council of Arles in 314 the African
Church accepted its ruling.[66] In the east it was not the laying on
of hands but the unction which was used in the act of reconciliation.[67]

Thus the sacrament of baptism, as it had been known, was
split into two parts, the one known as baptism and the other as
confirmation, a name quite unknown in the New Testament or
the writings of the Fathers of the first three centuries.[68] To them,
as to many in our century, the argument as to whether the gift of
the Spirit is conveyed in immersion or in the laying on of hands
would have seemed meaningless. A distinction originally made
for the reconciliation of heretics and schismatics was then
applied where children had been baptised in infancy and only
admitted to communion in later years. 'There are various views,'
said St Thomas Aquinas,

> 'regarding the institution of the sacrament of
> confirmation. Some think it was instituted neither by
> Christ nor by the apostles, but by a council of the
> Church at some later period. Others that it was an
> institution by the apostles. These opinions cannot be
> sustained, for the founding of a new sacrament is
> reserved to that excellence of power which is Christ's
> alone. Let us say that Christ instituted confirmation,
> but by promising rather than by presenting it.'[69]

In other words, St Thomas ascribed its institution, not to the
incarnate Lord, but to his guidance in the Church, and the
Roman Church has consequently held that 'confirmation is not
a necessary sacrament in the same sense as baptism, that it
confers further graces, but nothing other in kind or in essential
principle from what baptism has always given.'[70]

Notes to Chapter 7

1. Latourette, *A History of Christianity,* p.114.
2. Ignatius, *Philadelphians,* II, VIII.
3. Ignatius, *Smyrnaeans,* VI-VIII.
4. Kelly, *ECD,* p.191.
5. Greenslade, *SEC,* p.18.
6. Irenaeus, I, x.
7. Prestige, *FH,* pp.1-11.
8. *Joshua* 2:21; 6:25. Clement, XII. *Hebrews* 11:31. *James* 2:25.
9. Origen, *Third Homily on Joshua,* V. Bettenson, pp.336ff.
10. Cyprian, *De Catholicae Ecclesiae Unitate,* 6.
    Augustine, *De Baptismo,* IV, xvii.
11. *Romans* 8:32.
12. Origen, *De Principiis, Preface,* 4-6.
13. *ibid.*II, vi, 2.
14. Augustine, *On St John's Gospel: Tractate,* XXIX, vi.
15. A. Richardson, *Apologetics,* p.233.
16. Anselm, *Proslogion,* I. *cf. Cur Deus Homo,* I, ii.
17. A. Richardson, *Apologetics,* p.243.
18. Cyril of Jerusalem, *The Catechetical Lectures,* p.31.
19. Clement, VII, xxii. Ignatius, *Trallians,* ix. Justin, *Apology,* I, xxxi, 7.
20. Irenaeus, I, x. Tertullian, *De Praescriptione Haereticorum*, xiii.
21. Origen, *De Principiis,* III, i.
22. Kelly, p.43.
23. Hippolytus, *Apostolic Tradition,* xxi.
24. Kelly, *Early Christian Creeds,* p.101.
25. Wrongly attributed to St Augustine, *Sermon XXIV,* P.L. 39, col.2189.
26. Kelly, *ECC,* p.4.
27. Cyril of Jerusalem, p.76.
28. *ibid.* p.90.
29. *ibid.* pp.95ff.
30. *ibid.* p.110.
31. C.E. Pocknee, *Water and the Spirit,* pp.17-20.
32. Lietzmann, I, p.64.
33. *Romans* 6:3.
34. *Acts* 18:24; 19:7.

35. Origen, *De Principiis,* I, iii, 27.
36. Jeremias, *Infant Baptism in the First Four Centuries,* pp.43-58.
   K. Aland, *Did the Early Church Baptise Infants?* pp.29-37, 87-99.
37. Basil the Great, *Protreptic on Holy Baptism.*
   A. Hamman, *Baptism: Ancient Liturgies and Patristic Texts,* pp.78, 108, 142.
38. *Didache,* VII. Justin, *Apology,* I, 60.
39. Tertullian, *De Baptismo,* 18.
40. Tertullian, *Against Marcion,* IV, xi.
41. Hippolytus, *AT,* xxi, 4.
42. Origen, *Commentary on Romans,* V, ix.
43. Tertullian, *De Paenitentia,* IV-VII.
44. Tertullian, *De Baptismo,* xvii-xx.
45. Tertullian, *De Corona Militis,* iii. The pomps are the theatrical shows associated with pagan worship. *Apology,* XV.
   De Spectaculis, ii-iv.
46. J.G. Davies, *The Architectural Setting of Baptism,* p.47.
   van der Meer and Mohrmann, *Atlas of the Early Christian World,* p.46.
47. Eusebius, *Ecclesiastical History,* VI, 43.
48. Tertullian, *De Baptismo,* vii.
49. Hippolytus, *AT,* xvi-xxii.
50. *Didascalia Apostolorum,* xvi.
51. Paulinus of Nola, *Letters,* 32, 5.
   van der Meer and Mohrmann, *Atlas of the Early Christian World,* p.131.
52. *II Corinthians* 1:21. *I John* 2:20. *Revelation* 7:2-4.
53. Kelly, *Early Christian Doctrines,* pp.193-196.
54. St Thomas Aquinas, *Summa Contra Gentiles,* IV, 60.
55. Tertullian, *De Baptismo,* xvii.
56. *ibid.* xv. *Contra Marcion,* I, xxviii.
57. Cyprian, *Epistles,* LIV, 10.
58. *ibid.*
59. *ibid.* IX.
60. Cyprian, *The Unity of the Catholic Church,* VI.
61. Eusebius, *Ecclesiastical History,* VI, 39, 43.
62. Cyprian, *Epistles,* LXXIV, 3, 6, 9.
63. *ibid.* LXXIII.
64. *ibid.* LXXI, i.
65. *ibid.* LXXII, ix. LXXIV, viii.
66. Stevenson, p.323.
67. C.H. Hefele, *History of the Church Councils,* II, p.302.
68. Pocknee, pp.16, 30.
69. St Thomas Aquinas, *Summa Theologica,* 3A, LXXII, i ad i.
70. O.C. Quick, *The Christian Sacraments,* pp.180ff.

Chapter 8

The Eucharist

8

Israel had observed the seventh day of the week, the sabbath; but the Church assembled for the liturgy upon the first day of the week, the day of resurrection. Whereas the first requirement of the sabbath was abstinence from work, the first requirement of the Lord's Day was worship.[1] Circumstances did not make it possible for most Christians to abstain from work on that day before the time of Constantine, and it is a moot point as to how far the Church would have given the day a sabbatical character. Like the sabbath, the Lord's Day began, not at the previous midnight as in Roman and modern usage, but at 6 p.m. the hour of sunset, on the previous day,[2] so that it was during the hours of darkness that Christian worship at first took place. The pattern can be seen in the account of Paul's visit to Troas on his last journey to Jerusalem. Through the night he met with the congregation for preaching and prayer. Eutychus grew drowsy and fell from the window ledge where he had been sitting, but when he was found to be alive Paul went upstairs again to celebrate the Eucharist.[3] At its close he resumed his journey. In the first instance this time of worship was a remembance that Christ rose at dawn on the first Easter day, but it must also have been convenient when so many Christians were in servile conditions of employment. From time to time the custom is mentioned in Christian literature. 'In meetings before daybreak,' said Tertullian, 'we take the sacrament of the eucharist.'[4] Christian women should therefore marry none but Christian husbands, he urged, for suspicion was bound to be aroused by a weekly departure for nocturnal worship.[5]

For some time after the resurrection the apostles continued to be present at the temple services[6] but it was the Eucharist, the fulfilment of our Lord's command at his last supper, which was the worship of the Church. The books of the New Testament were written for converts for whom the weekly Eucharist was the background of life; they knew its details by heart; and because of this the New Testament accounts do not tell us about the early manner of celebration as we might have wished. Only outlines are given. Apart from the accounts of the last supper in *Matthew, Mark* and *Luke* the eucharistic elements in *John, Hebrews* and *Revelation*[7] all tell that these books were written to be read in the setting of worship and to be understood in its light. Participation in the Eucharist was participation in the Church, and a share in the life of Christ. The incarnate Lord had shared the meals of publicans and sinners: he had broken the bread to the thousands on the hillside; and his last supper was the final one of those great signs which had preceded his atoning death.

'How I have longed to eat this passover with you before my death,' said Jesus to his disciples.[8] Casual reading might suggest that the last supper was a passover meal on the passover night, but this is far from clear and scholarly opinion is divided.[9] It certainly took place at the passover season, but *Matthew, Mark* and *Luke* apparently tell that it took place on the actual night of the passover, while *John* implies that it took place a night earlier and that Christ — 'the Lamb slain before the foundation of the world' — suffered on the cross at the time when the passover lambs were being killed.[10] It may be that *John* is correct and yet that the last supper was a passover meal but held, uniquely, before the actual night by anticipation, and not a *kiddush* or common meal between a rabbi and his disciples, despite the arguments in favour of this last.[11] As the first passover heralded Israel's deliverance from Egypt and the giving of the covenant, so the Eucharist spoke of Christ's blood of the new covenant,[12] and it was held therefore, not on the passover night, or whichever night the last supper may have been held upon, but at the weekly commemoration of Christ's rising from the dead.

For a time there existed two Christian acts derived from the last supper. There was the *agape,* a common meal capable of being abused as early as the time of St Paul.[13] Next came the Eucharist. The one, it seems, opened the night's fellowship; the other concluded it; but the agape was doomed to decline into little more than a charitable act.[14] Clement of Rome's letter to the Corinthian church, written about 96, has an incidental reference to the Eucharist and towards the close breaks out into a long prayer which has parallels with later liturgies and may well have been part of his eucharistic intercession or, at least, representative of it.[15] Pliny's letter to Trajan, written about a decade later, apparently refers both to agape and Eucharist but not in any detail. Our fullest early account may well be that in the *Didache*. Unfortunately any attempt to date this must be largely a matter of guesswork. Some have placed it as early as 100 and others about half a century later, but there is general agreement that it is a composite document where a writer of limited ability has brought together older material, much of it primitive.

'Concerning the eucharist,' it says,

> 'give thanks in this manner. First, concerning the cup. We thank thee, our Father, for the holy vine of David, thy son, which thou didst make known to us through Jesus, thy Son. Glory be to thee for ever. As this bread that is broken was scattered upon the mountains, and gathered together, and became one, so let thy Church be gathered together from the ends of the earth into thy kingdom; for thine is the glory and the power through Jesus Christ for ever. And let none eat or drink of your eucharist but they that have been baptised into the name of the Lord; for concerning this the Lord hath said, "Give not that which is holy to the dogs."
>
> And after you are filled, give thanks thus. We thank thee, Holy Father, for thy holy name, which thou hast made to dwell in our hearts, and for the knowledge, faith, and immortality, which thou didst make known to us through Jesus, thy Son, Glory be to thee for ever.
>
> Thou, Almighty Lord, didst create all things for thy name's sake, and gavest meat and drink for men to enjoy, that they might give thanks unto thee, and to us didst vouchsafe spiritual meat and drink and life eternal, through thy Son. Above all we thank thee because thou art mighty. Glory be to thee forever. Remember, Lord, thy Church, to deliver her from all evil, and to perfect her in thy love, and gather together from the four winds her that is sanctified into thy kingdom which thou didst prepare for her. For thine is the power and the glory for ever. Let

> grace come, and let this world pass away. Hosanna to
> the Son of David. If any is holy, let him come; if
> any is unholy, let him repent. Maranatha. Amen. But
> suffer the prophets to give thanks as much as they
> will. ... And on the Day of the Lord come
> together and break bread and give thanks, having
> first confessed your transgressions, that your
> sacrifice may be pure. But whoso hath a dispute with
> his fellow, let him not come together with you, until
> they be reconciled, that your sacrifice be not
> polluted. For this is that which was spoken by the
> Lord, "In every place and time offer me a pure
> sacrifice; for I am a great King, saith the Lord, and
> my name is wonderful among the Gentiles." '[16]

In spite of the apparent reference to the Eucharist, it seems
likely that the opening sentences concern an agape celebrated in
more or less private fashion in a family home. In the New
Testament accounts of the last supper and in later liturgies the
consecration of the bread comes first, whereas here it is the cup.
Again, the phrase, 'after you are filled', suggests a substantial
rather than a symbolic meal. Probably it is only in the mention
of worship on the Lord's Day, where no details are given, that
we have a reference to the Eucharist.[17]

Fuller information about the agape comes from Hippolytus.
If possible the bishop was to preside or, failing him, one of the
lesser clergy. Evidently the meal took place in the house of
whoever provided it as a gift. The bishop said grace and shared
the bread with each guest. Each gave thanks for himself as he
received the wine. Catechumens ate at a separate table. Guests
were to pray for their host; each was to eat sufficiently, and
what remained over was to be sent away as a gift; the meal was
to be in silence, apart from an exhortation by the bishop or his
answer to questions.[18] The agape was an act of generosity and
hospitality given by a wealthier member of the Church for the
good of the poorer members, for fellowship and encour-
agement. Such gatherings were noticed by unbelievers.

> See, they say, how these Christians love one another.
> ... They are wroth with us, too, because we call each
> other brethren. ... Our feast explains itself by
> its name. The Greeks call it love. Whatever it costs,

our outlay in the name of piety is gain, since with the
good things of the feast we benefit the needy.[19]

Tertullian, who tells this, adds that at the close the participants
wash their hands, lights are brought in and the feast closes with
prayer. Like many other details in Christian worship, the
lighting and blessing of the lamp came from a Jewish source,
long survived, and the fourth-century hymn for the occasion is
well known today through its English version by John Keble.

> Hail, gladdening light, of his pure glory poured
> Who is the immortal Father, heavenly, blest,
> Holiest of holies, Jesus Christ our Lord!
> Now we are come to the sun's hour of rest,
> The lights of evening round us shine,
> We hymn the Father, Son, and Holy Spirit divine.
> Worthiest art thou at all times to be sung,
> With undefiled tongue,
> Son of our God, Giver of life, alone,
> Therefore in all the worlds thy glories, Lord, they
> own.[20]

The Eucharist existed because of our Lord's command at his
last supper, but its form is not exactly that stated in the New
Testament sources, where seven distinct acts are listed: our Lord
took bread, gave thanks over it, broke the bread, and distributed
it to the disciples; he then took the cup, gave thanks over it, and
handed it to the disciples.[21] The liturgical tradition, on the other
hand, with absolute unanimity reproduced four points: the
offertory, in which the bread and wine were taken and placed
upon the table; the prayer in which the presiding cleric gave
thanks to God over the bread and wine together; the fraction, or
breaking of the bread; and the communion in which the bread
and wine were distributed together.[22] This striking unanimity
confirms that the eucharistic practice of the Church preceded the
writing of the New Testament documents. It had been created by
the apostles and not by the literary tradition.

Already the act of worship, the Eucharist, was being
distinguished from the act of fellowship, the agape, but since
our Lord had eaten his last supper in the setting of a Jewish act,
traces of this remain in the Christian Eucharist. As participants
in the Jewish rite had brought their contributions, so the

Christian communicants brought their offerings, the bread and wine in particular, though by the end of the first century the Church had come to interpret the offertory in a more limited and liturgical sense. In the Jewish precedent there had been a grace at the beginning; properly this belonged to the agape. In the Eucharist the breaking of the bread and the thanksgiving over the cup now came together and the blessing of the cup now became the great eucharistic prayer, said over bread and wine together. In the Jewish meal the bread had been broken simply for distribution and not symbolically; so, in the 'four action' shape of the liturgy it was broken at once after the prayer of thanksgiving for the communion which followed immediately. In the Jewish precedent the bread had been received sitting, or rather, reclining at the table, while the cup had been received standing, but in the Church of the first three centuries all received communion standing.[23] On days other than Sunday, said Tertullian,[24] Christians knelt for prayer with bowed heads and clasped hands; but at the Eucharist they stood, while some even held that all prayer on Sundays should be said standing. On early sepulchral monuments Christians are commonly shown with outstretched arms in prayer to the risen Lord, an attitude conventionally known as *orans*.[25]

These factors, the Jewish background and the apostles' following of our Lord's command, shaped the eucharistic rite so that a unity pervaded later developments. When Polycarp visited Rome about 140 the Bishop, Anicetus, could invite him to celebrate without fear that his people might be surprised by an unfamiliar rite.[26] As we have seen, Clement of Rome was accustomed to a rite where scope for free prayer by the celebrant in the intercessions remained. Only with Justin in the middle of the second century do we learn more details. His account, though brief, involves duplication since he tells first of the Eucharist to which the newly baptised processed immediately after the baptism, and next of the normal Eucharist on the Lord's Day.[27] From this and references in the *Dialogue with Trypho* we learn the pattern of the rite.[28] The *Synaxis* or *missa catechumenorum*[29] began with readings from the Old and New Testaments read by a lector and followed by a homily or sermon from whoever presided. Then the congregation stood in prayer of intercession. About this point, where formerly as catechumens they had been obliged to leave, the new Christians, if there had been baptisms that day, would be brought from the baptistry and introduced to the congregation. Then began the *missa fidelium* or Liturgy of the Upper Room. First came the kiss of peace as confirmation of their prayer that all might be reconciled as children of the heavenly Father. Then came the *offertory,* the giving of the bread, of the cup of wine mixed with water, and of gifts for the poor, while those newly baptised and present at their first communion also received a cup of cold water.[30]

Next in the eucharistic prayer the celebrant, speaking to some extent extempore but on set lines, gave thanks over the elements as he consecrated them, praised God for the creation of the world and the redemption of mankind in Christ's passion, offered the elements before God and invoked the Holy Spirit. The congregation responded 'Amen'. The bread was broken and the elements shared among the congregation by the deacons, who afterwards took them to any who were absent. 'This food,' says Justin,

> 'we call eucharist, of which no one is allowed to partake except one who believes that the things we teach are true, and has received the washing for forgiveness of sins and rebirth, and who lives as Christ handed down to us. For we do not receive these things as common bread or common drink; but as Jesus Christ our Saviour, being incarnate by God's Word, took flesh and blood for our salvation, so also we have been taught that the food consecrated by the word of prayer which comes from him, from which our flesh and blood are nourished by transformation, is the flesh and blood of that incarnate Jesus.'[31]

Our next source of information is Hippolytus. Writing about 215 he makes it plain that the wording was largely his own, but he claims to represent the liturgical tradition of the Greek-speaking church in Rome of at least a generation before his time. Some parts of the service, such as the threefold *Sanctus,* are missing, and the document is open to controversy among liturgical scholars, but it is generally accepted that we have in it the only extant eucharistic prayer surviving unrevised from the first three centuries, an instance of the weekly act of worship which stated and shaped the faith of the ordinary Christian.[32]

After the kiss of peace the deacons presented the bread and wine at the holy table; the bishop laid hands upon the elements and gave the salutation and the *Sursum Corda,* while the people responded

> The Lord be with you.
>   And with thy spirit.
> Lift up your hearts.
>   We lift them up unto the Lord.
> Let us give thanks unto the Lord.
>   It is meet and right.

Then followed the eucharistic prayer:

> We give thanks to thee, O God, through thy beloved Son Jesus Christ, whom thou didst send to us in the last days, a Saviour and a Redeemer, and Messenger of thy will; he is thy Word, inseparable from thee; through him thou didst create everything, and in him thou wast well pleased. Thou didst send him into the Virgin's womb and, being conceived within her, he was incarnate and revealed as thy Son, being born of the Holy Spirit and the Virgin. And fulfilling thy will and acquiring for thee a holy people, he stretched forth his hands when he suffered that he might deliver from sufferings those who had believed in thee.

Now came the words of institution:

> Who also, when of his own free will he was betrayed to suffering that he might destroy death, broke the chains of the devil, trod down hell, gave light to the righteous, established the end of the time and revealed the resurrection; He took bread and, giving thanks to thee, he said, 'Take, eat; this is my body which will be broken for you.' In the same way also he took the cup, saying, 'This is my blood which is shed for you; as often as you do this you make my memorial.'

After this came the *oblation* and *epiclesis*:

Remembering therefore his death and resurrection we offer to thee the bread and the cup, giving thanks to thee that thou hast counted us worthy to stand in thy presence and to minister to thee. And we beseech thee that thou wouldest send thy Holy Spirit on the oblation of thy holy Church. Do thou gather into one and grant to all the saints who partake the fulness of the Holy Spirit for the confirmation of faith in truth, that we may praise and glorify thee through thy servant Jesus Christ, through whom be glory to thee and honour, to the Father, and to the Son, and to the Holy Spirit, in thy holy Church, both now and for evermore.

The people responded, 'As it was, is, and ever shall be, world without end, and for evermore. Amen.'

Then followed three brief prayers by the bishop for worthy reception with true benefits. He elevated the elements while a deacon said, 'Let us attend.' The bishop said, 'Holy things to the holy,' and the people replied, 'One holy Father, one holy Son, one is the Holy Spirit.' The bishop said, 'The Lord be with you all,' and they responded, 'And with thy spirit.' Then all received the elements, and the service ended with a prayer said by a presbyter and a blessing given by the bishop with outstretched hand:

Almighty God, the Father of our Lord and Saviour Jesus Christ, we give thee thanks, because thou hast imparted to us the reception of thy holy mystery; let it not be for guilt or condemnation, but for the renewal of soul and body and spirit, through Jesus Christ our Lord.

'Amen.' 'The Lord be with you.' 'And with thy spirit.'

Eternal God Almighty, the Father of the Lord and our Saviour Christ, bless thy servants and thy handmaids; protect, help, and prosper them by the power of thine archangel. Keep and confirm in them thy fear by thy greatness; provide that they shall both think what is thine and will what is thine; grant to them peace without sin and anger; through Jesus Christ our Lord.

'Amen.' 'The Lord be with you all.' The people replied, 'And with thy spirit,' and the deacon said, 'Go in peace.'

As given by Hippolytus, the eucharistic prayer is supremely one of solemn thanksgiving for our redemption through Christ[33] and the work of Christ is seen, as is common in the early fathers of the Church, as one of conflict and victory.[34] Baptism had not merely initiated the convert into the Christian society; it had made him a member of the body of Christ. In the Eucharist Christ himself, the head of the body, and his members were united with God and with one another. Every Christian knew it to be essential that he should participate in the weekly celebration. But many Christians were slaves, or otherwise restricted in their freedom, and provision was therefore made for them to receive the elements so that their union with Christ would be maintained. This is recorded as early as Justin. One of the dangers for a Christian woman married to a heathen husband, said Tertullian, was the suspicion with which he might see her take the consecrated bread which she had not been able to receive with the congregation.[35] Eusebius tells how an old believer named Serapion who lapsed in time of persecution obtained no response to his plea for forgiveness and reconciliation until he was at the point of death. He then sent his grandson to a presbyter who, however, was too ill to go to the dying man. Instead he sent a portion of the reserved sacrament to the boy, telling him how to moisten the dry bread and place it in the mouth of the dying man in token of forgiveness.[36]

It is said that Dean Inge was once asked if he was interested in liturgical studies. 'No,' he replied, 'and neither do I collect stamps.' This modern indifference to liturgical history — which is widespread — fails to understand how much these acts meant for the ordinary Christian of the early days who had no knowledge of the theological disputes to which historians give space. The liturgy was heard week by week until every word burned itself into his memory and thought. It told him the faith and upheld him in Christ, making him a member of the one body. He saw the life-giving bread and the saving cup offered to God the Father, and gave thanks that he had been counted worthy to stand in God's presence and serve him, and prayed that all who shared in the body and blood of Christ might be brought together in unity by the Holy Spirit.

Notes to Chapter 8

1. G. Dix, *The Shape of the Liturgy*, p.336.
2. A. McArthur, *The Evolution of the Christian Year*, pp.14-16.
3. *Acts* 20:6-12.
4. Tertullian, *De Corona Militis*, iii.
5. Tertullian, *Ad Uxorem*, II, iv.
6. *Acts* 3:1.
7. T.S. Garrett, *Christian Worship*, p.35.
8. *St Luke* 22:15.
9. Oesterley, *The Jewish Background of the Christian Liturgy*, pp.158-192.
    Jeremias, *The Eucharistic Words of Jesus*, pp.15-84.
10. R.H. Lightfoot, *St John's Gospel*, p.354.
    Manson, p.139.
11. W.D. Maxwell, *An Outline of Christian Worship*, pp.5-7.
12. *St Matthew* 26:28.
13. *I Corinthians* 11:20-22.
14. Duchesne, I, p.385.
    Dix, pp.90-93.
15. Maxwell, pp.7-9.
16. Stevenson, pp.127-129.
17. J.A. Jungmann, *The Early Liturgy*, pp.35-37.
18. Dix, p.82.
19. Tertullian, *Apology*, XXXIX.
20. Dix, p.87.
21. *St Matthew* 26:26-29. *St Mark* 14:22-25. *I Corinthians* 11:23-26.
22. Dix, pp.48ff.
23. *ibid.* pp.78-81.
24. Tertullian, *De Oratione*, XVII, XIX, XXIII.
25. van der Meer and Mohrmann, *Atlas of the Early Christian World*, p.41.
26. Eusebius, *Ecclesiastical History*, V, 24.
27. Justin, *Apology*, LXV-LXVII.
28. Justin, *Trypho*, XLI.
29. Dix, pp.36ff.
30. Maxwell, pp.11-14.
    J.H. Srawley, pp.30-35.

31. Justin, *Apology,* LXXXVI.
32. Maxwell, pp.21-25. Garrett, pp.51-55.
33. Jungmann, pp.64-73.
34. Gustav Aulen, *Christus Victor,* pp.32-76.
35. Tertullian, *Ad Uxorem*, II, v.
36. Eusebius, *Ecclesiastical History,* VI, 44.

Chapter 9

The Christian Ministry

9

It was from the bishop or his deputies that early Christians received baptism and the Eucharist. Even the pagans, as the assault on the bishops in time of persecution revealed, knew that the life of the Christian community revolved around them. But the early history of the Christian ministry is far from clear, partly because of the limitations of the New Testament evidence, partly because the transition to the second-century episcopate is obscure, and partly because the waters have been muddied by later controversialists anxious to vindicate the practices of the different branches of the Church to which they belonged.

Not least among the many ways in which the Church stood apart from the ethnic religions was the fact that she had no sacerdotal system.[1] The concept of a priest in Israel differed little from that of a priest in pagan religion; he was an intermediary between God and man, one who offered sacrifices to God on behalf of those who could not make the approach themselves. The word *priest* which is now widespread in Christian usage is derived from the Greek *presbyteros*, which simply means an older man, and the use of it to describe both the Christian ministry and these other priesthoods is a misfortune; for in the New Testament, priesthood in the Old Testament sense is never ascribed to individual servants of the Church but only to Christ and his body, the Church.

But within the fellowship of the Church various forms of service appeared. 'You are Christ's body,' wrote Paul,

> 'and each of you a limb or organ of it. Within our community God has appointed in the first place, apostles, in the second place prophets, thirdly, teachers; then miracle workers, then those who have gifts of healing, or ability to help others or power to guide them, or the gift of ecstatic utterance of various kinds.'[2]

Later he wrote,

> These were his gifts; some to be apostles, some prophets,
> some evangelists, some pastors and teachers, to equip
> God's people for work in his service, to the building up
> of the body of Christ.[3]

The rightful insistence of the Church that her ministry is a divine institution has led Christians to argue that its shape and pattern were given to her intact and have remained unchanged, but what Paul describes here are not stated offices so much as functions and services contributing to the common life,[4] not parts of a hierarchy but personal gifts. 'Christ first endowed the men,' wrote Bishop Westcott, 'and then gave them, thus endowed, to the Church. Through their work the character of permanent offices became revealed.'[5]

This awareness that the whole Christian community shares the priestly office of Christ is found in the early writers. 'We are the true high-priestly people of God,' said Justin. [6]'All the righteous', said Irenaeus, 'possess the sacerdotal rank.'[7] But by choosing twelve and sending them to preach as his representatives Christ had founded a ministry within his Church.[8] On them he conferred that authority which men had seen in himself, the authority which creates obedience rather than prescribes it and which exists not for power but for service.[9] They were to be the patriarchs of the new Israel.[10] Though he named them apostles, men sent as messengers, the Gospels do not state that he instructed them to become leaders of the community after his death; but after his resurrection they immediately did so, and showed their awareness that the ministry was to be perpetuated by promptly filling the vacant place of Judas. They did so by drawing lots and from this, it would seem, came the word *clerici*, derived from the Greek word, *cleros,* a lot.[11] The phrase, 'the Twelve' became standard and has almost a symbolical character in the New Testament, but the name of apostle was more loosely used. In *I Corinthians* Paul appears to speak of their number as considerably more than twelve: 'Christ appeared to Cephas and afterwards to the Twelve. ... Then he appeared to James, and afterwards to all the apostles.'[12] Paul and Barnabas are called apostles.[13] In the last chapter of *Romans* Paul[14] speaks of Andronicus and Junias as 'eminent among the apostles'. It is plain that he considered that the chief work of an apostle was to preach the Gospel, especially where it had not been known before.[15] yet the great name of apostle soon disappears from the normal use of the

Church except in an historical sense, and instead we find reference to pastors or shepherds, to bishops, presbyters and deacons. These words describe functions, emphasise responsible authority, and possibly imply more. The first dropped out of general use, but the three others became permanent and specific. The Church regarded her ministry as apostolic but reserved the name of apostle for men of the first generation.

Whatever place each had in the service of the Church, the whole of the ministry derived its nature from the person and work of Christ. 'I am among you as a servant,' he said to the Twelve at the last supper,[16] and all the Christian ministry, the *diaconia* of the Church, is to be understood in the light of this. The Church accepted the fact that her ministry had come down from Christ through the apostles. 'The apostles,' wrote Clement at the close of the first century,

> 'received the Gospel for us from the Lord Jesus Christ: Jesus the Christ was sent from God. Thus Christ is from God, the apostles from Christ; in both cases the process was orderly and derived from the will of God. The apostles received their instructions; they were filled with conviction through the resurrection of our Lord Jesus Christ, and with faith by the Word of God; and they went out full of confidence in the Holy Spirit, preaching the Gospel that the Kingdom of God was about to come. They preached in country and town, and appointed their first-fruits, after testing them by the Spirit, to be bishops and deacons of those who were going to believe. . . . Our apostles also knew, through our Lord Jesus Christ, that there would be strife on the question of the bishop's office. Therefore . . . they appointed the aforesaid persons and later made further provision that if they should fall asleep, other tested men should succeed to their ministry.'[17]

Irenaeus saw the succession of the bishops from the apostles not so much as a guarantee of the validity of the sacraments which they ministered as proof of the truth of the doctrine they taught and preached. Whereas heretics spoke as individuals the bishops spoke as the authentic voice of the Church, teaching the faith as it had been handed down to them by the apostles.

> It is within the power of all, in every church, who may wish to see the truth, to contemplate clearly the tradition

of the apostles manifest throughout the whole world; and we are in a position to reckon up those who were instituted bishops in the churches by the apostles, and to demonstrate the succession of these men to our own times. . . . Since, however, it would be tedious in a book like this to reckon up the succession in all the churches . . . we do it by indicating that tradition derived from the apostles of the very great, the very ancient, and universally known church founded and organised at Rome by the two most glorious apostles, Peter and Paul; as also the faith preached to men, which comes down to our time by means of the succession of the bishops. For it is a matter of necessity that every church should agree with this church on account of its pre-eminent authority, that is, the faithful everywhere, inasmuch as the apostolical tradition has been preserved continuously by those faithful men who exist everywhere. The blessed apostles then, having founded and built up the church, committed into the hands of Linus the office of the episcopate. Of this Linus, Paul makes mention in the epistles to Timothy. To him succeeded Anacletus; and after him, in the third place from the apostles, Clement was allotted the bishopric. This man, as he had seen the blessed apostles and had been conversant with them, might be said to have the preaching of the apostles still echoing in his ears and their tradition before his eyes. Nor was he alone in this. . . . [18]

Irenaeus then lists the successors, Evaristus, Alexander, Sixtus and Eleutherius who now 'in the twelfth place from the apostles holds the inheritance of the episcopate.' He spoke also of Polycarp of Smyrna, who had not merely spoken with men who had seen Christ, but had been appointed a bishop by apostles.

The same argument is found in Tertullian:

Let the heretics produce the original records of their churches; let them unfold the roll of their bishops, running down in due succession from the beginning in such a manner that their first distinguished bishop shall be able to show for his ordainer and predecessor some one of the apostles or of apostolical men — a man, moreover, who continued steadfast with the apostles.

> For this is the manner in which the apostolic churches transmit their registers; as the church of Smyrna, which records that Polycarp was placed therein by John; as also the church of Rome, which makes Clement to have been ordained in like manner by Peter. In exactly the same way the other churches likewise exhibit their names of those who, having been appointed to their episcopal places by apostles, are regarded as transmitters of the apostolic seed.[19]

When the time came, probably soon after the middle of the second century, that the Church wished to demonstrate the apostolic succession of the episcopate, lists of the bishops were compiled.[20] For the most part they were mere lists of names with occasional references to events of importance in the history of the Church. Dates were not given, since the compilers lacked a good system of chronology and were mainly interested in demonstrating the continuity of the see. Lists existed at other important churches, but for Eusebius the representative lists, or *fasti,* were those of the four great churches of Jerusalem, Antioch, Alexandria and Rome.[21] 'Peter, James, and John,' he quotes Clement, 'after the ascension of the Saviour, did not claim pre-eminence because the Saviour had specially honoured them, but chose James the righteous as Bishop of Jerusalem.'[22] Until the siege of Jerusalem, he tells us, 'most of the apostles and disciples, including James himself, the first Bishop of Jerusalem, known as the Lord's brother, were still alive.'[23] When James was martyred, Simeon, the son of Cleopas, the son of that Mary[24] who stood by the cross and possibly of the Cleopas who met the risen Lord on the road to Emmaus, was elected in his place. 'I have failed to find any written evidence of the dates of the bishops at Jerusalem,' wrote Eusebius. 'It is well known that they were very short lived — but I have received documentary proof of this, that up to Hadrian's siege of the Jews there had been a series of fifteen bishops there. All are said to have been Hebrews in origin.'[25] Elsewhere he tells that the first Gentile bishop was named Mark and that, by the time of Narcissus, the thirtieth from the apostles, there had been fifteen Gentile bishops.[26]

When so much time had passed it was inevitable that those lists should be defective; yet they seem to have been substantially correct, and there can be no doubt that there had been a continuous succession in each see. But this leaves much untold. It merely means that one bishop succeeded another and gives us no information — until the time of Tertullian — on who consecrated them. Nor are we told the precise nature of the office they held, its character, rights and authority. In particular, we are left without clear information on the passage from the situation seen in the pages of the New Testament to the appearance in the second century of the threefold ministry of bishop, presbyter and deacon.

Let us look first at the lowest of these three orders. The New Testament contains two words describing service, each originating in general use but later becoming specific; the one, *leiturgia,* comes to be applied to worship, the service of God, while the other, *diaconia,* applies to service of one's neighbour. The two, of course, are linked in Christian life, but a time came when the apostles found their responsibilities too great to be carried without aid: they chose for themselves the primary duty and asked that the congregation should choose seven men 'to serve tables'. [27] Since their task was part of the *diaconia* which pervades the life of the Church they have commonly been identified with the office of deacon since the time of Irenaeus. [28] Consequently the church of Rome, despite its great responsibilities, limited its deacons to seven [29] and early in the fourth century a council of the Church made this a general rule. [30] This identification has been described as 'a very old error' [31] but it seems clear from the emphasis placed on their appointment that Luke saw it as the initiation of a new order in the Church. [32]

Possibly Paul refers to deacons in *I Corinthians* 12:28 when he speaks of 'helps'. In *Romans* 16:1 he speaks of Phoebe, a deaconess of the church at Cenchreae, and when writing to the Philippians he greets their bishops and deacons. *I Timothy* 3:9 states the qualities required in these two orders. Deacons must be men of a clear conscience and a firm hold on the deep truths of the faith. According to Ignatius deacons were servants of the sanctuary, carrying the food and drink to the people at the celebrations as servants of God's Church. [33] Theirs was a practical service to the widow, the orphan and the prisoner. At their ordination the bishop alone laid hands on them, said Hippolytus, as they were ordained for his service. [34] Deacons did not have a primary part in the sacraments of the Church; instead they took care of the sacred vessels, received the offerings of the people, and kept order in the congregation; they distributed the eucharistic elements to the people and carried them to the absent; and in some churches they read the Gospel. [35] There were times when the deacons called the people to prayer, and it was the deacon's cry, 'Ite, missa est'(Go, it is finished), which dismissed the people from the Eucharist and gave it in time the popular name of the Mass,[36] a simple word which, as has so often happened in the Church, later became loaded with doctrinal meaning.

Always in the early Church the order of the diaconate was one to which men — or women, as the case might be — were ordained for life; but the development in Church law in the fourth century led to their integration into the clerical hierarchy in a different way. In the eastern Church they became secretaries and administrators, working for the bishops; in the western Church they were included as the lowest of the three major orders, no more than a stage on the way to the priesthood.[37] In other words, the name remained but the content vanished, and it is hard to see how, in the Roman and Anglican Churches, where the name is still used in other than the primitive sense, the order of deacons, as known in the early Church, can be said to exist. On the other hand, in the Reformed Churches, though the deacons of Baptist and Congregational Churches are reckoned laity, they fulfil much of the original intent, and the elders of Presbyterian Churches, also regarded as laity and in this case called by an equally misleading name, perform many of the functions of the early deacons.

But the problems raised by the diaconate are small compared with those attached to the place of bishops and presbyters in the Church, a subject of such keen historical controversy that it is virtually impossible to write without bias; indeed, in view of its ecumenical importance, it is desirable that anyone who wishes to pursue it should consult the sources for himself. He will discover that if as much weight was put on every word of Scripture as has been done in this debate, it would be argued on the strength of his reference to Timothy as 'his own son'[38] that Paul was a married man. Originally the word *episcopos* meant an overseer, supervisor, or inspector, and the word *presbyteros* an older man. Neither, in the beginning, had ecclesiastical associations. *Episcopos* is used in the Septuagint to describe a foreman artificer at the building of the temple.[39] On the other hand the office of the elders had a precedent for the disciples in the Jewish elders of the synagogue.

At the start the apostles had complete responsibility; a part of this was devolved on the seven; and it has been suggested that the introduction of presbyters, as distinct from the apostles, came from the dispersal of the apostles after the death of James and the arrest of Peter.[40] From then on all official communications with the mother

Church were carried on through them. They were named with the apostles but distinct from them.[41] This was repeated in the daughter Churches. Paul and Barnabas appointed elders or presbyters in every congregation and with prayer and fasting committed them to the Lord in whom they had put their faith.[42] Oversight of the congregation and teaching of the faith were their main duties[43] and the fact that they are always spoken of in the plural indicates that they acted jointly.

From early times it has been noted that in the New Testament the words *presbyteros* and *episcopos* are synonymous.[44] As he was about to leave Asia, Paul called for the elders of Ephesus and told them to care for the flock over which the Holy Spirit had made them bishops.[45] At the beginning of *Philippians* Paul saluted the bishops and deacons and, in Lightfoot's words, 'it is incredible that he should recognise only the first and third orders and pass over the second.... It seems therefore to follow of necessity that the "bishops" are identical with the "presbyters".'[46] The same identification is found in *I Peter*.[47] Similarly in *I Timothy* Paul describes the qualifications required in a bishop and those of a deacon, but without mentioning presbyters; yet later, in a passage speaking of Christian ministers, he calls them presbyters.[48] He instructs Titus to appoint elders in every city and then goes on to speak of them as bishops.[49] This fact has often been acknowledged and discreetly evaded,[50] but only special pleading[51] and an urge to interpret the New Testament to suit later circumstances can avoid the obvious conclusion.

Probably the germ of later developments is found in the distinction that whereas presbyters shared a joint responsibility with others, the word *episcopos* stood for personal action and direct initiative. Therefore while the presbyters are described collectively, the functions of the bishop are spoken of in the singular in the Pastoral Epistles, because this side of the office required independence.[52] Only one celebrant could lead the people in the Eucharist; in a small community such leadership cannot have been available in large numbers; and perhaps it is not unfair speculation to see in Justin's description of the celebrant as 'the president' a sign of how one presbyter came to take his place above the rest.[53] Two elements are found in the leadership of the early Church and its ministry, the first, a collective responsibility, congregational or conciliar, and the second personal.[54] Peter acted personally to baptise a gentile, but had to justify himself to the apostles and members of the church in Judaea. The argument that the leaders of the Church were first known as apostles and later as bishops is dismissed by Lightfoot as baseless, for while the apostles had a roving commission the bishops had each a local flock and seat, and the origin of their office must therefore be sought in the presbytery. 'The episcopate', he wrote, 'was formed not out of the apostolic order by localisation but out of the presbyteral by elevation; and the title, which originally was common to all, came at length to be appropriated to the chief among them.'[55]

Accordingly the earliest traces of this development are to be sought, and are to be found, at Jerusalem, where James, the brother of our Lord, can be said to have been regarded in apostolic times as an example of a bishop in the later sense of having authority over his presbyters, a member of the governing body and yet its recognised leader in sacrament, doctrine and discipline. In common justice it must be admitted that there are limits to our knowledge in this obscure field, that a single apostolic ministry existed from the start, that at an early date it devolved certain responsibilities to the diaconate, that it was exceedingly fluid and adaptable, especially as congregations came to exist further away from the apostles or as the apostles died, and that the Church adapted the ministry to her needs by reserving particular responsibilities to a single bishop in each congregation and assigning lesser ones to his presbyters. This last is the situation as it appears in the second century.

Early Christians acted for themselves and did not always wait on instructions. No one asked Ananias what right he had to baptise Saul of Tarsus, though he was no more than a disciple. The Church at Antioch appears to have been founded by 'some natives of Cyprus and Cyrene'[56] and since the Church could not exist without baptism and Eucharist presumably these unnamed men celebrated them. At Colosse the church seems to have been founded by Epaphras, with whom Paul only later became acquainted, and there is no information on who appointed Archippus to be a deacon there.[57] Though preaching and teaching were among the functions of a bishop, there was never any question in the first few centuries that they were open to any layman. Ordinary Christians, said Origen, 'made it their business to itinerate not only through cities, but even villages

and country houses, that they might make converts to God.'[58] In
more formal circumstances Origen himself lectured on biblical
exegesis at Caesarea at the request of the bishop.[59] Similarly,
though baptism was normally reserved to the bishop, the validity
of baptism by a layman was unqestioned as is still the case in
most branches of the Church today. 'The word of the Lord,'
said Tertullian, 'ought not to be hidden by any; in like manner
baptism ... can be administered by all.'[60]

The insistence of Ignatius[61] that Christians should participate
only in the bishop's Eucharist reveals that some were doing
otherwise; and the common responsibility for discipline which
appears as early as Paul's first letter to the Corinthians,[62] can be
traced as late as the time of Cyprian in the middle of the third
century.[63] But there was every reason why the Church should
control acts of such vital importance and should restrict them to
those whom she had commissioned in orderly fashion. Thus the
spontaneous prophetic ministry which had once existed in the
Church disappeared or found a place among rigorist sectarians.
The Church perpetuated the apostolic ministry but assigned its
functions to different servants as she saw fit. In this she acted, as
in her acceptance of the first day of the week for Christian
worship, upon the actions of her Lord though not on explicit
and detailed instructions.

> For communication instruction and preserving public
> order, for conducting religious worship and for
> dispensing social charities, it became necessary to
> appoint special officers. But the priestly functions
> and privileges of the Christian people are never
> regarded as transferred or even delegated to these
> officers. They are called stewards or messengers of
> God, servants or ministers of the Church, and the
> like; but the sacerdotal title is never once conferred
> upon them. The only priests under the Gospel,
> designated as such in the New Testament, are the
> saints, the members of the Christian brotherhood.[64]

Clement of Rome had seen the ministry as a divine and
apostolic institution but he knew no threefold ministry, only
that of bishop and deacon. But in every letter of Ignatius, save
one, we find reference to the bishop, presbyters and deacons.
Here, for the first time, is that pattern which was later to be

standard, though in not one of the three orders is there the exact field of duties which in time was to be seen. Presbyters were not in charge of congregations and, for the most part, did not baptise or celebrate the Eucharist. Ignatius did not mention the bishop's apostolic succession, though he probably took it for granted; and the bishop had a congregation rather than a diocese. By contrast, in the second half of the second century Irenaeus saw the episcopal succession as a guarantee of the authenticity of his teaching and evidence for the unity of the Church, and Tertullian, in his orthodox days, was of the same mind. Yet there is one important respect in which he set the course for a different way of thought. The earlier Fathers of the Church who wrote in Greek had not used the classical word for a priest to describe the Christian clergy; but Tertullian accepted the Latin *sacerdos,* a priest, to describe the Christian ministry.[65] However, the comment of Archbishop Bernard[66] that this shows that the distinction between layman and priest was fully recognised is misleading. There was no doubt that such a distinction existed, but Tertullian did not question that the laity had a part in the priesthood of the Church. It was no clerical monopoly. 'Are not we laymen also priests?' he wrote. After he became a Montanist he wrote that it was only the authority of the Church which made a difference between the clergy and the people.

> Where there is no bench of clergy, you present the eucharistic offerings and baptise and are your sole priest. For where three are gathered together, there is a church, even though they be laymen. Therefore if you exercise the rights of a priest in cases of necessity, it is your duty also to observe the discipline enjoined on a priest.[67]

Though he wrote this after he had become a Montanist his words refer, not to the practice of heretics but of the orthodox. The New Testament doctrine of the whole people of God was common ground to him and the orthodox, and had not yet been obscured by a sacerdotal view of the Christian ministry.

However, the word had been introduced from pagan sources and the concept was to be increasingly accepted. No pagan words could be used to express the Gospel without imperilling a fully Christian understanding of the faith. In this case the understanding of the Eucharist as the pleading of Christ's eternal sacrifice was liable to be seen exclusively as the act of the celebrant rather than that of the people of God. It might have been better, said Lightfoot, 'if the later Christian vocabulary had conformed to the silence of the apostolic writers, so that the possibility of confusion would have been avoided.'[68]

It is with the name of Cyprian that the next developments are associated. Like Tertullian, he was born in Africa, and probably in Carthage, once the great rival of Rome but now the capital of one of her richest provinces, no further away than a ship running before the wind could reach on the second day from Ostia, the port of Rome. Born and brought up a pagan, Cyprian practised as a lawyer and became wealthy and landed. Converted by a presbyter named Caecilian he was baptised, probably at Easter 246.[69] First a deacon and then a presbyter, this convert held such a place in the city and church, that on the death of the bishop he was elected his successor by public acclamation. Cyprian at first declined and suggested an older man. A number of the clergy were of the same mind, but for different reasons, and at this point first appeared the opposition with which Cyprian later had to deal. At the close of 248 or the opening of 249 he was consecrated.[70] Little more than a year later the Decian persecution broke upon the Church and at Carthage Cyprian's conduct renewed the criticism of his appointment. No sooner had he hid himself than the Roman presbyters and deacons, then holding the administration of the see in commission, wrote to him telling of the glorious martyrdom of their own bishop and making the obvious implication; simultaneously they wrote to his clergy urging them to supply by their devotion the void thus created.[71] Cyprian at once wrote a reply which satisfied his critics at Rome, if not those at Carthage.

Beset with practical problems, Cyprian lacked the philosophical mind of the eastern Fathers, and his temper was like that of Tertullian. Jerome had once known an old man who told him that he had heard Cyprian say that he never passed a day without reading Tertullian. 'Hand me the master,' he used to say, meaning Tertullian. Apart from personal criticism Cyprian had to face three major crises. First came the question of how to treat those who had lapsed under persecution but later repented and sought readmission to the Church. His own inclinations were merciful, but he deferred action until a council of the African Church could meet after Easter 251. Meantime his decision had been anticipated by a group of his presbyters who on their own initiative gave letters of recommendation to penitents asking that the bishop would restore them.[72] Secondly, when Cornelius became Bishop of Rome in March 251 a rival and opponent, who stood for unyielding discipline against the lapsed, secured his own consecration.[73] Though so contrary in outlook, the two dissident parties in Carthage and Rome made common cause and consecrated their own nominee, Fortunatus, as Bishop of Carthage.[74] Thus Cyprian had to deal with schism. Thirdly, when the schismatics began to drift back to the fold there was dispute as to whether those baptised in the schism should be rebaptised. For Cyprian there was no ministry, no sacrament and no salvation outside the Church: and schismatics were outside. Stephen, the Bishop of Rome, could not accept the conclusion that they must again be baptised; the laying on of the bishop's hands was, he held, sufficient. Cyprian could claim precedents,[75] but those who had previously been rebaptised in Africa seem to have been Gnostics of some sort; those now to be admitted, as Stephen understood, were Christians of the same faith but outside the fellowship.

The story of these disputes and the principles involved may be found in Cyprian's letters, but the most comprehensive statement of his teaching is in the tract *On the Unity of the Catholic Church,* a tract which he revised in the light of experience and of which, in one chapter, two texts survive.[76] No abstract document, it springs from the working experience of a bishop in a struggling Church and reflects his daily problems. Irenaeus knew heresy mainly from books, but Cyprian dealt with a divided flock. The mark of his legal training still lay upon his mind, and for all his awareness that the Church was a spiritual community, his approach was practical and legalistic, logical to an extreme. All commences in the conviction that the Catholic Church not merely should be a unity, but is; whoever, therefore, is not within her fold is an outsider, with all the consequences.

> If you leave the Church of Christ you will not come to Christ's rewards; you will be alien, an outcast, an enemy. You cannot have God for your Father unless you have the Church for your Mother. If you could

escape outside Noah's ark, you could escape outside
the Church.[77]

The intensity of Cyprian's conviction that no one could be a
Christian outside of the Catholic Church drew strength not only
from Scripture and tradition, but from his awareness that,
however violent the persecution, the strength of paganism had
now been shaken.[78] He glimpsed that the Church in its moment
of adversity stood poised upon the verge of victory. Enemies
from within were therefore more dangerous than enemies from
without.

> When the adversary reveals himself our minds are
> prepared for the encounter. There is more to fear
> from an enemy who creeps upon us.... When he
> saw the idols abandoned and his seats and temples
> deserted through the multitude of believers our
> enemy thought of a new trick. He invented heresies
> and schisms.[79]

Unfortunately for Cyprian he was faced, not with defectors
from the faith such as Irenaeus and Tertullian had in mind, but
with men whose faith was beyond question and whose record as
confessors was honourable[80] and possibly better than his own.
He therefore turned to the episcopate as the divinely given centre
of unity springing from the apostles.

Any appeal to the authority of the episcopate in a Church now
as troubled as it was widely scattered involved that of her
principal see.

> The Lord said to Peter, 'I say unto thee that thou art
> Peter, and upon this rock I will build my Church ...
> and whatsoever thou shalt loose on earth shall be
> loosed in heaven.' He builds the Church upon one
> man. True, after the resurrection he assigned the like
> power to all the apostles. ... Despite that, in order to
> make unity manifest, he arranged by his own
> authority that this unity should, from the start, take
> its beginning from one man. ... It is particularly
> incumbent upon those of us who preside over the
> Church as bishops to uphold this unity firmly and to
> be its champions, so that we may prove the
> episcopate also to be itself one and undivided. ...

> The episcopate is a single whole, in which each
> bishop's share gives him a right to, and a
> responsibility for, the whole.[81]

At this point, however, there is a second text of Cyprian's tract which specifically states that primacy belongs to the see of Rome. 'He who does not hold this unity of Peter, does he believe he holds the faith? He who deserts the chair of Peter, on whom the Church was founded, does he trust that he is in the Church?' Much controversy has arisen from the existence of these two texts, each apparently genuine. Cyprian's relations with the Roman see were not always consistent, and it has been suggested that he possibly revised what he originally wrote when the Bishop of Rome failed to support him in his African disputes.[82]

As Cyprian asserted ever more strongly the role of the bishop as the focus of unity in the Church, so he began to look to the place of the Church of Rome in the universal Church. In the controversy over the lapsed it would seem that he first turned to the Church of Rome for support and then saw fit to remember his own independence of it, somewhat modifying his earlier statements. To him the chair of Peter was the basis of the unity of the Church,[83] but neither in this tract nor in his letters did he concede that the Roman Church had any right to legislate for other sees. Each bishop was independent.

> So long as the bond of friendship is maintained and
> the sacred unity of the Catholic Church is preserved,
> each bishop is master of his own conduct, conscious
> that one day he must render account of himself to his
> Lord.[84]

Neither Peter[85] nor his successors had been given power over their colleagues. For Cyprian the criterion of membership in the Church is no longer, as for Irenaeus, the acceptance of the apostolic teaching, but submission to the bishop.[86] To turn against the bishop was to turn against God, to be without sacramental grace, and to be without hope. Stern logic, combined with a passionate conviction that the Church was the body of Christ, drove Cyprian into the harsh conclusion that men who called themselves by the name of Christ were, in fact, outside of his fold. The Church gave heed to him and many consequences followed in time. Paradoxically, the unity of the

Church had come to be asserted more dogmatically and exclusively as unity had shown signs of becoming lost. Had the
episcopate failed to develop and a bishop remained no more than
the pastor of a single congregation the Church would have had no
stronger organisation than an elementary congregationalism, ill-
equipped to meet the problems of growing numbers and the
pressures of the state, first hostile and persecuting, and then
protective and dominating. There had been both gain and loss.

The Church at large had refused to follow Cyprian in his
repudiation of heretical and schismatic baptism, but his respect
for the see of Peter nourished the growing sense of authority in
the Roman Church. As the numbers of Christians continually
grew in every city and its surrounding countryside the bishop
became more exalted and more remote. Cyprian declared his
spiritual power. He was the first to apply to the Christian
priesthood those Old Testament texts which enjoined respect for
the priesthood in Israel. So uncompromising was the tone in
which he asserted sacerdotal principles 'that nothing was left to
his successors but to enforce his principles and to reiterate his
language.'[87] In practice the consent of the laity was still a strong
element in the exercise of discipline, but Cyprian had moved far
from earlier concepts of the episcopate and its relation to the life
of the Church, and in this he set the tone for the thought and
practice of the Church in the coming centuries.

Here and there writers of the fourth century observed that
bishops and presbyters had been identified in the New
Testament.[88] In particular, the name of Jerome, a great scholar
but also an eccentric, a frustrated and in some ways most
unlikeable man, was associated with this judgement. In the
epistles of St Paul to Timothy and Titus, he wrote, bishops and
presbyters were identified, the one bearing a title of dignity, the
other of age.[89] He cites *Philippians* 1, *Acts* 20, *Titus* 1, and *I
Timothy* 4 as showing this and *I Peter, II* and *III John* to show
that apostles could call themselves presbyters. At a later date, he
wrote,[90] one was elected to be above the others for the sake of
avoiding schism, and traces of this were long found at
Alexandria.[91] Apart from ordaining, he asked, what was there
that a bishop could do but a presbyter could not? All bishops
had the same rank, the Bishop of Rome as the Bishop of
Gubbio; all were equally successors of the apostles. But the
Church paid no heed, in this respect, to his voice. In regions

where the Church had gained a strong footing in early times, such as parts of Greece and southern Italy, the dioceses remained small and the bishops poor, but the survival of the bishops above the wreckage of the Roman empire in the west, their superiority to the barbarians, and their integration into the feudal system of the early Middle Ages as great landlords, increased this tendency until a great gulf lay between the village priest and a bishop who was one of the lords of the realm. 'Once upon a time,' wrote St Thomas Aquinas,

> 'there was no difference of style between bishops and priests. Bishops were those who superintended, as Augustine notes,[92] while priests, or presbyters in Greek, meant elders. ... Nevertheless a real distinction of rank existed between them. The *Gloss*, commenting on the text, "After these things the Lord appointed also other seventy-two,"[93] says that the form of bishops was found in the apostles, the form of priests of the second rank in the disciples. The difference was afterwards expressed in name and style, and the denial of the difference is reckoned a heretical tenet by Augustine.'[94] [95]

Notes to Chapter 9

1. J.B. Lightfoot, p.184.
2. *I Corinthians* 12:28.
3. *Ephesians* 4:11ff.
4. A. Richardson, *Word Book,* p.147.
5. Westcott, *Ephesians,* p.171.
6. Justin, *Trypho,* cxvi.
7. Irenaeus, IV, viii, 3.
8. *St Mark* 3:13ff.
9. *St Luke* 9:1. *St Matthew* 7:29. *St Mark* 10:41-45.
10. *St Luke* 22:29ff. K.E. Kirk, *The Apostolic Ministry,* pp.118-124.
11. St Jerome, *Ep.* LII, P.L.22, col.531.
12. *I Corinthians* 15:5ff.
13. *Acts* 14:14.
14. *Romans* 16:6ff. Kirk, p.130.
15. *Galatians* 1:16. *I Corinthians* 1:17.
16. Irenaeus, III, iii.
17. Clement, XLII, XLIV.
18. Irenaeus, III, iii.
19. Tertullian, *De Praescriptione Haereticorum,* XXXII.
20. A. Erhardt, *The Apostolic Succession,* p.60.
21. *ibid.* p.36.
22. Eusebius, *Ecclesiastical History,* II, i.
23. *ibid.* III, vii. For the death of James, probably in 62, *cf.* II, xxiii.
24. *St John* 19:25. *St Luke* 24:18. Eusebius, *Ecclesiastical History,* III, xi; III, xxxiii; IV, xix.
25. Eusebius, *Ecclesiastical History,* VI, v.
26. *ibid.* V, xii. Erhardt, pp.37ff.
27. *Acts* 6:1-6.
28. Irenaeus, III, 10.
29. Eusebius, *Ecclesiastical History,* VI, xliii.
30. Stevenson, p.313.
31. Kirk, p.138.
32. H.B. Swete, *Early History of the Church and Ministry,* p.82. J.B. Lightfoot, p.189.
33. Ignatius, *Trallians,* II.
34. Hippolytus, *AT,* xxxiii.

35. J. Bingham, *Antiquities of the Christian Church,* II, xx.
36. *ibid.* I, pp.567-570.
37. World Council of Churches, *The Ministry of Deacons,* pp.12, 26.
38. *I Timothy* 1:18.
39. H. Burn-Murdoch, *Church, Continuity, and Unity,* pp.82-84. Swete, pp.82ff.
40. J.B. Lightfoot, pp.192ff.
41. *Acts* 15:2-6, 23; 16:4.
42. *Acts* 11:24.
43. J.B. Lightfoot, pp.194ff.
44. *ibid.* pp.96ff.
45. *Acts* 20:17, 28.
46. J.B. Lightfoot, pp.96ff.
47. *I Peter* 5:1ff.
48. *I Timothy* 3:1-13; 5:17-19.
49. *Titus* 1:5-7.
50. H. Daniel-Rops, *The Church of Apostles and Martyrs,* I, p.306. Duchesne, I, p.65.
51. Kirk, pp.170ff.
52. Swete, p.84.
53. Justin, *Apology,* lxv.
54. Ehrhardt, pp.170ff.
55. J.B. Lightfoot, p.196. For the opposite judgement, *cf.* Kirk, pp.170ff.
56. *Acts* 11:20.
57. *Colossians* 1:7; 4:17.
58. Origen, *Against Celsus,* III, ix.
59. Eusebius, *Ecclesiastical History,* VI, xix.
60. Tertullian, *De Baptismo,* xvii.
61. E. Hatch, *Organisation of the Early Christian Churches,* p.118.
62. *I Corinthians* 5:4.
63. Cyprian, *Epistles,* XI, i; XIII, ii; LIV, v.
64. J.B. Lightfoot, pp.184ff.
65. Tertullian, *De Virginibus Velandis,* ix. *De Exhortatione Castitatis,* vii. von Campenhausen, *Tradition and Life in the Church,* pp.220ff.
66. Swete, p.221.
67. Tertullian, *De Exhortatione Castitatis,* VII.
68. J.B. Lightfoot, p.254.
69. E.W. Benson, *Cyprian,* p.13.
70. *ibid.* pp.25-27.
71. *ibid.* p.87.
72. *ibid.* p.92.
73. Eusebius, *Ecclesiastical History,* VI, xliii.
74. Benson, p.227.

75. Cyprian, *Epistles*, LXXIII, ii.
76. Quasten, II, pp.349-352. Benson, pp.180-221; 549-551.
77. Cyprian, *De Unitate*, VII.
78. Cyprian, *Epistles*, LI, xxiv; LXXV, ii.
79. Cyprian, *De Unitate*, I, iii.
80. *ibid*. XX, xxi.
81. *ibid*. IV, v.
82. Greenslade, *Early Latin Theology*, pp.122ff.
83. Quasten, II, p.376.
    K. Baus, *From the Apostolic Community to Constantine*, p.360.
84. Cyprian, *Epistle*, LI, xxi.
85. Cyprian, *Epistle*, LXX, iii.
86. Kelly, *ECD*, p.206.
87. J.B. Lightfoot, p.257.
88. Burn-Murdoch, p.138.
89. Jerome, *Epistle*, LXIX, P.L.22, col.656.
90. Jerome, *Epistle*, CXLVI, P.L.22, col.1192-1194.
91. Duchesne, I, p.69.
92. Augustine, *Civitas Dei*, XIX, 19.
93. *St Luke* 10:1. The Vulgate reads 'seventy-two' instead of 'seventy'.
94. Augustine, *De Haeresibus*, LIII.
95. Thomas Aquinas, *Summa Theologica*, 2a-2e, clxxxiv, 6 ad I.

Chapter 10

The End of Roman Persecution

10

As the Wars of the Roses decimated the older nobility of England and prepared the way for the authoritative rule of the Tudors, so the anarchy of third-century Rome destroyed much of the power of the former ruling classes. Along with this went a shifting of power within the lands of the empire, the beginning of the slow decline in the predominance of Italy, and the resurgence of the east. Further, while it was still considered essential to uphold the traditional cults of the gods by which the power of Rome was supposed to be maintained, the religion of the temples, as Pliny had noted long before, steadily counted for less. It was a survival rather than a living force. There was a growing inclination to be interested in oriental religions of all sorts, and a growth of monotheistic belief which saw the names of all the Olympians as no more than titles or aspects of one divine power.[1] When Juvenal complained a century earlier that the Orontes had flowed into the Tiber, the idea may have had the startling originality of Canning's declaration in 1826 that he had 'called the New World into existence to redress the balance of the Old,' but by the middle of the third century the influence of the east was as obvious as the military superiority of America over Spain and Portugal today. Immigrants from strange places were found in every rank of what was still called Roman society. When the emperor, Septimius Severus, was returning from his Scottish campaign in 211 he took it as a bad omen that the first legionary to meet him as he entered Carlisle was a negro. He himself was a native of North Africa and his second wife, Julia Domna, a woman of great personality, was a Syrian from Emesa. Caracalla and Geta, her two sons, were thus half oriental and partly Punic, and had even less Roman blood in their veins than George I had British when he came over from Hanover. Elagabalus, the grandson of Julia Domna, had been a priest of the sun until he became emperor in 219 and brought an explicitly oriental regime to hold court in the city of Augustus.[2]

This produced a violent reaction, so that Gibbon is probably correct in suspecting that the list of his follies and obscenities in the *Historia Augusta* has, at least, been exaggerated.[3]

Alexander Severus, his cousin and successor, conformed more to Roman conventions but again the Syrian background was apparent in a monotheism of sorts which took the sun as a symbol of that one divinity to which all religions, under different names, paid homage. A statue of Abraham and, surprisingly, one of Christ stood among the figures of the classical gods in his private chapel. Whatever form it took, it is most unlikely to have been a crucifix, for this displayed the element in the faith least apparent to pagans. Alexander Severus, it was later told, had thought of building a temple to Christ.[4] His mother Mamaea, who dominated him, took an open interest in the Church. About 232, when she was at Antioch, she sent for Origen and listened to him expounding the faith.[5] This pagan syncretism, the urge to find one common end in all religions, was far removed from the exclusiveness which the Church had inherited from the older Israel, but when Alexander and his mother were murdered by the military in 235 most of those members of his entourage who perished with him, according to Eusebius, were Christians.

Philip the Arabian, emperor from 244 until 249, also had an interest in the Christian Church which tradition possibly exaggerated. Origen wrote both to Philip and his wife. On Easter Eve, Eusebius tells, Philip asked to share in the worship of the Church, but the bishop refused until he submitted to the accepted discipline for the admission of catechumens. But the story is qualified by the significant phrase, 'it is said'.[6] Part at least of the story looks like a pious fiction, but it is a sign that the Church was now living in a changed climate of opinion. Imperial circles had a syncretistic outlook. They were far from being Christian but were far from unfriendly. Why should not polytheism absorb yet another divinity? Alexander Severus was remembered as frequently quoting a garbled version of one of the sayings of Christ.

These things reflected the outlook of society as a whole. On both sides there were signs that the Church and the empire might come to terms. Converts multiplied as the aristocratic families which had once controlled the establishment declined and their ranks were permeated by newcomers from the provinces and the proletariat. What would Queen Victoria have thought had she known that Edward VII would have a Prime Minister who was the grandson of a Scottish farm labourer and George V another who was the son of one? What would the Romans of Antonine times have said had they been told that the child of a liaison between an army sergeant and a barmaid would rule the empire and make it Christian? By the middle of the third century Christians were entering the moneyed classes.[7] Even in the far west of the empire there was an advance by the Church in the countryside, probably because of the movement of moneyed townsmen and their dependents from the cities to the country villas. At Lullingstone, some eighteen miles to the south-east of London, a farmhouse was extended to a country house by some wealthy Roman about the close of the first century. For a time it was then abandoned until reconstructed on a larger scale. Excavation has revealed that a room in the villa had been transformed into a Christian chapel, probably about the close of the third century, and that when the house fell into disuse a door was opened into the garden to permit the chapel to become the place of worship for the surrounding country people.[8] Social change, the decay of the old order, and the rise of new classes to power and prosperity had brought expansion for a Church rooted in the rising classes.

If anything, this renewed the ancient hostility of the stalwarts of the old regime, for the Church had now risen for the first time to be a major social challenge which could not be ignored. She was on the verge of power and, one way or another, must be dealt with, must be acknowledged or suppressed. In September 249 Decius succeeded Philip the Arabian in the rule of an empire teetering on the brink of collapse. In what is now Rumania the barbarians from across the frontier had begun a mass irruption like that of the Helvetii which Julius Caesar met in Gaul; but this time the empire was incapable of repelling the invasion. All the questions asked by historians as to why a once great empire had fallen to this sorry pass must have pressed upon the mind of Decius. He was convinced that military decline and social disorder came from the loss of the ancient moral basis of the Roman state. Cato, he believed, should be living at this hour. He therefore revived the obsolete office of censor and, since no Cato was available, bestowed it upon the future emperor Valerian.[9] Simultaneously, he decided to launch a comprehensive attack upon the Church 'which was the master-institution of the internal proletariat and at the same time was not, as the barbarians were, beyond the physical reach of the dominant minority's now distractedly vindictive arm.'[10] This marks an epoch in the history of the Church under Roman rule. Previous persecutions, though the result of government policy, had been sporadic and local; but this was an ordered, deliberate, and comprehensive attempt to exterminate the Church like that which almost completely destroyed the Japanese Church in the seventeenth century.

In the first phase, which began in December 249, action was taken against the leaders. Alexander, Bishop of Jerusalem, died in his prison cell at Caesarea after interrogation, and so did the Bishop of Antioch. Dionysus, Bishop of Alexandria, who had been rescued against his will, wrote to his successor to say that the imperial edict was not the prime cause of the persecution since action had been taken against Christians at Alexandria almost a year before. 'No road, no highway, no alley was open to us, either by night or by day . . . for a long time the terror was intense.'[11] Many renounced their faith, as — to the shame of the Church — did Euctemon,[12] Polycarp's successor at Smyrna, but Dionysus records case after case where Christians accepted martyrdom by official action or by mob violence. Others fled to the recesses of the countryside. At Carthage, Cyprian went into hiding, but Fabian of Rome was martyred on 20 January 250, and the situation of the Church at Rome was so grave that the see lay vacant for fifteen months. In 1854 the papal burial vault in the catacombs was discovered with the simple fragments of the epitaph of Fabian. Against the back wall had been the memorial tablet erected by Pope Damasus in the fourth century.

> Here — if you would know it — there rests in crowded company a multitude of holy men. Venerable tombs contain the bodies of martyrs but the royal citadel of heaven received their lofty souls. Here lie the companions of Sixtus who overcame the enemy, here the host of princes who keep vigil before the altar of Christ; here lies the Bishop who lived during the long time of peace; here the holy confessors sent by Greece. Here lie youths and boys, old men and their chaste grandchildren who chose to

> preserve their chastity. Here, it must be confessed, I,
> Damasus, would have wished to lay my bones to rest,
> yet was loth to disturb the ashes of these holy ones. [13]

In June 250 the second phase began. Now that the leadership
had been broken or driven underground a general recantation
was demanded of all Christians through the time-honoured
medium of a sacrifice to the genius of the emperor. To every
citizen who sacrificed a certificate was then issued, and one of
the surviving Egyptian examples testifies by its detail to the
comprehensiveness of the persecution.

> To the commission chosen to superintend the
> sacrifices at the village of Alexander's island. From
> Aurelius Diogenes, son of Sabatus, of the village of
> Alexander's island, aged 72 years, with a scar on the
> right eyebrow. I have always sacrificed to the gods,
> and now in your presence in accordance with the
> edict I have made sacrifice, and poured a libation,
> and partaken of the sacred victims. I request you to
> certify this below. Farewell. I Aurelius Diogenes,
> have presented this petition. [14]

Two witnesses added their names and the document was dated
26 June 250.

Decius was killed in Thrace in battle against the Goths in
November 251, and persecution then lapsed for a while.
Christians began to reassemble for worship. But the pause was
only due to the temporary disorganisation of the troubled state.
Gallus, the successor of Decius, was reduced to the dangerous
expedient of buying off the Goths. During their brief and
troubled reigns he and his successor Aemilianus were hostile to
the Church, if restricted in their actions. [15] Preoccupied with the
Goths on the Danube frontier and then with the Persians on the
Euphrates, Valerian, the next emperor, had little opportunity at
first to deal with Church and was mistakenly credited with some
partiality towards her, [16] but, possibly suspecting that some
Christians were looking for relief to the foes of the empire, he
issued an edict against the clergy in 257. [17] Rash defiance brought
martyrdom, but the government was not anxious to proceed to
extremes, for suppression and recantation would have met its
needs. Dionysus, Bishop of Alexandria, was banished to a

country village and Cyprian of Carthage was exiled to one on the
bleak Libyan coast.

A further edict followed in the summer of 258, this time
threatening death to clergy and upper class Christians. Christian
workers on the great imperial estates were to have their property
confiscated and to be sent to the mines. Under this edict Xystus,
Bishop of Rome, and four of the seven deacons of the Roman
Church were seized in the catacombs and executed on 6 August
258, and the remaining deacons a few days later.[18] All were
buried by the faithful in the vault where Fabian and the other
martyred bishops of Rome already lay. On 13 September 258
Cyprian was interviewed by two senior officials of the
proconsul. He refused to sacrifice and next day was put to death
'under the emperors Valerian and Gallienus, but in the reign of
our Lord Jesus Christ.' From Spain to Palestine there were
martyrdoms until suddenly a respite came.

While Rome declined, Persia had recovered strength and in
260 Valerian was obliged to march beyond the Euphrates. Near
Edessa he was outnumbered, surrounded, and forced to
surrender. On the heels of this great disaster the Persian armies
rapidly overran Syria and penetrated far into Asia Minor.
Valerian, robed in purple but in chains, was carried back into
Persia; whenever the Persian king wished to mount on
horseback his imperial captive was made to kneel on the ground
while the victor put his foot on his shoulders to use him as a
mounting block. Even death brought no end to the humiliation
of Valerian; the scene was carved on a rock face, and his corpse
was treated with preservative, painted, stuffed with straw, and
exhibited as a trophy.[19] All Asia knew of the disaster and of the
humiliation of the master of the world. In this extremity the son
and successor of Valerian had no alternative save to halt the
persecution. Its maintenance over several reigns is clear evidence
that Dionysius of Alexandria was right in tracing its origins
beyond the personal decision of Decius. Classical historians
were prone to ascribe to the personal decisions of rulers actions
determined by social and economic pressures and the needs of
the ruling circle. Over a decade the resources of the empire had
deliberately been pitted against the Church; and the effort had
failed. It would be difficult to overstate the importance of this
great event. Henceforth, though as yet there was no official
recognition, the Church had to be accepted as a fact.

Christians now became prominent in imperial circles and among the educated. In some instances whole towns became Christian and the leaders of the Church began to emerge as the leaders of the community. Persecution, though it had yet to make its last and fiercest onslaught, had proved futile. 'In the third century,' says a secular historian, *Rostovtzeff*

'the Christian Church acquired enormous strength. As a state within the state, its organisation steadily improved in proportion as that of the state deteriorated. Oppression, compulsion, persecution were the mottoes of the state; love, compassion, consolation were the maxims of the Church. The Church, unique in this respect among other religious communities, not only administered spiritual relief but promised and gave practical help in the miseries of actual life, while the state oppressed and persecuted the helper.'[20]

As the anarchy of the third century destroyed the economic, social and intellectual life of the ancient world it was replaced by a new type of state nurtured like the old in violence and compulsion, a brutal autocracy brought to power by the despair of the masses, a dictatorship of the proletariat; simultaneously there multiplied beside it a new community which also had arisen among the poor but which acknowledged a very different way of life.

So great was the confidence of the Church in its new-found security that when the Emperor Aurelian destroyed Palmyra, which had virtually established itself as an independent kingdom in Syria after the capture of Valerian, the surrounding bishops took the astonishing step of appealing to him to depose the heretical Paul of Samosata and to evict him from his Church.[21] Aurelian responded, not because of any interest in Christian orthodoxy, but because Paul had been a henchman of Zenobia, the defeated queen of Palmyra. This, and the emperor's known inclination towards monotheism, may have deceived the Church. If so, the illusion was soon destroyed for, as Lactantius told in bitter words, only assassination prevented Aurelian from mounting a new persecution.[22] A man of great vigour, he had restored the frontier of the empire, though within narrower bounds, and had had the courage and foresight to acknowledge the changed position of Rome in the world by defending the imperial city with massive walls, still standing, which she had not required in the years when her might was beyond challenge.

On his death seven rival emperors rose and fell within nine years until there came to the throne on 20 November 284 a soldier from Dalmatia who had risen from the ranks to become commander of the imperial bodyguard.[23] For the modern reader Diocletian's name has a classical ring, but to the contemporary Roman it spoke of barbarism, for it was no more than a latinised form derived from the village on the Adriatic coast from which he had been recruited. Nevertheless, he proved himself an administrator of such remarkable qualities that he practically reorganised the empire. Not the least of his achievements was that after holding power for twenty-one years he was able to resign it and still remain alive.

His great palace built for old age on the Adriatic shore of his boyhood, which now encloses the town of Split within its walls, was classical and traditional in many respects, but its architectural detail exhibits a range of motifs totally alien to the art of Augustan times. Anyone who looks carefully at a building by Robert Adam can see this mixture of classical and barbarian motifs which the great architect brought back to Britain after his visit to the palace of Diocletian. This is a symbol of the achievement of his reign, since he restored the framework of the Roman state but gave it a new character, part oriental and part totalitarian. Ennius had said of Fabius, the Roman general who opposed Hannibal, that he saved the state by delay. Diocletian saved it by action. Living in seclusion when not on campaign, he assumed the quasi-divine status of an eastern ruler.[24] To deal with the insecurity of the throne he divided the imperial power among four emperors, two Augusti with two Caesars as their junior colleagues, and in their nomination he broke away from the hereditary principle to revert to the second-century system of adoption. Provinces were subdivided to enable governors to cope in more detail with finance, administration and justice. Civil servants were therefore multiplied, as were also requisitions in kind and taxes. To relieve the burden of central administration, provinces were grouped together into dioceses while a complete military reorganisation took place, with systematic strengthening of the frontiers.

Thus efficiency was regained, but at a cost which had to be

met. Barbarians were recruited from beyond the frontier and settled within the empire to fill the ranks of the legions. Peasants lost such nominal freedom as they still possessed and were bound to the soil on which they laboured. In 301 Diocletian endeavoured to curb the distress caused by inflation of the currency through his *Edict on Prices,* a prices and income policy which, like most such, dealt with the symptoms but left the causes untouched. And so the economic malaise continued unchecked.[25] In choosing military commanders and civilian administrators he showed that he had no use for the old senatorial families, so that from his time rather than from that of Constantine may be said to date the decline of the senate to little more than a town council for the city of Rome. Finally, he recognised the declining importance of Rome itself. Even when drawn from distant provinces previous emperors had upheld the prestige of Rome as the imperial residence and the centre of power, but Diocletian and Maximian, whom he had made his colleague as Augustus, established their courts at Nicomedia and Milan. From Nicomedia, Diocletian ruled Thrace, Asia Minor, Syria and Egypt, the wealthiest and most populous provinces. From Milan, Maximian ruled Italy and North Africa, while the Caesar Galerius was responsible for the Danube frontier, and the other Caesar, Constantius, for Spain, Gaul and Britain.[26] it amounted to a radical reshaping of the government.

It remained only to deal with the Church. Unwonted security had given Christians unwarranted confidence. Christians held high appointments in provincial administration and had been allowed to evade the demands for official sacrifices. Others served within the imperial household itself. Most significantly, Diocletian's wife, Prisca, and his daughter, Valeria, the wife of Galerius, whether baptised or not, were reckoned Christians.[27] In all the cities crowded congregations met for worship and great churches were being built for the first time. Prosperity also showed itself in dissension among Christians.[28] In some respects Diocletian and his colleagues had always been conservative, aiming at the restoration of the ancient ways, and as the position of the empire became re-established on the frontiers there came the first signs of action against the Church. Given his outlook, it is strange that he waited so long; but the answer probably lies in this shrewd man's recognition of the magnitude of the step and the failure of previous attempts to suppress the rival of the state.

It was in the army that action was first taken: Some Christians under the command of Galerius suffered death, but others were merely dismissed from the service.[29] Diocletian had already shown his resentment against Christians, and it was later remembered how furious he had been when some of his Christian subordinates, present when auguries were being made, frustrated the augurs by making the sign of the cross.[30] Lactantius, who held a position of importance at Nicomedia and was well informed, if prejudiced, tells that discussions went on between Diocletian and Galerius all through the winter of 302, that the older man commended restraint and the younger man demanded action, until a reply from the oracle of Apollo at Didyma clinched the matter. 'It was the just on the earth,' the oracle declaimed, 'who prevented a truthful response from the tripod.' Diocletian turned to his attendants to ask who were 'the just' and a priest replied, 'The Christians, of course.'[31]

On 23 February 303, the feast of Terminalia, a date chosen, according to Lactantius, as an appropriate one to terminate the Christian Church, action commenced. As dawn broke in the sky, soldiers and police burst open the doors of the great church at Nicomedia and searched, in vain, for an image of the Christian God. Copies of the Scriptures were burned and the building was ransacked. From the roof of the imperial palace Diocletian and Galerius watched the onslaught. Galerius wished the church to be set on fire but Diocletian forbad it lest the blaze should spread to the adjoining houses and so rage through the city. Next day an edict was published commanding the destruction of churches and the Scriptures, the dismissal of Christians in public service, and the loss of privilege and legal status for all of the faith. When posted up in Nicomedia it was immediately pulled down by a Christian official named Evethius, who was at once arrested and roasted alive.[32] Anthimus, the Bishop of Nicomedia, was executed and leading Christians from the imperial households were brutally tortured to death. Two outbreaks of fire in the palace within a fortnight provoked an intensification of persecution. The empress Prisca and her daughter Valeria were compelled to sacrifice and thus to apostasise. Prisons built for criminals, says Eusebius, were filled with clergy. Bishops were singled out, arrested, and tortured to compel them to sacrifice. Nor did these actions fail to meet with some considerable success.

'I saw with my own eyes,' says Eusebius, 'Churches thrown down. ... Scriptures committed to the flames in the public squares ... pastors hiding disgracefully.' There were those who apostasised, 'but it is not for me,' he wrote, 'to describe their wretched misfortunes. ... I am determined to say nothing of those who made shipwreck of their salvation.' Instead he tells of the martyrs, of abominable brutality and heroic constancy. 'What could I say that would do full justice to them? I could tell of thousands.' 'Things were done,' he added, 'that would make the hearers shudder.' But this must not mislead. Bishops and other clergy, along with Christians in high position, were singled out and hunted down; Christians who displayed their faith were seized and killed; but many, as the example of Eusebius himself can tell, were left untouched. In particular, the great majority of tortures and executions took place in the east where the Church was strongest;[33] in Italy and North Africa it appears that Maximian enforced only the first edict and not its successors,[34] and in the west under Constantius church buildings were destroyed but, if the chroniclers who wrote in the time of his son can be trusted, Christians were otherwise left in peace. It was not the death of all Christians which was desired — their numbers were too great for that — so much as their recantation and the breaking of the Church. After some time executions slackened. Instead, Christians were blinded in the right eye, lamed on the left ankle with a branding iron, and sent to the copper mines.

Late in 303 Diocletian paid a brief visit to Rome but on 20 December, when setting out for Ravenna, he took ill. He managed to reach Nicomedia in the spring, but was so desperately ill that the rumour went round the city that he had died and that the fact was being concealed. Periodically he was delirious. Galerius, intent on taking full control, urged him to resign. On 1 May 305 a great military parade was held some miles outside Nicomedia.[35] Diocletian, who still had many years of life before him, looked like an old man. He wept as he addressed his soldiers, told them of his illness, and his decision to abdicate. Under his reconstitution of the empire his colleague Maximian was also obliged, reluctantly, to follow suit. At that point, to the astonishment of all, Diocletian announced that while their successors as Augusti were to be Galerius and Constantius, the sons of Maximian and Constantius were to be passed by and the new Caesars were to be Maximin Daza, a nephew of Galerius, and Severus. Diocletian doffed the purple, assumed his former name, entered a carriage and set off for Dalmatia where he recovered his health and enjoyed his time with gardening and trout-fishing.

In the following spring, ignored, suspect, and in danger, Constantine escaped by night[36] and crossed Europe with such speed, changing horses at every post-house, that the legend sprung up that he ordered the horses, as he left them behind him, to be hamstrung to prevent his pursuit and arrest. At Boulogne he joined Constantius and when his father died at York on 25 July 306 his legions proclaimed his son as Augustus in his place. Making the best of a bad situation, Galerius recognised him. Almost at the same time Maxentius, the other son who had been ignored, was proclaimed at Rome. An army sent against him under Severus was defeated and thus a new quadrumvirate was formed, not as Diocletian had announced, but consisting of Constantine in Britain, Maxentius in Rome, Galerius and Maximin in the east.

Thus the greatest of Diocletian's constitutional innovations had proved too cumbrous and impractical to survive its inventor, so that for a time it seemed that a return to the anarchy of the third century was imminent. When the empire was at odds with a sizeable and determined minority of its subjects the imperial contestants on the one side were likely in time to become aligned with, or against, the persecuted minority; but for the moment this had yet to appear. Meantime the complicated relationship of the emperors deteriorated. Maximian, who had reluctantly been retired, came to an accord with Constantine which was sealed by the younger man's marriage to his daughter Fausta. Somewhat ominously the panegyric[37] delivered at the wedding made no reference to the fact that this now made Constantine a brother-in-law to Maxentius at Rome. On 11 November of that year a new contender, Licinius, was named as Augustus of the west, but Maxentius reasserted his authority and by 310 was in control of Italy and North Africa. Thus the empire, nominally one, was divided; Constantine ruled on the Atlantic seaboard, Maxentius in Italy and North Africa, Licinius further east, Galerius in Thrace and Asia Minor, and Maximin in Egypt. Constantine and Maxentius showed themselves not unfriendly to Christians but as one went east the persecution of the Church grew more severe; such an unstable situation could not last.

In the spring of 311 Galerius became ill with pediculosis or phthiriasis,[38] an offensive disease of his bowels, 'the symptoms of which,' Gibbon says, 'Lactantius and Eusebius describe with singular accuracy and apparent pleasure,'[39] and on 30 April he issued an edict, in which the other emperors were associated with him, calling the persecution to a halt. His well-meaning efforts, it declared, had failed to recall Christians to the religion of Rome; they were therefore permitted, provided they otherwise observed the law, to rebuild and use their churches.[40] Regarded by Eusebius as a death-bed repentance, this was no more than an act of policy forced upon the dying man by the evident failure of the persecution.[41] It was a remarkable admission. When Diocletian had invested Galerius as Caesar he gave him his daughter Valeria as his wife. Having no family of her own Valeria adopted Candidianus, the illegitimate son of her husband, and at his father's death this son, being still in his teens, was considered too young for sovereignty in the rough atmosphere of the times. Before he died on 5 May 311 Galerius, knowing only too well that they would need protection, commended his wife and son to Licinius, whose previous record ill-qualified him for such a trust.

No mention was made in the edict of Galerius of any return of confiscated church property, but when published in Asia Minor it was welcomed with general thanksgiving among Christians. In Egypt Maximin received it with mixed feelings. His prefect Sabinus informed the provincial governors of their emperor's intention in unenthusiastic words, but Christians were jubilant. 'It was,' says Eusebius,

> 'as if suddenly a light had shone out of a dark sky. In every town could be seen crowded churches, overflowing congregations, and the appropriate ceremonies duly performed. This confounded all the unconverted heathen. ... Of our own people, those who had faithfully and manfully fought through the ordeal of the persecutions again held their heads high in the sight of all; those whose faith had been sickly and their souls storm tossed made earnest efforts to be well ... beseeching God to be merciful to them. Then, too, the gallant champions of true religion

were released from the misery of the mines and
allowed to return to their homes, exulting and
beaming as they passed through every town, full of
joy unspeakable and a confidence beyond
description. Long columns of men and women went
on their way, singing psalms and hymns of praise to
God in the middle of the highways and city squares.
Those who a little while ago had been prisoners ...
could be seen with happy smiling faces regaining
their own hearths.'[42]

In the east this new-found liberty was brief, for Maximin, a
pagan who looked for support from pagans in the dynastic
dispute for the empire, began to impose restrictions on
Christians in October 311. Cities were encouraged to petition
against Christians and their requests were granted. But it was in
another quarter of the empire that a decision was to be forced.
Constantine, whose position had been the weakest among the
contenders, steadily increased his strength while the position of
Maxentius in Italy deteriorated. In 312 Constantine invaded
Italy, defeated the armies of Maxentius outside Turin, and
occupied the imperial palace of Milan. It was an expedition
calling for great courage; for the army of Constantine was far
outnumbered by that of his opponent, while Maxentius[43]
enjoyed reliable supplies from Africa, the granary of the empire,
the impregnable walls built by Aurelian for the defence of
Rome, and the knowledge that previous attacks upon him had
failed.

Constantine marched rapidly on Rome, but as he approached
the city and the crisis of his career he had, as he later told
Eusebius, a vision. However controversial this famous incident
may be, there can be no doubt that Constantine himself accepted
it as divine guidance and that, as a consequence, for good or for
ill, he determined to associate the outcome of his cause with that
of the Christian Church. On his way to Rome, Constantine
prayed for divine aid and a sign. Then with his own eyes, he told
Eusebius, on the following day he saw the trophy of the cross
against the sun, with the words, '*Hoc vince*' (By this sign,
conquer). His soldiers also saw the sign, he said, and were
astonished. In the following night Constantine dreamed that
Christ appeared to him and commanded him to adopt the

Christian symbol known as the *labarum*. At daybreak he did so, placing a cross-piece against a spear, with a crown above and a hanging with the Christian symbol below.[44] Misled by a characteristically ambiguous utterance of the Sybilline oracle, Maxentius decided not to stand a winter siege, however difficult this might be for his opponent, but to meet Constantine outside the walls. By now an atmosphere of superstition attached itself to both sides and as he marched out it was noted as an ill-omen that the owls perched on the city wall above him. He was defeated at the battle of the Milvian Bridge on 28 October 312, and as he sought to escape back across the bridge into the city, the press of fugitives broke the bridge and threw him into the water. Weighed down by his armour he sank at once, and on the next day it was with some difficulty that his body was dragged from the mud, not for any reason of affection or respect. Constantine entered Rome as victor to be acclaimed by an obsequious senate as first among the three Augusti of the Roman world.[45] Constantine did not need their acclamation; he had secured the position for himself.

This victory immediately tranformed the position of the Church in the west and, in the course of the following months, throughout the empire. An edict of toleration and restitution[46] for the Church appears to have been issued at once, but the text is not extant. It was from the perspective of later times and not from that of contemporary observers that Constantine's victory was seen to be epoch-making. Men did not at once realise that the whole course of the world's history had been changed. On receipt of Constantine's edict Maximin in Egypt gave a lengthy instruction to his prefect in which a measure of freedom was grudgingly conceded to Christians but, warned by past experience, his Christian subjects were wary of resuming public worship.

> The letter merely permitted us to be protected from deliberate cruelty, and gave no encouragement to the holding of meetings or building of churches or performance of any of our normal practices. And yet the advocates of peace and true religion had sent him written instructions to allow these very things, and by laws and decrees had committed them to all their subjects. But this unprincipled scoundrel had made up his mind not to budge an inch.[47]

In February 313 Constantine met Licinius at Milan. Their partnership was cemented by the marriage of Licinius to the sister of Constantine and evidently he concurred in Constantine's new religious policy. It has been commonly said that an edict of Milan[48] was jointly issued but this, at the very least, is open to question. Learning that Licinius was preoccupied with his wedding celebrations, Maximin at once marched his army out of Syria through the Cilician Gates in bitter weather.[49] He had made a vow to Jove that, if victorious, he would exterminate the Christians, but on 30 April Licinius defeated him near Byzantium. Maximin's speed in advance was excelled by his flight, for, leaving his broken army behind him, he was said to have covered 160 miles in twenty-four hours.

On 13 June Licinius issued an edict at Nicomedia in terms of the Milan agreement to enforce throughout the east that toleration for Christians which Constantine had instituted in the west. It expressed monotheism, but no sign of Christian faith. 'Complete and unrestricted liberty' was extended to Christians and confiscated Church property was to be restored. Back in his native countryside of Cilicia, Maximin granted the Church full toleration and in fury began to execute the priests of pagan gods, thus confirming the judgement that a religious or more accurately, a superstitious character had now been given to the conflict by all the contestants. He died within a month or so and Eusebius, using a word which the twentieth century was to make conventional, reported that his sons and lieutenants were then 'purged'.

Valeria, the widow whom Galerius had commended to the care of Licinius, had fallen into the hands of Maximin, and had attracted his attentions though he already had a wife. As she refused to consent to him her estates were confiscated and her servants executed or scattered. She herself and her mother, Prisca, the wife of Diocletian, were exiled to a remote village in Syria while Diocletian, in vain, sought their release. On the death of Maximin, Prisca and Valeria escaped to the court of Licinius but, finding it no improvement, they fled again and for fifteen months wandered in disguise and obscurity. Already condemned to death, when discovered, they were beheaded and their bodies thrown into the sea.[50] Licinius who, like Constantine, had his eyes set on the prospect of sole rule, was a man prepared to eliminate any possible rivals without mercy; he had killed the two boys, Severianus and Candidianus, because they were the sons of emperors; but these two women offered no threat to him and a further explanation is needed to account for the vindictive treatment they received. Their original offence had been the confession of the Christian faith, and Valeria's refusal to consent to Maximin is in keeping with the contemporary attitude to sex. In the end, Diocletian's daughter was less fortunate than Stalin's daughter who escaped to America. Within months of the meeting at Milan, Licinius had quarrelled with Constantine and had again begun to harass the Church.[51] Prisca and Valeria belonged to that tragic class of Christians known as the *lapsed* since they had consented, or been forced, to sacrifice, but their humiliation and suffering were almost certainly a consequence of their faith. Their conversion, if this reading of the story is correct, had therefore more in common with the standards of the New Testament than had that of Constantine; but history has been slow to remember this.

What Diocletian began, Constantine completed. Though much of the work of the older man was to be lasting, by now it was plain that his plans for a tetrarchy were impractical and that the empire was to revert to the rule of one man. Constantine made it an autocracy with more in common with oriental rule than the regime which once acknowledged Augustus. Whatever posterity has associated with his name, it was probably this which he saw as his greatest achievement, with the acceptance of the Church as an essential element in it.

After years of troubled relations Constantine and Licinius came to open war, and in 324 Constantine eliminated his rival to reign alone.[52] For long the city of Rome had counted for less in the empire. Even in Diocletian's time its status was something of an anachronism.[53] It had no particular claims on Constantine who had been born on the Danube, brought up in Asia, and invested with the purple in Britain. At this point he made a decisive breach with tradition. As the United Nations Organisation after the second world war made its headquarters in New York and not, as would have happened during the nineteenth century, in a European city, so Constantine showed his recognition of the fact that Rome was no longer the centre of power by selecting Byzantium, on its strategic site between the Aegean and the Black Sea, between Europe and Asia, as the site

of his new capital. Rome, its senate, and its traditions belonged
to the past. Similarly Constantine made far-reaching changes in
military and civil administration[54] to create a new type of
authoritarian state and, even though the claims of his eulogist
are exaggerated, he did much to restore the frontiers of the
empire.[55] Before he died in 337 he had created a new Byzantium
which was to bear his name to be the foremost of the world's
cities for a thousand years.

Those emperors who sought to strengthen the Roman state
during the first three centuries after Christ persecuted, while
bad emperors neglected action against the Church along with
many other duties; or so it has been argued. Behind such a
conclusion lies the fact that the senatorial families, though
incapable of dealing with living emperors, could make or mar
the reputation of dead ones, that Roman historians shared the
outlook of the senatorial class[56] where pagan traditions were
most tenacious and converts fewest, and that the clash between
the senate and the provincial armies and the peasants in the third
century produced the anarchy through which Christians enjoyed
no small measure of immunity. At the close of this long crisis
Diocletian salvaged the imperial structure only by commencing
its transformation. That social revolution, of which he was both
an instance and a product, now controlled the establishment;
but the lower classes had no possible machinery available to
enforce their control and so, as in France long after, a non-
commissioned officer from the Mediterranean litoral emerged
from the turmoil in supreme control. Never again were there to
be emperors in the city of the seven hills in the Antonine
tradition to represent the standards of the older ruling classes,
for a new generation had risen to control society; and the
Church was strong among the newcomers. When Diocletian
failed to suppress the Church a rapprochement between Church
and state must have seemed unavoidable to men greedy for
power. What had been the great spiritual adventure of classical
antiquity had reached its end[57] and was to be replaced, in the
west, by the chaos of the Dark Ages and, in the east, by the new
culture of the Byzantine empire which had decided to absorb the
Church.

Cochrane

Notes to Chapter 10

1. M. Grant, *Climax,* p.163.
2. Dio Cassius, LXXX, xi. Toynbee, V, p.407.
3. Gibbon, vi. Lampridius, *Elagabalus,* V-VIII, XII.
4. Lampridius, *Alexander Severus,* XXII, XXIX, XLIII.
5. Eusebius, *Ecclesiastical History,* VI, xxi; VI, xxviii.
   Frend, *Martyrdom,* pp.329-335.
6. Eusebius, *Ecclesiastical History,* VI, xxiv. Duchesne, I, p.336.
7. Origen, *Against Celsus,* III, ix.
8. G.W. Meates, *Lullingstone Roman Villa.*
9. *Historia Augusta, Valeriani Duo,* V, VI.
10. Toynbee, V, p.408.
11. Eusebius, *Ecclesiastical History,* VI, xxxix-xl.
12. Frend, *Martyrdom,* p.406.
13. van der Meer and Mohrmann, *Atlas of the Early Christian World,* p.52.
14. Stevenson, p.228.
15. Eusebius, *Ecclesiastical History,* VII, i; VII, xi.
16. *ibid.* VII, x.
17. Frend, *Martyrdom,* p.423.
18. *ibid.* pp.426ff.
19. Lactantius, *De Mortibus Persecutorum,* V.
    Widengren, P1.2 opp. p.72.
20. Rostovtzeff, p.456.
21. Eusebius, *Ecclesiastical History,* VII, xxx.
22. Lactantius, VI.
    P.R. Coleman-Norton, *Roman State and Christian Church,* I, pp.16ff.
23. A.H.M. Jones, *Constantine and the Conversion of Europe,* p.26.
24. Jones, *The Later Roman Empire,* I, pp.40-70.
25. *ibid.* I, p.438.
26. Gibbon, xiii.
27. Lactantius, XV.
28. Eusebius, *Ecclesiastical History,* VIII, i.
29. *ibid.* VIII, iv.
30. Lactantius, X. Constantine, *De Falso Cultu,* III, P.L.8, 273.
31. Lactantius, XI. Frend, *Martyrdom,* pp.498ff.

32. Eusebius, *Ecclesiastical History,* VIII, ii; VIII, v.
    Lactantius, XIII.
33. Frend, *Martyrdom,* p.508.
34. Jones, *Constantine,* p.64.
35. Lactantius, XIX.
36. *ibid.* XXIV.
37. *Panegyrici Veteres,* P.L.8, col.609-620.
    Jones, *Constantine,* pp.69ff.
38. Coleman-Norton, I, p.20.
39. Gibbon, XIV.
40. Eusebius, *Ecclesiastical History,* VIII, xvii. Lactantius, XXXIV.
41. Lietzmann, III, p.72.
42. Eusebius, *Ecclesiastical History,* IX, i.
43. N.H. Baynes, *Constantine the Great and the Christian Church,*
    p.8.
    Jones, *Constantine,* pp.80-84.
44. Eusebius, *De Vita Constantini,* I, xxviii, xxxi. P.L.8, col.22-23.
    Lactantius, XLIV.
    Baynes, pp.60-65.
45. Eusebius, *DVC,* I, xxxviii-xxxix. P.L.8, col.25-26.
46. Frend, *Martyrdom,* pp.534ff.
47. Eusebius, *DVC,* X, ix.
48. *ibid.* X, v. Jones, *Constantine,* p.93. Frend, *Martyrdom,*
    pp.518ff.
49. Eusebius, *DVC,* X, viii.
50. Lactantius, XL-XLI, L-LI.
51. Jones, *Constantine,* pp.126-134.
52. Eusebius, *DVC,* II, xvii-xix.
53. Jones, *LRE,* II, p.687.
54. *ibid.* I, pp.97ff., 367-372.
55. Eusebius, *DVC,* IV, v-viii. P.L.8, col.71ff.
56. Popper, I, p.180.
    Jones, *LRE,* I, p.7.
57. Cochrane, p.152.

Chapter 11

The Conversion of Constantine

11

Constantine talked about his conversion. He told Eusebius[1] with
great earnestness that it had been in two parts; in the first, which
took place in broad daylight, he saw the cross set against the sun
— a significant conjunction for him since it identified the
Christian faith with the monotheism which underlay current
paganism — and in the second, by night, he dreamed that Christ
appeared to him and commanded him to mark his soldiers with
the Christian symbol in the coming battle. Interpretation of this
controversial event has been obscured, firstly, by Constantine's
assumption that it was a miracle and, secondly, by the later
assumption that miracles do not happen. But there is no need to
deny the story or to place other than a natural interpretation
upon it.

a mock sun — I have myself seen one.

Constantine's army is said to have seen the first part, which
may well have been a solar phenomenon.[2] Something of this sort
is needed to explain why, in a superstitious age, an army in
which stray Christian sympathisers may have been found but in
which active and committed Christians must have been almost
non-existent should suddenly accept a Christian symbol which,
until then, had been banned. It was almost, if not quite, like
asking the Brigade of Guards or the U.S. Marines to put on the
Hammer and Sickle. But Constantine alone, as is usual in these
matters, had the dream; and it reveals the outlook of a man
whose understanding of the Christian faith was superficial.
Lactantius, writing before 318, tells of the dream and of the
acceptance of the Christian symbol by the troops.[3] It is beyond
doubt that Constantine displayed this symbol in the battle, and
for the first time in a Roman army, and that his action was
common knowledge. It was an action which would have shaken
to the very core of his being, not merely Marcus Aurelius, but
Tertullian. Public monuments, the coinage, edicts of
Constantine and his correspondence all confirm that, however
limited his first understanding of the faith may have been, from

this time Constantine presented himself in public as a Christian.[4] Maxentius had treated Christians mildly. Constantine and he had been at war because of personal ambition alone and not because of religion, but when the senate economically erected a triumphal arch in honour of Constantine out of fragments of the arch of Trajan, his victory was ascribed to divine inspiration.[5] There was an ambiguity in the phrase which is not immediately apparent to the modern reader, for it was open to understanding by Christian and non-Christian alike, but when his statue was erected a cross was placed in one hand,[6] not too prominently but unavoidably. For what it is worth, there is no reason to question the sincerity of his action. At a later stage it was to bring him great advantages in the east, but Constantine then was absorbed in the problems of the west and at the time the only advantage offered him must have been the prospect of supernatural aid. Recruited largely from the frontier regions where they were stationed, the legions of the west can have had little direct acquaintance with the Church, and Rome, whatever the strength of the local church, was the traditional centre of paganism.[7] When Constantine first marched in, weary and battle-stained if triumphant, his conversion must have been more of an embarrassment than a help.

What then did it mean to him? How far did he understand the community to which he committed himself or, if we may so put it, which he decided to take over? 'Had I seen a miracle, men say, I should have been converted,' Pascal wrote.

> How can they be sure they would do a thing of the nature of which they are ignorant? They imagine that this conversion consists in a worship of God which is like commerce, and in a communion such as they picture to themselves.[8]

Constantine took this great step when he was largely ignorant of what it involved. He was prepared to learn, and the evidence of his writings shows that in many respects he did so; but, like other converts, he carried into his membership of the Church strong traces of his outlook in unconverted days. Others had done so before and many were to do so afterwards, but there was no other convert of comparable importance capable of so influencing the community into which he had come. This great decision which tipped the scales of history was his own, and it was made as the result of a dream; but this is only superficially true, for the dream and the decision reflected the crisis in society. What his conversion meant for Constantine was equally true for many of his contemporaries. He was a child of his time, and his mind moved with the drift of the age even if others did not. He had decided to become a Christian, but he was not, and never became, a twice-born Christian. What has been called his conversion was the collapse of a culture and a society, the disintegration of an exhausted civilization and the first struggles of a new one as seen in the life of one man.

His decision meant not merely the end of persecution but the commencement of support by the state. Immediately after his capture of Rome, Constantine wrote to Caecilian, the Bishop of Carthage, to say that he had instructed his accountant in Africa to pay him a large sum for the maintenance of clergy from the Libyan bounds to the Atlantic seaboard. More would be available from officials should this prove inadequate, but the money was to go only to clergy of the Catholic Church and not to sectarians. All this seems to have been under the supervision of Hosius, the Bishop of Cordova, who had been with Constantine on his campaign, and of whom we might wish to have been much better informed. At the same time two letters went to Anullinus, the proconsul of Africa, ordering the restitution of any property previously confiscated from the Church and relieving the clergy of the Catholic Church from all public burdens. Interference with Christian worship, the proconsul was told, had proved ruinous for the Roman state, but the recognition of the Church had at once been attended with prosperity.[9] Evidently Constantine still saw the Church in a pagan light but with this difference, that he had now identified the true God more correctly, and expected to be rewarded accordingly. Similarly he had still to learn that the God of the Christians was as jealous a God as the Jehovah of the Old Testament: over the next five years his coins continued to carry inscriptions to Hercules the Victorious, Mars the Preserver, Jupiter the Preserver, and, above all, the Unconquered Sun. A set of gold medallions struck to commemorate the Milan meeting carried the head of Constantine and the Sun side by side.[10] Presumably an earlier generation of bishops might have instructed the emperor on the error of his ways but Hosius and his colleagues had learned prudence in the school of adversity. They accepted what they had got, and were thankful.

In the years of her sufferings the Church had depended upon a group of resolute Christians who knew in whom they believed and were ready, and often anxious, to die as martyrs. Next to these came the very considerable number of Christians who shrank from martyrdom, or even the loss of property and freedom or who, had the test come, would have done so. One must draw the unheroic conclusion that since these did not attract official attention and evaded it whenever they could, they must have been responsible for the continuance of many struggling congregations. Next came those such as Pliny knew, who had tacitly abandoned polytheism and were monotheists of a sort with respect for Christian morals, but could not be classed as active members. They did not take part in the weekly Eucharist. One group must have tailed off into the other, unless human nature has changed since then. As paganism declined, the third category shows signs of having grown steadily, and its presence in the circle of the Syrian emperors in the decades before Decius is easily seen. For them the sun was merely a convenient symbol of that divine power from which all things derived; Apuleius, no Christian, spoke of Isis similarly, as,

> the chiefest of the heavenly ones, the inclusive manifestation of gods and goddesses ... whose unique divinity the whole world adores under manifold forms, with varied rites and by multifarious names.[11]

What separated most of them from the Church was their interpretation of the divine nature, their classification of Christ as one teacher among many, and a certain indifference to strict Christian morals.[12] Yet they must not be underestimated. Periodically in time of persecution they threw up men prepared to speak as Christians and to pay the price, to the surprise both of the state and of the Church.

Something like this last category had been the background of Constantine's family, and in his Christian days he was inclined to exaggerate their sympathy with the Church, and a grateful Church was not disposed to argue the point. Christ's Church had called on men to break with the strong ties of the pagan family as they entered the new community. 'I am come,' said

Jesus, 'to set a man at variance with his father, and the daughter against her mother.'[13] But Constantine was aware of no breach; he was devoted to his father's memory and spoke of him as sympathetic to the Church.[14] Perhaps he was right; perhaps he was not; but the family had been a happy one. It is significant that Helena, Constantine's mother, was disliked by pagan writers and given a dubious reputation. St Ambrose had heard the report that she had been a servant girl at an inn before she married and, as the Abbé Duchesne discreetly says, 'considering the customs of that age in matters of hospitality, this implies a great many things.'[15] Her daughter Anastasia was given an indubitably Christian name,[16] and after Constantine's rise to power, though Helena had had to surrender her place to an aristocratic rival[17] whom Constantius had married for dynastic reasons, she was recalled to a place of dignity by her son and showed great enthusiasm in tracing and restoring the holy places of the faith.[18] On the Mount of Olives she built a church with a great opening in the roof to mark the place of the Ascension, and at Bethlehem the visitor to the Church of the Nativity built by the Crusaders can look down through a grill in the floor of the nave to see the mosaic floor of an earlier church built by Helena. In public Constantine preferred to speak of his great father, but it may well be that in the household, as in that of Diocletian, the Christian influence was on the distaff side, though Eusebius, who became something of a courtier, credited his hero with the conversion of his mother. Thus Constantine, in becoming a Christian, had no awareness of breaking with his family tradition or, for that matter, with his own earlier worship.

Previously Christians had made an explicit contrast between religion and the Christian Church. They broke with the one to enter the other. But Constantine saw no discontinuity between his worship before conversion and his worship afterwards. Two words in the New Testament describe religion; neither is particularly respectful unless when used in contrast;[19] and in the Authorised Version one is accurately translated as *superstition*. In earlier days Constantine had rebuilt temples as part of his public duty, but if he had been a religious man it had only been in this latter sense. He was superstitious, and continued to be so. He looked for signs and wonders. In a panegyric delivered before him at Trier in 310, Eumenius described a former vision granted to Constantine, but this time of Apollo offering him a laurel crown with an omen of thirty years of power.[20] It turned out to be a remarkably good forecast. Presumably Constantine had regarded Apollo as merely one manifestation of the supreme divine power. Through the honours paid to the immortal gods, it had long been held, the might of Rome stood firm, but the disasters of the preceding century gave this little confirmation. Constantine, at the crisis of his life, identified the traditional monotheism of his family, not with the gods of Olympus or the Pantheon, as in the earlier vision, but with the God of the Christians; he decided to back him, and the outcome convinced him that he had put his money on the right horse. This is not to detract from his sincerity, his consistency, or his large measure of success; it is merely a recognition of his mental limitations — as distinct from his capacity for management — and the mixed character of the result.

With the notable exception of Tertullian, the Fathers of the Church had respected philosophy but dismissed the pagan cults. Constantine did not understand this distinction. He and the two writers closest to him, Eusebius and Lactantius, used the word *religion,* though usually with the criterion of *true* or *false,* to describe both Christian faith and paganism.[21] A lengthy passage[22] on the testimony of the Sibyl and Virgil to Christ has probably been inserted into one of his speeches, but it represents his mind. Christians had always exploited such passages, but Constantine hardly realised that the Scripture and these were different in kind. This marks a change in Christian thinking. Similarly, though it has been said that St John Chrysostom 'is perhaps the earliest Christian author to employ *philosophia* with a purely Christian connotation'[23] Eusebius spoke of Constantine as 'a true philosopher'.[24]

Constantine brought into the Church a degree of magical thinking. As a young man he heard Diocletian blame the silence of the oracle on the sign of the cross made by Christians present; and he fully agreed.[25] When displayed in battle the trophy of the cross, he held, was potent to bring victory. When one of the fifty men deputed to bear it took fright and fled he was killed, but his companion who retained it was uninjured.[26]

He was confident that the service of God made a man prosperous and, like pagans, saw the service of God in terms of formal worship rather than daily conduct. Attention to religious

duties always paid. Earlier generations of Christians had good
reason to know that the service of Christ was the way of the
cross and brought no mundane rewards,[27] but Lactantius and
Eusebius accepted the outlook of Constantine. In *De Mortibus
Persecutorum* the whole thesis of Lactantius is that God visibly
rewards the righteous in terms of this world's goods and
penalises the evildoers. 'God was the giver of prosperity to
Constantine,' Eusebius wrote, 'the source of his victories and of
his long life.'[28] Divine justice was seen in the misfortunes of the
persecuting emperors, while Constantine was rewarded.[29] Even
his good health was part of this.[30] Constantine had no doubt
about it. 'The neglect of religious observances,' he wrote to a
provincial governor soon after his conversion, 'has brought
great dangers upon the community, and the lawful restoration
of it has conferred the greatest good fortune on the Roman
name.'[31] Sudden prosperity convinced many that he was right,
but it stuck in the gullet of Augustine. Yet it was grafted into
Christian thinking by writers like Salvian.[32] More temperately,
Augustine wrote that Constantine had been favoured in order to
undeceive the pagans, but that his successors had not been
attended by such success lest men become Christians for hope of
gain.[33]

Constantine's education had been restricted,[34] and so was his
grasp of the content of the faith. In his vision he had seen the
cross surrounded by the victor's laurel crown. It portrayed the
victory over sin and death and its interpretation in the Church
had been '*Hoc signo vici*' (By this sign I have conquered). Julian
the Apostate understood this when he said on his deathbed,
'You have conquered, Galilean,' but Constantine interpreted it
by the words, '*Hoc signo vince*' (By this sign, conquer). If the
vision had indeed been a divine revelation then he who died at
Calvary must certainly have changed if he extended his Kingdom
as the result of a battle.
Yet Constantine was willing to learn. Hosius, the Bishop of
Cordova, was with him as he entered Rome and probably had a
part in his conversion. From then onwards bishops continually
shared the counsels of Constantine. He received instruction and
learned to read the Bible.[35] In many ways his faith deepened and
he became something of an amateur theologian. He was strongly
aware of the unity of God and the power of providence. Had not
God called him from the shores of distant Britain to overthrow

the oppressors of the Roman world?[36] He was deeply convinced that God cared for him and guided him.[37] He had a keen sense of responsibility to God and of the judgement and possible wrath of God,[38] and was determined to do all in his power to serve him. Yet with all this there went misunderstanding. As with so many of those now flocking into the Church, it was monotheism which drew him. Even when he spoke of Christ, his mind was on the tokens of divine power and the divine revelation rather than atonement and redemption. Christ, for him, was the divine Word by whom all things were made and by whom God was revealed, rather than the Saviour. This was true of his age, and it casts some light on the later appearance of Arianism and the rise of Islam.

Until now the Church had repudiated violence. One cannot completely discount the claim of the Apologists that Christians can be seen to practise the precepts of the Sermon on the Mount. Soldiers who confessed Christ can be traced in the half century before Constantine, but it is doubtful if they had been baptised into the Church. Tertullian treated with ridicule the idea that there was any place for a Christian in the army. How could a man who had taken the sacrament of Christ swear an oath of allegiance to any man? How could he use the sword and take part in battle when he was not even allowed to sue in the courts, to put men in chains, or even in prison? If a soldier believed and was baptised he must either abandon his faith or be involved in continual evasion. Desertion or martyrdom was the only real choice before him.[39] It is small wonder if any Roman official who read this regarded the Church as no other than an anarchist society.

Half a century later than Tertullian, at the close of his long answer to Celsus, Origen could not avoid the charge that if all behaved like the Christians the empire would be overwhelmed by the barbarians.[40] He made the customary Christian reply that prayer was the best defence and that the conversion of the barbarians would secure peace, but did not deny that Christians refused to take part in the administration of justice and to fight in the army. They owed a loyalty, not to the state, but to a higher community. Totally divorced from the state, the Church had made no attempt to solve the problems of a secular society which knew neither the law of God nor the grace of Christ. Pacifism in the modern world implies rejection of the society to which a man belongs, but in the early Church it implied adherence to his community, which was the Kingdom of God and not the kingdom of Caesar; for the Church was a non-violent society, neither defending her people against the state nor the state against its neighbouring states.

'What would happen if an emperor became a Christian?' Celsus asked in a prophetic moment.[41] His implicit answer was that society would collapse. Certainly, society as the Roman world knew it would have collapsed; but when this very situation arose the consequences did not follow. Celsus had assumed that a Christian emperor would practise the commands of Christ as he saw the Church of his time doing. When the time came the Church found herself committed to a course of action contrary to all her past principles. Constantine came into the Church impulsively on his own terms as the result of a battle. He bypassed all the discipline of the Church for the training and initiation of converts. It never occurred to him to question his action by Christian standards. He did not know what he was doing and the Church did not know what she was getting.

In private life Constantine's temper remained uncontrollable and he was always liable, as had been his pagan predecessors on the throne, to outbursts of fearful cruelty. There is a strange contrast between the terrible story of the execution of his wife Fausta and the death of his son Crispus,[42] and the indifference of Marcus Aurelius to his nymphomaniac wife and his monstrous son. Rome had treated marriage as a social contract. She had been the model for the permissive society of the twentieth century in her acceptance of prostitution, concubinage, homosexuality, lesbianism, pornography, paederasty, divorce and abortion, even if it has not yet occurred to any modern Chancellor of the Exchequer to follow her example in taxing prostitution. Forgetting his mother's previous occupation, Constantine classed barmaids and prostitutes together by exempting them from penalties under the laws regarding adultery. He tightened the law on divorce. A woman could now divorce her husband for being a murderer, a poisoner, or a tomb robber, but if she did so on such grounds as drunkenness, gambling, or sexual vices, she lost her dowry. A man might divorce his wife if she was guilty of adultery, poisoning, or procuring, but if he did so on other grounds he had to restore her dowry and could not remarry. In irregular divorce the guilty party was penalised but the innocent could remarry. Constantine discouraged concubinage, but possibly not for moral reasons, by making invalid all gifts and legacies from the man to his companion or their children.[43] Though his acts against paganism were restricted he prohibited the survivals of ritual prostitution.[44] A law of 1 April 320 threatened savage penalties for fornication, and one of 31 July 336 recognised the rights of those who chose to stay celibate.[45]

These are signs of the beginning of a general change of mind on matters of sex. In pagan Rome the attitude to it had been crude. Acute difficulty had been found at times in filling up the ranks of the Vestal Virgins. Horace taunted the lover who rejected him with the sneer that she was growing old and would soon be soliciting in back alleys.[46] Under the empire, and probably long before it, Rome had tolerated every kind of sexual vice and perversion, but there are elements in human personality which resent these abuses and a reaction had set in. There is no mistaking the contempt and disgust of their historians for the orgies of men like Tiberius and Eligabalus. Within the Church there had been a growing ascetic preference for virginity and on its fringes a condemnation of sex as evil in itself. Roughly contemporary with Constantine, the *Pervigilium Veneris* is thoroughly pagan, but its attitude to the love of young people has more in common with the romanticism of mediaeval love-poetry than with anything from the classical world. Whether from within the Church or from the general temper of the age, Constantine had absorbed something of a more puritan attitude to sex.

As Constantine's position grew stronger he increased his support for the Church in public matters.[47] He legislated for Sunday observance, prayed regularly himself, and prescribed a prayer for general use in the army.[48] Other traces of Christian influence began to appear. A law of 21 March 315 prohibited branding on the face 'because it is fashioned after the image of the heavenly beauty', and this suggests that he had learned that man was made in the image of God but that his conception of God was still the pagan conception of an old man in the sky rather than that of a Spirit, infinite and eternal. An act of 14 May 316 commanded that drivers in the public posts should avoid cruelty to their animals. Another of 17 April 331 shows more clearly the breach between Christian and pagan morals by providing for the rearing of foundlings rather than their exposure. In 326 the gladiatorial combats were prohibited,[49] but this was not observed except in the east and they continued at Rome till 402. Prudentius appealed to the emperor to stop them, and the end came when the monk Telemachus ran between the gladiators to part them and was killed by the stones hurled at him by the spectators.[50] *— Is this factual? THEODORET is the source.*

It was said that Constantine, superstitious as ever, continued to consult the omens for some time after his conversion, and this may well have been true; but in 318 he forbad the practice except in private houses. Paganism was still so strong that he could not completely abolish time-honoured superstitions even if, as is not always clear, he had wished to do so. It has often been noted that he continued to use the pagan title of *Pontifex Maximus* but this was still a political office of practical importance. Its achievement had been a critical step in the advance to power of Julius Caesar.[51] After the clash with Licinius, Constantine's actions against paganism increased, and when he became sole emperor he became markedly pro-Christian. Wherever he went he associated with bishops and in 325 he gave the city of Rome her first Christian governor.[52]

After Easter 337 Constantine took ill and realised that he was about to die. In the suburbs of Nicomedia he met the bishops and told them that he now sought baptism, the seal of immortality. It had been his intention, he said, to be baptised in Jordan where Christ had been baptised, but God had seen otherwise. His baptism then took place. Long delayed, it had been left so late not because of any reasons of policy or uncertainty, but because of the desire to avoid post-baptismal sin once he had passed through the waters of regeneration. After saying farewell and making provision for the succession he died at noon on Pentecost, perfect in timing right up to the end. In Constantinople, the former Byzantium and the New Rome where no pagan temple was permitted, he had prepared his own burial place in the Church of the Twelve Apostles. Within it stood the cenotaphs for each of the Twelve and, in the centre, the tomb made ready for himself. As this suggests, he had not underestimated his own achievement. Nor was he without justification. He had changed the course of history . . . and the course of the Church.

With his conversion a flood of others began the transformation

of the Church from a restricted body of the convinced, like the
Baptists in the Soviet Union today, into an accepted part of the
social order with a core of conviction and a fringe of adherents.
Gradually the word *conversion* was so devalued that it became
difficult to distinguish the active from the nominal Christians.
For the first time the law began to be accommodated to the
Church, but it is significant that the changes were usually
directed to matters of secondary importance, such as Sunday
observance. Even had Constantine's grasp of the faith been
perfect, he was not a free man. Pagans were very numerous and,
in Rome itself, probably well in the majority. In every field they
held posts of administrative power. Everywhere he turned
he must have met that faceless but effective resistance which
confronts every reformer from the forces of reaction installed at
every official level of government. When he revisited Rome his
troops still marched up to the Capitol to pay their dues at Jove's
eternal shrine. There survives an account of his fury when the
legions enthusiastically but tactlessly hailed him with a pagan
greeting on 1 March 326.[53] Too often a tribute was paid to
Christian ways while the substance was rejected, as when
crucifixion, for obvious reasons, was abolished but torture
retained.

Until the second half of the third century Christians had
worshipped in private houses. It has been said that Clement of
Alexandria was the first to use the word *ecclesia* to describe a
building and not a congregation, but this is questionable.[54] At
Dura-Europos, a Roman frontier city on the Euphrates,
excavation in 1934 revealed a house-church built after 232 and
abandoned when the ramparts were rebuilt in 256. Nothing
distinguished it from other houses; only those who worshipped
there could know its purpose. In time of persecution Christians
in Rome worshipped in the catacombs. As numbers grew in the
second half of the third century, churches began to be built in
Egypt, Syria, and Asia Minor. From early times the word
ecclesia had described both the universal Church and her
congregations and to this day it is the root from which the name
for a place of worship is derived in some languages such as
French and Gaelic. But a name for buildings was now needed,
and the edict of Maximin in 312 refers to the buildings which
'Christians call *oikoi kyriakoi* (the Lord's houses)'.[55] This seems
to be the root from which the English *church,* the German

Kirche, and the Scots *kirk* have come.

Before the persecution of Diocletian Christians had been bold enough to erect churches such as the great church at Nicomedia, the burning of which marked the opening of their ordeal, and under Constantine new and beautiful churches arose.[56] Known as *basilicas* from the secular model on which they were based, these were great open halls, with two or three aisles on each side, separated from the main aisle by colonnades. At Rome Constantine built the basilica of St John Lateran, the churches of St Peter on the Vatican and St Paul's outside the Walls on the Ostian Way, and the Church of St' Laurence. Other great churches were built at Jerusalem, Bethlehem, Mamre, Nicomedia, Antioch and Constantinople. At Rome the new churches could not occupy the central sites of a city already dominated by its great temples, but in the new capital the churches held pride of place. These churches and their clergy were next endowed, for they were no longer to be supported by their congregations. Rich altar vessels were bestowed. For the first time the arts of the ruling culture, as distinct from the folk culture, were brought into the service of the Church on a massive scale. In 331 Constantine wrote to Eusebius ordering fifty copies of the Scriptures and providing for the cost.[57] Probably the *Codex Sinaiticus,* written in four columns of forty-eight lines on sheets of vellum, is one of these. As Eusebius knew well when he preached an exultant sermon at the dedication of the great church at Tyre, these splendid fabrics and their adornments told Christian and pagan alike that a new order had arrived.[58]

A bishop had once been no more than the devoted pastor of a threatened minority group, but by the middle of the third century the bishops of churches like Alexandria, Antioch and Carthage were men of high standing. With the coming of Constantine bishops who, not long before, had been in danger of martyrdom in the arena, found themselves raised to unforeseen honours. Human nature being what it is, the change cannot have been unwelcome. When the Council of Nicaea met, men who had suffered persecution stood in the hall of the imperial palace, blind in one eye and lame on one leg from the days when they had slaved in the copper mines while Constantine, robed in purple, entered, bowed his head, and stood beside his chair till the bishops beckoned him to be seated.[59] He kissed the empty

Eusebius

eye-socket of one such saintly ex-convict. A time had been when bishops got a variable allowance from their people and supplemented it as they could. Spiridon, Bishop of Trimithus in Cyprus under Constantine, continued to earn his living as a shepherd after his consecration.[60] Zeno, Bishop of Majuma, was a linen weaver all his life.[61] But now the bishops were fast becoming wealthy, independent, and privileged.[62] A bishop's sphere of pastoral care spread far beyond the city into the countryside, and the change was now seen in the fact that while his sphere had previously been known as his *parochia* or *ecclesia,* his parish or congregation, it was now known as his diocese, a name taken from one of the larger Roman areas of civil administration.

As the bishop's status suddenly rose there came the beginnings of clericalism; the laity counted for less in the Church;[63] there was a loss of intimacy as numbers grew, and a subtle change in authority within the Church. Things had changed greatly from the time when Cyprian had written that such matters as the restoration of the lapsed must be decided only 'with the consent of the whole people'.[64] Yet the corporate nature of the Church was still declared by the fact that, as soon as freedom came to her, she made her decisions, not by personal acts, but through councils.

Other changes followed. Great as were the services of Constantine to the Church, his well-meaning actions hindered it in the lands of Rome's great enemy beyond the Euphrates. Constantine once said that the bishops had jurisdiction within the Church but that he, too, was a bishop, since God had ordained him to be an overseer of those who were outside the Church.[65] Such an outlook, and this new and intimate relationship between the Church and the empire made all Christians beyond Rome's eastern frontier suspect in Persian eyes. Owing a loyalty to the Kingdom of God, and under suspicion of owing another to the kingdom of Caesar, they were doubly suspect as potential dissidents.

From the start the Church had been a community living her own life in the midst of secular society and bearing the responsibility for the poor and the elderly of her flock, apart from any help given to outsiders. Charity was not now forgotten, but the responsibility of the congregation for her own poor became a thing of the past. Christian charity set out on the

road to that parody which, until recently, surprised so many
tourists on seeing the squalid array of beggars around the portals
of some vast and overdecorated cathedral in southern Europe.
Within the Church the familiar secular indifference to the
injustices of wealth and poverty became accepted, and with this
the diaconate, as it had long functioned, became irrelevant.[66] It
was deprived of its original duties and was reduced to the minor
one of service to the celebrant at the altar. While the name
remained, the function had gone; instead of being an order in
which men spent their lives it became a stage on the way to the
priesthood.

Similarly the Church had enforced her own discipline through
confession, penance, excommunication and absolution; these
did not cease, but they came to be related to the life after death
rather than Christian obedience in this world. At the same time
the authority and standards of secular justice became accepted
among Christians, not only because it was taken for granted that
criminals should be tried and punished by the civil courts, but
because the Church permitted the concept of justice to enter her
own thought and practice to the detriment of her understanding
of love and grace. Augustine was to quote Cicero as his
authority for the nature of justice since he could not quote the
Gospels.[67]

However sudden the great transformation may have seemed
to those who lived through it, all this was merely the culmination
of a process which had been going on for many years, for if the
Church is the body of Christ her humanity is still far short of his
perfect manhood. If the Church began by calling in the outcasts
of society, in time she became too respectable by secular
standards and increasingly conformist. All the signs are that
Clement and Origen came from a Church which may still have
had many from the lower classes in her ranks but was now
gathering in those from the more comfortable and prosperous
classes.[68] She was accepting society rather than challenging it,
coming to be seen as a potential support for the state rather than
a menace to it. 'Whosoever he be of you that forsaketh not all
that he hath,' said Jesus, 'he cannot be my disciple.'[69] Men did
not always need to give up too much. Membership was strictly
defined by confession of the faith, baptism, regular
participation in the Eucharist and acceptance of the discipline of
the Church; but it was becoming easier. As early as the start of

the third century the distinction between those within and those without the Church was, occasionally, blurred.[70] Compromise was all too easy.

In its first beginnings the divine community owed its being to an authoritative word from God. Nor did Christ offer any vindication for his commands other than his own authority and person. Yet it had seemed necessary for defenders of the faith to meet contemporary intellectuals on their own ground. Justin had regarded philosophy as a preparation for the Gospel, but by the time we come to Origen we find the faith vindicated on grounds other than its own content. What had been presented as consistent, when truly understood, with the reasoning mind, was coming to be by definition subject to it. Greatly as Origen is to be respected, he has not infrequently been under suspicion of having surrendered too much in the endeavour to find common ground with those outside the faith. In time he was followed by others who, less consciously, allowed their thought of God to be shaped by a guide from outside the Church. Plotinus had gathered many strands of Platonic thought into a system which, during the long centuries of the Dark Ages when Plato himself was almost unknown, transmitted the heritage of classical thought to the theologians and mystics of the early Middle Ages. At times it was a stronger influence than the Bible, expressing the soul's quest for the divine rather than the unsought grace of God to men. In its purest form the thought of Plotinus,

> helped to give theological expression to Christian dogma regarding the Godhead ... it provided a theological formulation of mysticism. ... In its deeply religious tone, its tendency to emanationism and pantheism, and its negation of the supernatural gift of God it is an ambivalent influence, now good, now dubious, in the history of Christian theology.[71]

Constantine's conversion was seen by Eusebius, and by most Christians at the time and since, as the triumph of the Church;[72] yet it may be asked whether in the acceptance of Constantine on his own terms and, by implication, of that society which he represented and of its world of thought, she had not gone, in some respects, strangely wrong. At this point the wheel had come full circle and the Church, which looked back to Pontius Pilate as the representative of the state which had crucified her

How Much is fullah Conditions by our post-Constantinian world.

Lord, looked up to Constantine, the head of that state, as her deliverer and protector.

Neither the beginnings of the process nor its culmination passed entirely without protest. Tertullian's absorption in Montanism can be seen not only as an expression of his own fanatical personality but as a reaction against the growing conventionality of the Church. And this can also be said of the rise of monasticism. Many great movements, both inside and outside the Church, have begun with most attractive features and later degenerated. Monasticism is one of the few instances to the contrary. Christians had always formed a community apart, but if they were not of the world, as Tertullian says in his *Apology,* they were certainly in it. If any early Christian might have been expected to admire the monastic ideal it was he, but Tertullian explicitly stated that Christians had no intention of seeking a life apart.[73] Monasticism found its antecedents in pre-Christian days among the Essenes, the men of Qumram, and the Therapeutae described by Philo whose poverty, asceticism and discipline induced Eusebius to regard them as Christians;[74] its origins were in Egypt and among the Copts, the indigenous inhabitants least touched by Greek influence.

Later monasticism was normally a communal life but the Egyptian beginnings were solitary, or eremitical. St Jerome, who was fascinated by it, admitted that the origins of monasticism were debatable, but he himself reckoned St Paul of the Thebaid to be the first instance.[75] At the time of the Decian persecution Paul was a boy of fifteen who inherited considerable wealth through the death of his parents. He was not one of those who sought martyrdom, but went for safety to his sister's farm and then, when threatened with denunciation by his brother-in-law, fled to the mountains for safety. There he discovered a remote opening in the rocks which led him to a tiny oasis with a palm tree and a spring. Here he spent the remainder of his life in prayer and meditation, living on dates and cold water until, like many of the early hermits, he was rumoured to have reached a fabulous old age. Jerome's account of Paul is more colourful than credible. When he was visited by St Anthony, we are told, a crow flew in and dropped a loaf of bread and Paul rejoiced that he who had not eaten a loaf for years could now share it with a guest. This anecdote proved very popular in Celtic monasticism and was portrayed on its sculptures.

St Anthony is said to have been born in 251 in Middle Egypt, and some twenty years later to have sold his property, placed a younger sister in a house of consecrated virgins, and adopted the ascetic life, first at his own village, and then in a remote spot.[76] About 305 he was joined by others; Paul had fled from persecution, but Anthony and his companions went to meet it. In 338 he paid a second visit to Alexandria to greet Athanasius after his return from his first exile and to aid him against the Arians. When he died in 356 at the age, it was said, of 105, he showed his regard for Athanasius by leaving him his sole possessions, an old tunic of sheepskin and the mantle on which he had slept. Such solitaries multiplied in Egypt. At Nitria, west of the delta and south of Alexandria, they established a colony, each living in his own hut and meeting only for worship and discipline.[77] Their asceticism was not wholly Christian in origin and their retirement was a denial of the communal nature of the Church, probably provoked by reaction against a fellowship which had lost its first zeal. But these were only the beginnings of monasticism and to pursue it further would take us beyond our bounds.

Social and racial alienation may possibly have been factors in the appearance of monasticism among the Copts of Egypt, and in the Melitian and Donatist schisms it certainly was so.[78] Yet in each case the basic cause was the reaction of dissidents who rejected a Church which had compromised with classical concepts, social order and the state. Each was an appeal to the life of the primitive and uncorrupted Church and each, unfortunately, was far from perfect and had made a compromise of its own in the acceptance of disunity and the use of violence.

Once again, to follow the story of these would take us far beyond our period, but their beginnings are within it, for each arose out of persecution and Christian heroism, or rather, the absence of it. In 304 a dispute on the future treatment of the lapsed broke out among a number of bishops imprisoned at Alexandria and when release came the different parties put their principles into action.[79] Melitius, a bishop from Upper Egypt stood for rigorous treatment, and Peter of Alexandria for a measure of compassion, but more personal issues were also involved. Four other bishops wrote to Melitius in 305 to protest that he was ordaining clergy in dioceses other than his own.[80] He had condemned Peter, the Bishop of Alexandria, for going into hiding and even after the martyrdom of Peter in 311 the schism continued.

Though troublesome enough, this was a minor schism; a far greater one was that of the Donatists. In date and character of origin it was almost identical but the factors involved were more complex and the consequences more lasting. Racial, social and cultural differences and personal rivalries accentuated a division of opinion within a troubled Church. As early as her wars with Rome, Carthage had looked across the Mediterranean to Sicily rather than to a hinterland which was not too easily accessible. It is significant that while other great cities of the empire have survived their vicissitudes and are thriving to this day, Carthage disappeared. She was not securely rooted in her hinterland. Further inland in Numidia were small farmers and villagers, Berber in language and temperament, out of touch with Roman civilization, and prospering when the coastal towns went into decline.[81] In the second half of the third century resentment and desperation spread among them as their relative prosperity was subject to continual extortion and cruelty from tax-collectors, soldiers, those obliged to operate local government and great senatorial absentee landlords.[82] During the same years the Church made rapid progress in the villages, winning fanatical converts not altogether in harmony with the increasingly moderate churchmanship of the towns. Even there a tendency existed for Christians to be divided between a small Romanised group and a considerable native element.

On 19 May 303 during the great persecution of Diocletian, Paulus, the Bishop of Cirta, the modern Constantine and then the capital of the province of Numidia, was ordered to hand over the Scriptures.[83] He compromised, handed over a volume, and said that the readers had the others. They were fetched and, after some evasion, complied and handed over the possessions of the Church. No one was very heroic. At the end of 303 another bishop, Fundanus of Abitina, similarly handed over the Scriptures.[84] Out in the villages, however, Christians were made of sterner stuff and many died. Fundanus' congregation continued to meet in a house without him. One day they were arrested together, to the number of forty-seven. When charged they were more resolute than their bishop. While in prison, where it was later said they were left to starve to death, they

comprehensively condemned their bishop and all who had
surrendered copies of the Scriptures. Here we see the beginnings
of a party of popular opposition to the episcopate, waiting only
for leadership and a pretext.

Bishop Paulus had died. On 5 March 305 the Numidian
bishops gathered at Cirta to consecrate his successor. Secundus,
the presiding bishop, began to check the conduct of his
colleagues under persecution. Four of them had to confess their
evasive conduct until one, who had a particularly bad record,
brazenly retorted, 'Do you think that I am frightened of you like
the rest? What have *you* done? How did you come to be set free
unless you surrendered something?' At this the nephew of
Secundus said, 'Do you hear what he is saying against you? He is
ready to leave and make a schism; and not only he, but also all
who are accused by you.' Secundus took the hint and broke off
his enquiry. By this time the threat of schism was evident to all.
Early in 312 Caecilian, a man with many enemies since he had
earlier been charged with refusing food to the imprisoned
members of Fundanus' congregation, was consecrated as Bishop
of Carthage. Secundus and seventy Numidian bishops descended
on the Church of Carthage and appointed an administrator of the
see, who was promptly murdered. Majorinus was consecrated in
the place of Caecilian and, when he died in 313, Donatus of
Casae Nigrae. He was a remarkable man with a vast popular
appeal who lived for another forty years and gave his name to
the schismatic Church.[85]

Donatism proved both endemic and tenacious in North
Africa, not only because of the passionate memories surviving
from the days when persecution revealed the inconstancy of
some who held office in the Church but because, as in Northern
Ireland, a religious difference coincided with a racial and social
cleavage. Constantine was scarcely converted before he was
drawn into the dispute. Already earlier bishops had been ill-
advised enough to appeal to the pagan Aurelian to deal with
Paul of Samosata, and now the Church took the perilous step of
asking the Christian emperor to intervene against a schismatic
bishop. Constantine's lack of success — one of the few failures
of his reign — did not make the step any less momentous.
Donatism survived the hostility of the state and the controversial
zeal of Augustine to maintain itself in North Africa until the
coming of Islam.[86] No doctrine of the faith was involved in the

schism. If anything, the Donatists were more orthodox than the orthodox, like those alienated from the Roman Church by the abandonment of the Tridentine Mass. No one emerged with credit. On both sides the North African bishops conducted themselves discreditably and the congregations followed their example. While ostensibly the Donatists protested against compromise with a secular society which had absorbed and corrupted the Church, in practice they accepted a policy of bitterness and violence far removed from the commands of the Sermon on the Mount. If the Church was involved in a betrayal of the Kingdom of God, the Donatists were equally guilty of a departure from the way seen in Christ.

Though the Egyptian monks soon began to gather in ordered settlements, monasticism was essentially the protest of individuals against a secularised Church. No matter how much respect it acquired, it never had any prospect of gaining the Church as a whole to its way of life. Schismatics who formed sects of their own, by that very act forfeited any hope of persuading other Christians. But in another field of compromise where doctrine was concerned it was the protest which, after some uncertainty, won the support of the Church. Other movements of protest had been against social and moral compromise between the Church and the secular world, but the condemnation of Arianism was a refusal to compromise on the essentials of the faith.

Arius was the priest of a large and important Church in Alexandria who, if he had not been born in Antioch, had at least been educated there, and who in 318 became a party to a debate with his bishop on the nature of Christ. It was a subject on which the Church, whatever her faith might be, had made as yet no authoritative theological statement. Some theologians had stressed the kinship of Christ with God the Father, while others had followed Origen who, while teaching the unity of the Father, Son and Holy Spirit, had taught that in the strictest sense the Father is God alone, while the Son possesses the Godhead by participation or derivatively.[87] In the late fifties of the third century Origen's pupil Dionysius, Bishop of Alexandria, became involved with his namesake, the Bishop of Rome. He was charged with making a sharp division, amounting to a separation, between the Father and the Son, with denying the Son's eternity, with speaking of the Father and Son as though they were separable, with failing to describe the Son as being 'of one substance with the Father', and with speaking of the Son as a creature. By this time east and west were speaking different languages to the point of misunderstanding one another. In the west theologians were so concerned with the divine unity that they could only speak haltingly of the 'persons' of the Trinity, while in the east theologians moved in an intellectual climate impregnated with Neo-Platonic ideas about the hierarchy of being.[88] From the time of Philo through the teaching of Plotinus and Origen, the east had learned to think of the Word as proceeding from the ineffable and inaccessible God but as falling, in certain respects, within the category of the created.

In 318 Alexander, the Bishop of Alexandria, addressed his clergy on the subject of the Trinity and provoked a reply from Arius. 'If the Father begat the Son,' he said, 'he that was begotten has a beginning of existence, and from this it is evident, that there was a time when the Son was not.'[89] Arius' position has been summed up by Duchesne:

> God is one, eternal, and unbegotten. Other beings are his creatures, the Logos first of all. Like the other creatures the Logos was taken out of nothingness and not from the Divine Substance; there was a time when he was not. He was created, not necessarily, but voluntarily. Himself a creature of God, he is the Creator of all other beings, and this relationship justifies the title of God, which is improperly given to him. God adopted him as Son in prevision of his merits, for he is free, susceptible of change, and it is by his own will that he determined himself on the side of good. From this sonship by adoption results no real participation in the Divinity, no true likeness to it. God can have no like. The Holy Spirit is the first of the creatures of the Logos. The Logos was made flesh, in the sense that he fulfilled in Jesus Christ the functions of a soul.[90]

Arius set out to canvass support from prelates like the Bishop of Caesarea and returned to Alexandria where he had great popular support among those inclined to despise the Bishop's authority.[91]

He had, however, a younger and more persistent opponent than the Bishop in Athanasius, who succeeded Alexander in 328.[92] Some ten years earlier Athanasius had published a little book, *On the Incarnation of the Word of God.* Arius had been concerned with a philosophical understanding of the nature of the divine Word. There are passages in Athanasius' tract which might well have been acceptable to Arius, but throughout it ran the conviction that in Christ there had come among men no subordinate being but the fullness of the divine nature.

> He cleansed lepers, he made the lame to walk, he opened the ears of the deaf and the eyes of the blind. . . . Even the most casual observer can see that these were acts of God. The healing of the man born blind, for instance, who but the Father and Artificer of man, the Controller of his whole being, could thus have restored the faculty denied at birth? He who did thus must surely be himself the Lord of birth. . . . Did not that prove him none other than the very Lord whose mind is over all?[93]

Athanasius was concerned, not with a philosophical understanding of the Logos, but with the nature of God's redemption of mankind.

In the east Arius had strong support among the bishops, their congregations, and at the court, while Athanasius found his most consistent support in the west. At the Council of Nicaea in 325 he won a temporary and precarious victory by a hair's breadth. Subsequently his cause appeared to be lost, but before the close of the century it had won the support of the Church. It is notorious that this great debate has been contemptuously narrowed to an argument about a single letter, the *iota* which makes the difference between two Greek words, one meaning of the same nature, and the other, of the like nature, and it is difficult to find a dispute to which the average modern mind could be more indifferent. Yet vital issues were at stake. At the height of the dispute Athanasius had to face the support of the emperor for his adversary's position and even in the lifetime of Constantine to defend the independence of the Church against the full power of the state. Even more important was his recognition that the Arian reduction of Christ to a created being was the betrayal of all that the Church had taught for three centuries. He knew and respected 'the supremely learned and diligent Origen', but he had broken with a tradition which was too ready to accommodate the faith of the Church to the philosophy of the classical world. Only on the faith of the true God and Saviour Jesus Christ, declared in her preaching and presented in her sacraments, could the Church survive.[94] A compromise at this point would have been at the expense of her whole being, but she had already compromised on a great deal else and in these respects the conversion of Constantine had been a Pyrrhic victory. Too much had been paid.

Despite her faults and betrayals the Church is still the body of Christ, the witness for him in a hostile world. In her faith, her fellowship, charity, and unity, her sacraments, her ministry and continuity she is his primary creation, the earthly face of the Kingdom of God. 'In the world ye shall have tribulation,' said Jesus as his death drew near, 'but be of good cheer; I have overcome the world.'[95] It is fashionable in critical circles to discount the discourses of Jesus in *St John* as his, but the word here translated as 'the world' is, in fact, the cosmos, and it is difficult to imagine such an outrageous saying in that setting as coming from other than his imperial mind. But 'the world' is also secular society, human society as it organises itself apart from God, a system of co-operative guilt with limited liability,[96] and the outcome of the first clash was the crucifixion of Christ on the orders of Pilate. Less than three centuries later the Church came to terms with secular society in the person of Constantine. Had his conversion been one in the full sense of the word the logical course would have been that the state should have been allowed to wither away and its place be taken by the divine community which used neither power nor violence and was indifferent to property. Instead the Church co-operated in the creation of the Byzantine Empire which was to last for a thousand years and then in the reconstruction of the state in mediaeval Europe.

There were great gains. 'No one who has not lived under persecution,' the writer once heard an Asian Christian say, 'has any right to criticise the Church for accepting Constantine with all his imperfections.' It would be wrong to ignore the great and good contributions to human life which have flowed from what is called Christendom and the heroic and unselfish service continually given to the state, but they have not been won without cost. From Roman times the Church accepted slavery. Even when its severity was first tempered and afterwards abolished other forms of human exploitation were tolerated. Civil justice in crime and punishment, with all its attendant brutalities, was accepted, and, with time exceeded in religious persecution. War, too, was accepted, first with the limited weapons of ancient days, next in the vast slaughter of the First World War, and then in atomic warfare. At this point one might be tempted to write, finally, were it not that atomic fission is unlikely to be the culminating achievement of science.

Even where, as in the United States, the Church is not formally associated with the state, she is intimately associated with the sources of economic and social power. Perhaps, in the twentieth century, it might be more accurate to word this in the past tense. But the damage has been done, and the quickening pace of technological advance in modern society has drawn the Church further into denial of the way of Christ, as centralised power brings the destruction of the simpler human relationships of family and neighbourhood, a depersonalised society, and an endless disparity between wealth and poverty. Hectic consumption of natural resources is followed by pollution of the air, the soil and the ocean.

In 1930 Charles Gore wrote,

> It is true — most lamentably true — that since the days of Constantine, by the recognition of indiscriminate baptism, by the abandonment of discipline, by the reckless adoption of the principle of established churches, the Church of Christ has dared absolutely to reverse the method of its Master, and thereby has lost its ethical distinctness and its moral power as a corporate body.[97]

Even today the Church does not seem to have heard that Constantine is a long time dead; and the time has long gone by when we should have asked whether she did not make her most desperate error when she accepted not only him but the secular order for which he stood.

Notes to Chapter 11

1. Eusebius, *DVC*, I, xxviii, xxix.
2. Baynes, p.58.
3. Lactantius, XLIV.
4. A. Alföldi, *The Conversion of Constantine and Pagan Rome*, pp.17ff.
5. Stevenson, p.302. Lietzmann, III, pp.75, 151ff. Jones, *Constantine*, p.95.
6. Eusebius, *DVC*, I, xl.
7. Jones, *LRE*, I, p.81; *Constantine*, p.85.
8. Pascal, *Pensées*, p.131.
9. Jones, *Constantine*, pp.86-88.
10. *ibid*. p.97.
11. Apuleius, *The Golden Ass*, XVII.
12. M. Grant, *Climax*, pp.172-179.
13. *St Matthew* 10:35.
14. Eusebius, *DVC*, I, xiii-xviii. Constantine, *De Falso Cultu*, P.L.8, col.272.
15. Duchesne, II, p.129.
16. Lietzmann, III, pp.154, 157.
17. A. Momigliano, *Paganism and Christianity in the Fourth Century*, pp.43, 45ff.
18. Eusebius, *DVC*, III, xlii-xlvii.
19. *James* 1:26-27.
20. *Panegyrici Veteres*, P.L.8, col.637-638.
21. Constantine, P.L.8, col.253, 272, 277, 401.
22. *ibid*. *Ad Sanctorum Coetum*, XVIII, XXI, P.L.8, col.449, 466.
23. Laistner, p.53.
24. Eusebius, *De Laudibus Constantini*, P.L.20, col.1336.
25. Eusebius, *DVC*, II, li.
26. *ibid*. II, ix.
27. Minucius Felix, *Octavius*, XII.
28. Eusebius, *DVC*, II, xxiii.
29. Eusebius, *Ecclesiastical History*, VIII, xvii.
30. *ibid*. X, iv.
31. *ibid*. X, vii.
32. Salvian, *De Gubernatione Dei. cf*. M. Montaigne, *Essays*, I, xxxi.

33. Augustine, *De Civitate Dei*, V, xxv.
34. Alföldi, pp.14, 20.
35. Eusebius, *DVC*, I, xxxii.
36. Constantine, *Ad Sanctorum Coetum*, P.L.8, col.405. *De Pietate*, P.L.8, col.257.
37. Constantine, *After the Council of Arles*, P.L.8, col.487.
38. Constantine, *To Aelafius*, P.L.8, col.485ff; *After the Council of Arles*, P.L.8, col.490.
39. Tertullian, *De Corona Militis*, XI.
40. Origen, *Against Celsus*, VIII, lxviii-lxxiii.
41. *ibid.* VIII, lxxv.
42. Gibbon, xviii. J.H. Smith, *Constantine the Great*, pp.206-212.
43. Jones, *LRE*, II, pp.972-976. Troeltsch, I, pp.129-131.
44. Socrates, I, xviii.
    Eusebius, *DVC*, IV, xxv.
45. Kidd, *History of the Church to A.D.461*, II, p.9.
46. Horace, *Odes*, I, xxv.
47. Jones, *Constantine*, p.103.
48. Eusebius, *DVC*, IV, xvii-xx.
49. *ibid.* IV, xxv.
50. Theodoret, *Ecclesiastical History*, V, xxvi.
51. Suetonius, *Julius*, XIII.
52. Alföldi, pp.76-79.
53. *ibid.* pp.101ff.
54. Clement, *Stromateis*, VII, v. Lindsay, p.43n. Dix, p.19.
55. Eusebius, *Ecclesiastical History*, IX, x.
56. van der Meer and Mohrmann, *Atlas of the Early Christian World*, pp.60-65, 135-139.
57. Eusebius, *DVC*, IV, xxxvi-xxxvii. C.R. Gregory, pp.326-328.
58. Eusebius, *Ecclesiastical History*, X, iv.
59. Eusebius, *DVC*, III, x.
60. Socrates, I, xii.
61. Sozomen, VII, xxviii.
62. Hatch, pp.144-155.
63. S. Neill and H.R. Weber, *The Layman in Christian History*, p.65
64. Cyprian, *Epistles*, XIV, XVII, LXIV.
65. Eusebius, *DVC*, IV, xxiv.
66. Harnack, I, pp.122, 161.
67. Augustine, *The City of God*, XIX, xxi.
68. R.M. Grant, *ELS*, pp.84-88.
69. *St Luke* 14:33.
70. Frend, *DC*, pp.125, 142ff.
71. D. Knowles, *The Evolution of Medieval Thought*, p.31.
72. von Campenhausen, *FGC*, pp.64ff.
73. Tertullian, *Apology*, XLII.

74. Eusebius, *Ecclesiastical History*, II, xvii.
75. Jerome, *Vita Pauli Eremitae.*
76. Duchesne, II, pp.387-390.
77. *ibid.* II, pp.391-394.
78. Greenslade, *SEC,* pp.58-61.
79. *ibid.* pp.51-55.
80. Stevenson, pp.290-293.
81. Frend, *DC,* pp.31, 38ff.
82. *ibid.* pp.62-69.
83. *ibid.* pp.5ff. Stevenson, pp.287-289.
84. Frend, *DC,* pp.8ff.
85. *ibid.* pp.11-24. Stevenson, pp.313-316.
86. Frend, *DC,* pp.308-315.
87. Kelly, *ECD*, pp.128-133.
88. *ibid.* p.136.
89. Socrates, I, v.
90. Duchesne, II, pp.100ff.
91. *ibid.* pp.107ff.
92. Lietzmann, III, p.128.
93. Athanasius, *De Incarnatione,* III, xviii.
94. von Campenhausen, *FGC,* p.72.
95. *St John* 16:33.
96. The definition is one casually made by Dean Inge.
97. C. Gore, *The Philosophy of the Good Life,* p.171.

BIBLIOGRAPHY

Aland, K. *Did the Early Church Baptise Infants?* London 1963.
Alexandrian Christianity, ed. Oulton, J.E.L. and Chadwick, H. London 1954.
Alföldi, A. *The Conversion of Constantine and Pagan Rome*. London 1948.
Ambrose. *Epistles*, cf. *Early Latin Theology*.
Anselm. *Cur Deus Homo?* London 1956.
  Proslogion. London 1903.
Apocrypha (N.E.B.). London 1970.
Apuleius. *The Golden Ass*. London 1950.
Aquinas, St. Thomas. *Summa Theologica*. 21 vols. London 1911-1935.
  Summa contra Gentiles. 5 vols. New York 1961.
  Theological Texts. ed. Gilbey. London 1955.
Aristotle. *Politics*. Oxford 1846.
Arnobius. *Adversus Gentes*. Edinburgh 1871.
Arnold, E.V. *Roman Stoicism*. Cambridge 1911.
Arrian. *Campaigns of Alexander*. London 1971.
Athanasius. *De Incarnatione*, cf. *Christology of the Later Fathers*.
Athenagoras. *Plea Regarding Christians*, cf. *Early Christian Fathers*.
Augustine. *Works*. 15 vols. Edinburgh 1871-1876.
Aulen, Gustav. *Christus Victor*. London 1940.

Baillie, J. *Our Knowledge of God*. London 1939.
Barnabas. cf. *Early Christian Writings*.
Barrow, R.H. *Symmachus, Prefect and Emperor*. Oxford 1973.
Basil the Great. *Protreptic on Holy Baptism*, cf. Hamman.
Baus, K. *From the Apostolic Community to Constantine*. Freiburg 1965.
Baynes, N.H. *Constantine the Great and the Christian Church*. London 1929.
Benko, S. and O'Rourke, J.J. *Early Church History*. London 1972.
Benn, A.W. *The Greek Philosophers*. 2 vols. London 1882.
Benson, E.W. *Cyprian*. London 1897.
Bettenson, H. *Early Christian Fathers*. London 1956.
  Documents of the Christian Church. London 1944.
Bevan, E. *Jerusalem under the High Priests*. London 1944.
Bigg, C. *The Christian Platonists of Alexandria*. London 1886.
Bingham, J. *Antiquities of the Christian Church*. 2 vols. London 1878.
Blinzler, J. *The Trial of Jesus*. London 1968.

Brandon, S.G.F. *The Fall of Jerusalem and the Christian Church (Fall of Jerusalem)*. London 1957.
> *The Trial of Jesus of Nazareth (Trial of Jesus)*. London 1968.
Brown, P. *Augustine of Hippo*. London 1967.
Buck, C. and Taylor, G. *St. Paul*. New York 1969.
Bultmann, R. *Theology of the New Testament (N.T. Theology)*. 2 vols. London 1952-1955.
Burkitt, F.C. *Church and Gnosis*. London 1932.
Burn-Murdoch, H. *Church Continuity and Unity*. Cambridge 1945.
Bury, J.B. *History of the Later Roman Empire*. 2 vols. New York 1958.
Butterfield, H. *The Origins of Modern Science*. London 1949.

Cambridge Economic History of Europe (CEHE), ed. Clapham, J.H. and Power, E. vol 1. Cambridge 1966.
Cambridge History of Later Greek and Early Mediaeval Philosophy (CHLGEMP), ed. Armstrong, A.H. Cambridge 1967.
Campenhausen, H. von. *Fathers of the Greek Church (FGC)*, London 1963.
> *Fathers of the Latin Church (FLC)*, London 1964.
> *Tradition and Life in the Church (TLC)*, London 1968.
Carr, E.H. *Karl Marx*. London 1934.
Case, S.J. *The Social Triumph of the Early Church*. London 1933.
Chadwick, H. *The Early Church*. London 1967.
Christology of the Later Fathers, ed. Hardy, E.D. London 1954.
Cicero. *De Divinatione*. London 19--.
> *De Natura Deorum*. London 19--.
> *De Officiis*. London 19--.
> *De Senectute*. London 19--.
> *Pro Sestio*. London 19--.
Clement of Alexandria. *Works*. London 1899.
Clement of Rome. *Epistle to the Corinthians*, cf. *Early Christian Fathers*.
II Clement. cf. *Early Christian Fathers*.
Cochrane, C.N. *Christianity and Classical Culture*. New York 1957.
Coleman-Norton, P.R. *Roman State and Christian Church*. 3 vols. London 1966.
Collingwood, R.G. *The Idea of History (IH)*, London 1963.
> *Roman Britain and the English Settlements (Settlements)*. London 1949.
Constantine. *Works (P.L.8)*. Paris 1844.
Crossman, R.H.S. *Plato Today*. London 1937.
Cullman, O. *Christ and Time*. London 1951.
> *The Early Church (Early Church)*. London 1956.
> *The State in the New Testament (State in NT)*. London 1957.
Cumont, F. *Oriental Religions in Roman Paganism*. Paris 1906.

Cyprian. *Works.* 2 vols. Edinburgh 1868-1869.
Cyril of Jerusalem. *The Catechetical Lectures.* London 1955.

Dampier, W.C. *A History of Science.* Cambridge 1966.
Daniélou, J. *Origen.* London 1955.
Daniel-Rops, H. *The Church of Apostles and Martyrs.* 2 vols. New York 1962.
Davey, N. cf. Hoskyns.
Davies, J.G. *Daily Life in the Early Church.* London 1952.
  Social Life of Early Christians. London 1954.
  The Architectural Setting of Baptism. London 1952.
Dickinson, G.L. *The Greek View of Life.* London 1941.
Didache. cf. *Early Christian Fathers.*
Didascalia Apostolorum. London 1903.
Dio Cassius. *Epitome.* 9 vols. London 1914-1927.
Dix, G. *The Shape of the Liturgy.* London 1945.
Dodd, C.H. *The Apostolic Preaching and its Development (Apostolic Preaching).* London 1936.
  The Parables of the Kingdom (Parables). London 1961.
  The Founder of Christianity (Founder). London 1973.
Duchesne, L. *Early History of the Christian Church.* 3 vols. London 1909-1924.

Early Christian Fathers, ed. Richardson, C.C. London 1952.
Ehrhardt, A. *The Apostolic Succession.* London 1953.
Eisler, R. *The Messiah Jesus and John the Baptist.* London 1931.
Engels, F. cf. Marx, K.
Epictetus. *Moral Discourses.* London 1910.
Epistle to Diognetus, cf. *Early Christian Fathers.*
Eusebius. *De Laudibus Constantini (DLC)* (P.G. 20). Paris 1857.
  De Vita Constantini (DVC) (P.G. 20). Paris 1857.
  Ecclesiastical History (Eccl. Hist.). Harmondsworth 1967.

Frankfort, H. and H.A. *Before Philosophy.* London 1951.
Frend, W.H.C. *Martyrdom and Persecution in the Early Church (Martyrdom).* Oxford 1965.
  Religion Popular and Unpopular in the Early Christian Centuries (Religion). London 1976.
  The Donatist Church (DC). Oxford 1952.
  The Early Church (EC). London 1965.
Frere, S. *Britannia.* London 1967.

Garaudy, R. *The Alternative Future.* Harmondsworth 1976.
Garret, T.S. *Christian Worship.* London 1961.
Gaster, T.H. *Scriptures of the Dead Sea Sect.* London 1957.

Gibbon, E. *Decline and Fall of the Roman Empire.* 6 vols. London 1905.

Gore, C. *The Philosophy of the Good Life.* London 1935.

Grant, F.C. *The Gospels.* London 1965.

Grant, M. *The Climax of Rome (Climax).* London 1976.
  The Jews in the Roman World (The Jews etc.). London 1973.

Grant, R.M. *Early Christianity and Society (ECS).* London 1978.
  Gnosticism and Early Christianity (GEC). London 1966.

Greenslade, S.L. *Schism in the Early Church (SEC).* London 1964.

Gregory, C.R. *Canon and Text of the New Testament.* London 1907.

Gregory of Nyssa. *De Vita S. Gregorii Thaumaturgi* (P.G. 46). Paris 1863.

Hamman, A. *Baptism: Ancient Liturgies and Patristic Texts.* New York 1957.

Hanson, R.P.C. *Allegory and Event.* London 1959.

Harnack, A. *The Mission and Expansion of Christianity.* New York 1962.

Harrison, J.E. *Prolegomena to the Study of Greek Religion.* Cambridge 1903.

Hatch, E. *Organisation of the Early Christian Churches.* London 1909.

Hefele, C.H. *History of the Church Councils.* vols 1-3. Edinburgh 1872.

Hermas. *The Shepherd.* London 1870.

Hippolytus. *Apostolic Tradition (AT).* London 1934.
  Refutation (R). Edinburgh 1869.

Historia Augusta. 2 vols. London 1922-32.

Horace. *Odes.* London 1929.

Hort, F.J.A. *The Christian Ecclesia.* London 1900.

Hoskyns, Sir E. and Davey, N. *The Riddle of the New Testament.* London 1958.

Ignatius. cf. *Early Christian Writings.*

Inge, W.R. *The Philosophy of Plotinus.* 2 vols. London 1918.

Irenaeus. *Against Heresies,* cf. *Early Christian Fathers.*

Jaeger, W. *Early Christianity and Greek Paideia (ECGP).* London 1969.
  The Theology of the Early Greek Philosophies. London 1967.

James, M.R. *The Apocryphal New Testament.* Oxford 1924.

Jeremias, J. *Infant Baptism in the First Four Centuries (Infant Baptism).* London 1969.
  New Testament Theology (NT Theology). London 1972.
  The Eucharistic Words of Jesus (Eucharistic Words). Oxford 1955.

Jerome. *Works* (P.L. 22-30). Paris 1865-1884.

Vulgate. Paris 1869.
Jones, A.H.M. *Constantine and the Conversion of Europe* (*Constantine*). London 1962.
The Later Roman Empire (LRE). 3 vols. London 1964.
Josephus. *Works*. London 1733.
Julius Capitolinus. cf. *Historia Augusta*.
Jungmann, J.A. *The Early Liturgy*. London 1959.
Justin. *Works*. Edinburgh 1867.

Kalthoff, A. *The Rise of Christianity*. London 1901.
Kautsky, K. *Foundations of Christianity*. London 1904.
Kelly, J.N.D. *Early Christian Creeds* (*ECC*). London 1951.
Early Christian Doctrines (*ECD*). London 1958.
Kidd, B.J. *History of the Church to A.D. 461*. 3 vols. *London 1922*.
Kirk, K.E. *The Apostolic Ministry*. London 1957.
Knight, G.A.F. *A Christian Theology of the Old Testament*. London 1964.
Knox, R.A. *Enthusiasm*. New York 1961.
Kümmell, W.G. *The Theology of the New Testament*. Nashville 1973.

Lactantius. *De Mortibus Persecutorum*. London 1873.
Laistner, M.L.W. *Christianity and Pagan Culture in the Later Roman Empire*. Ithaca 1951.
Lake, K. *Text of the New Testament*. London 1928.
Lampridius. cf. *Historia Augusta*.
Latourette, K.S. *A History of Christianity*. London 1955.
A History of the Expansion of Christianity. 7 vols. London 1938-1945.
Lawson, J. *A Theological and Historical Introduction to the Apostolic Fathers*. New York 1961.
Lecky, W. *A History of European Morals*. 2 vols. London 1899.
Lietzmann, H. *A History of the Early Church*. 4 vols. New York 1961.
Lightfoot, J.B. *Philippians*. London 1896.
Lightfoot, R.H. *The Gospel Message of St. Mark* (*St. Mark*). London 1962.
St. John's Gospel (*St. John*). London 1960.
Lindsay, T.M. *Church and Ministry in the Early Centuries*. London 1903.
Lucretius. *De Rerum Natura*. London 1951.

McArthur, A.A. *The Evolution of the Christian Year*. London 1953.
MacCoby, H. *Revolution in Judaea*. London 1975.
Machoveč, M. *A Marxist Looks at Jesus*. London 1976.
McIntire, C.T. *God, History and Historians*. Oxford 1977.
Manson, W. *Jesus the Messiah*. London 1948.

Marcus Aurelius. *Meditations*. London 1702.

Martyrdom of Polycarp, cf. *Early Christian Fathers*.

Marx, K. and Engels, F. *On Religion*. Moscow 1972.

Maxwell, W.D. *An Outline of Christian Worship*. London 1936.

Meates, G.W. *Lullingstone Roman Villa*. London 1955.

Meer, F. van der and Mohrmann, C. *Atlas of the Early Christian World*. London 1958.

Minucius Felix. *Octavius*, cf. Davies, J.G.

Mohrmann, C. cf. van der Meer. Oxford 1963.

Momigliano, A. *Paganism and Christianity in the Fourth Century A.D.* Oxford 1963.

Neill, S. and Weber, H.-R. *The Layman in Christian Society*. London 1963.

Niebuhr, R. *Faith and History*. London 1949.

Nock, A.D. *Conversion*. London 1961.

Oesterley, W.O.E. *A History of Israel*. 2 vols. Oxford 1934.

  The Jewish Background of the Christian Liturgy. Oxford 1925.

Ogg, G. *Chronology of the Public Ministry of Jesus*. Cambridge 1940.

Origen. *Works*. 2 vols. Edinburgh 1869-1872.

O'Rourke. cf. Benko.

Panegyrici Veteres (P.L. 8). Paris 1844.

Pascal, B. *Pensées*. London 1947.

Paulinus of Nola. *Letters*. Westminster Md. 1967.

Pfeiffer, R.H. *History of New Testament Times*. New York 1949.

Plato. *Republic*. London 1929.

Pliny. *Epistles*. London 1921.

Plutarch. *Works*. London 19 vols. 19--.

Pocknee, C.E. *Water and the Spirit*. London 1967.

Polybius. *Histories*. 6 vols. London 1922-1927.

Polycarp. *Epistle to the Philippians*, cf. *Early Christian Fathers*.

Popper, K.R. *The Open Society and Its Enemies*. 2 vols. London 1952.

Prestige, G.L. *Fathers and Heretics* (*FH*). London 1963.

  God in Patristic Thought. London 1963.

Quasten, J. *Patrology*. 3 vols. Utrecht 1950.

Quick, O.C. *The Christian Sacraments*. London 1941.

Raven, C.E. *The Gospel and the Church*. London 1939.

Richardson, A. *An Introduction to the Theology of the New Testament* (*Introduction*). London 1961.

  A Theological Word Book of the Bible (*Word Book*). London 1962.

  Christian Apologetics (*Apologetics*). London 1948.

Rist, J.M. *Stoic Philosophy*. Cambridge 1969.

Robinson, J.A.T. *Redating the New Testament*. London 1976.

Rostovtzeff, M. *Social and Economic History of the Roman Empire*. Oxford 1926.

Russell, B. *History of Western Philosophy*. London 1965.

Sallust. *Works*. London 1921.

Salvian. *De Gubernatione Dei*. Washington D.C. 1962.

Sandmel, S. *The First Christian Century in Judaism and Christianity*. New York 1969.

Scharlemann, M.H. *Stephen: A Singular Saint*. Rome 1968.

Schurer, E. *History of the Jewish People in the Age of Jesus Christ*. 5 vols. New York 1891.

Sherwin-White, A.N. *Roman Society and Roman Law in the New Testament*. Oxford 1965.

Smallwood, E.M. *The Jews under Roman Rule*. London 1976.

Smith, J.H. *Constantine the Great*. London 1971.

Socrates. *Ecclesiastical History*. Grand Rapids 1957.

Souter, A. *Text and Canon of the New Testament*. London 1935.

Sozomen. *Ecclesiastical History*. Oxford 1891.

Spartianus. cf. *Historia Augusta*.

Srawley, J.H. *Early History of the Liturgy*. Cambridge 1947.

Staniforth, M. *Early Christian Writings*. London 1968.

Stevenson, J. *A New Eusebius*. London 1957.

Streeter, B.H. *The Primitive Church*. London 1929.

Suetonius. *Lives of the Twelve Caesars*. 2 vols. London 1914.

Swete, H.B. *Early History of the Church and Ministry*. London 1918.

Tacitus. *Works*. 2 vols. London 1937.

Tatian. *Diatessaron*. Edinburgh 1894.

Temple, W. *Citizen and Churchman*. London 1941.

Tertullian. *Works*. 2 vols. London 1899.

Theodoret. *Ecclesiastical History*. London 1843.

Troeltsch, E. *The Social Teaching of the Christian Churches*. 2 vols. London 1931.

Virgil. *Works*. 2 vols. London 1930.

Weber, H.-R. cf. Neill, S.

Weiss, J. *History of Primitive Christianity*. 2 vols. New York 1947.

Westcott, B.F. *The Canon of the New Testament (CNT)*. London 1870.

Ephesians. New York 1906.

Whale, J.S. *Christian Doctrine*. Cambridge 1950.

Whitehead, A.N. *Adventures of Ideas*. London 1942.

Widengren, G. *Mani and Manichaeism*. London 1965.
Wilson, R. McL. *The Gnostic Problem*. London 1958.
Wisdom of Solomon, cf. *Apocrypha*.
Wolfson, H.A. *Philo*. 2 vols. Cambridge, Mass. 1948.
Woolley, Sir L. *Abraham*. London 1936.
World Council of Churches. *The Ministry of Deacons*. Geneva 1965.
Wright, W.C. *The Works of the Emperor Julian*. 3 vols. London
    1913-23.

INDEX